Lesbian Empire

D1340495

LESBIAN EMPIRE

Radical Crosswriting in the Twenties

GAY WACHMAN

RUTGERS UNIVERSITY PRESS
New Brunswick, New Jersey, and London

Library of Congress Cataloging-in-Publication Data

Wachman, Gay, 1943–
    Lesbian empire : radical crosswriting in the Twenties/Gay Wachman.
        p. cm.
    Includes bibliographical references and index.
    ISBN 0-8135-2941-7 (cloth : alk. paper)—ISBN 0-8135-2942-5
    (pbk.: alk. paper)
    1. English fiction—20th century—History and criticism. 2. Lesbians in
    literature. 3. English fiction—Women authors—History and criticism.
    4. Warner, Sylvia Townsend, 1893——Criticism and interpretation.
    5. Lesbians' writings, English—History and criticism. 6. Women and
    literature—Great Britain—History—20th century. 7. Feminism and literature—
    Great Britain—History—20th century. 8. Homosexuality and literature—
    Great Britain—History—20th century. 9. Lesbianism in literature.
    10. Radicalism in Literature.
    I. Title

PR888.L46 W34 2001
823'.912099206643—dc21

                                                                    00–045683

British Cataloging-in-Publication data for this book is available from the British
Library.

Manufactured in the United States of America

For Bonnie Gray

Contents

Illustrations

Acknowledgments

I owe particular thanks to Jane Marcus for her enthusiasm, erudition, and energy; she introduced me to the work of Sylvia Townsend Warner and Vernon Lee, encouraged me to find my own voice as a writer, and indefatigably read chapters and drafts. This book could not have been written without her.

Thanks to Wayne Koestenbaum for providing me with new ways of thinking about queer theory, and to Laura Doan for sharing her knowledge of sexology and history; I am indebted to them both for helpful readings, as well. I am especially grateful to Robin Hackett for years of collaboration and support. Thanks to Jane Bennett, Allen Bergson, Deirdre Bergson, Carolyn Ferrell, Tom Harrison, Illith Rosenblum, and Anna Wilson, and especially to Bonnie Gray for her expertise in all that pertains to lesbian representation.

I owe thanks to Ray Russell for sending me his unpublished bibliography of Sylvia Townsend Warner, and to Rosemary and Furse Swann, Elizabeth Savage, and Colin House for their hospitality and generosity in sharing their knowledge of Warner and Dorset. Thanks also to Deborah Phillips, Krystyna Colburn, Mary Joannou, and Nancy Berke for organizing panels and conferences where I was able to try out my ideas. I thank my colleagues in the English Language Studies Program at the State University of New York, Old Westbury for supporting my request for a leave of absence during the spring of 1997;

that respite was made economically feasible by the Constance Jordan Dissertation Year Award from the Center for Lesbian and Gay Studies and the Morton N. Cohen Dissertation Fellowship from the Ph.D. Program in English of the City University of New York Graduate Center. Special thanks for her enthusiasm and patience go to Leslie Mitchner, my editor at Rutgers University Press.

A version of "Pink Icing and a Narrow Bed" in chapter 4 was published in *Virginia Woolf and the Arts: Selected Papers from the Sixth Annual Conference on Virginia Woolf*, ed. Diane F. Gillespie and Leslie K. Hankins (New York: Pace University Press, 1997). A version of "Rewriting Lesbian Stereotypes in *Summer Will Show*" in chapter 5 appeared in the autumn 1998 issue of *Critical Survey* (Oxford: Berghahn Books). I am indebted to Sylvia Townsend Warner's literary executors, Susanna Pinney and William Maxwell, for access to the Warner/Ackland Papers in the Dorset County Museum and to Richard de Peyer, the museum's curator, for his help. I am grateful to Morine Krissdottir of the Dorset County Museum, Janice Mullin of the Imperial War Museum, and the helpful staff of both the New York Public Library and the Mina Rees Library at the Graduate Center of the City University of New York. I thank Bryan Fosten for his kindness in selling to me for a song plate 27 of his book, *The Thin Red Line*, and Ursula Milner-White for permission to quote from an unpublished letter from her uncle, Eric Milner-White, to George Townsend Warner, in the Warner/Ackland Papers of the Dorset County Museum.

Cherry Grove, Fire Island, N.Y.
August 2000

Lesbian Empire

INTRODUCTION

This book focuses on sexually radical fiction written by British women in the years following World War I. Its center is the achievement of Sylvia Townsend Warner in surmounting, sidestepping, and undermining the barriers of interdiction and inhibition that faced women writing about forbidden sexualities. Focusing primarily on her 1920s novels, I contextualize Warner's fiction alongside that of other writers of her time within and against imperialist sexual ideology, with its rigid enforcement of divisions and bigotries, whispers and silence. Drawing on the discourses of cultural studies, feminist historicism, queer theory, and literary analysis, I argue that Warner brought her oppositional feminist politics and her literary practice of crosswriting to an alternative modernist tradition of sexual radicalism.

Lesbian crosswriting transposes the otherwise unrepresentable lives of invisible or silenced or simply closeted lesbians into narratives about gay men. In the first half of the twentieth century, the most obvious examples are historical novels by women such as Marguerite Yourcenar, Mary Renault, and Bryher.[1] These writers free their imaginations from the sex/gender system of their time by writing about men's lives; when they set their novels in a time and place, such as ancient Greece, that tolerates homosexuality, they use that freer environment to celebrate homosexual romance. Crosswriting can be a strategy of ambivalence as well as of disguise, as it is, for example,

1

in Virginia Woolf's *Jacob's Room* (1922); it also reflects the identification with gay men that encouraged lesbians to acknowledge or act on their sexuality throughout the twentieth century. Above all, it is a tool for escape from one's specific, limited location within the rigid frames of imperialist society: Warner crosswrites the cultural boundaries of class, "race," and even species as well as those of gender and sexuality.

I am concerned neither with "high modernist" writing—although Woolf's *Mrs. Dalloway* (1925) is central to my chapter on the closet and the war—nor with the literature of exile that constitutes the sapphist modernist tradition sketched by Susan Gubar in "Sapphistries" and memorably historicized by Shari Benstock in *Women of the Left Bank*.[2] Instead, I connect Warner's three 1920s novels *Lolly Willowes* (1926), *Mr. Fortune's Maggot* (1927), and *The True Heart* (1929) with the work of a diverse group of writers who used fantasy as a means of escaping, reshaping, and critiquing a world fragmented by loss and pain. This work, from Vernon Lee's *The Ballet of the Nations* (1915) through Warner's *The True Heart*, forms a queer, primitivist, predominantly satirical, alternative modernist tradition that can be traced back to the aesthetics of excess in the art and literature of the 1890s.[3] Vernon Lee, Norman Douglas, T. F. Powys, Compton Mackenzie, Elinor Wylie, Ronald Firbank, David Garnett, Sylvia Townsend Warner—these writers span two generations, the Atlantic Ocean, and the sex/gender continuums. The books range from the sententious frivolity of Douglas's *South Wind* (1917) to the blistering pacifist allegory of war in Lee's *Satan the Waster* (1920), from Firbank's outrageous camp primitivism in *The Flower beneath the Foot* (1924) to Garnett's sadly ambivalent attack on British racism in *The Sailor's Return* (1925). These writers were sexual radicals who challenged conventional repression and hypocrisy through the breaking of taboos.[4]

Born in 1893, Sylvia Townsend Warner was part of the generation of modernists who began learning their sexual, social, and literary politics during the First World War. Between 1925 and 1978 she published seven novels, ten collections of short stories, seven volumes of poetry, a prize-winning biography, several translations, and numerous essays, articles, and political fables in periodicals ranging from *The Countryman* to *New Masses*.[5] The complexity of her writing—her crossings of genres and genders; her learned but seemingly offhand allusions to literature and history; her sexual, feminist, communist, anarchist radicalism—is perhaps a cause of the simplifications in much of the writing about her. In Britain, Warner has only recently been recognized by contemporary critics: men write mainly about her contribution to communist journalism in the periodicals of the thirties and forties; women emphasize her leftist politics and feminism but understate her radical representations of sexuality and her experimental conflations of genre. American writers, on the other hand, have focused almost exclusively on two novels, *Lolly Willowes* and *Summer Will Show* (1936). Because nobody—except perhaps Wendy Mulford, in her remarkable biography of Warner and Valentine Ackland's twenty most "political" years—has yet attempted an inclusive reading of Warner, she is still considered a minor figure, when she is considered at all.[6] And because her writing is not "difficult," she has not been admitted to the mainstream modernist canon and has rarely been read with the care required by her subtle irony, her shifts in narrative genres and tone, her intricate, musical poems, and her layered and nuanced literary and political intertextuality.

The writers whose novels I analyze—Warner, Woolf, and Radclyffe Hall, along with the less known Clemence Dane, Rose Allatini, and Evadne Price—were firmly based in England and enmeshed in the early-twentieth-century history and culture of the British Empire. All of them experienced as middle-class girls and young women the compulsory modesty of late-Victorian and Edwardian England, followed by the dislocations and losses of the war, and then the increased tolerance of gender and sexual difference in postwar London. They represent forbidden love in the idyllic countryside of English prewar pastoral and in the mud and pain behind the lines in wartime France, in a boarding school and in the consumer temple of the Army and Navy Stores, on the salt marshes of East Anglia and on a Polynesian island. Above all, they challenge or circumvent the rigid codes of expression and behavior on which imperialist patriarchy and capitalism depended. All of these writers (including Dane, whose first novel *Regiment of Women* [1917], is the earliest narrative I consider and the least oppositional to the dominant culture) break the rules of silence and propriety that muffled middle-class discourse—and, above all, the discourse of women—about class, "race," gender, and sexual differences.

It is because I see writing, however oppositional, as enmeshed in the dominant culture that I devote the entire first chapter to imperialist and lesbian history, congenital inversion theory, biography, politics, and the law. I have found it useful to discuss some specific legal cases of libel, slander, and censorship between 1917 and 1928; they reveal very clearly the devious practical politics of patriarchal nationalism. As Michel Foucault argues (and as Radclyffe Hall, for one, was exceedingly slow to learn), the law, like medicine, is a force of sexual oppression. I follow Foucault in arguing that the medical theory of congenital inversion, along with the interconnected evolutionist discourses of degeneration theory, primitivism, and eugenics, underpinned imperialist ideology.[7]

The second chapter focuses on Dane's *Regiment of Women* and Warner's *The True Heart* as particularly clear examples of imperialist sexual ideology in relation to lesbian modernism. Dane's *Regiment of Women* foregrounds eugenicist ideas as clearly and literally as Hall's presentation of congenital inversion: in these narratively conventional novels such effortless reproduction of the dominant ideology is predictable. The seemingly sentimental eugenicist childbirth that ends *The True Heart*, however, should be read as profoundly ironic in light of eugenicist horror at childbearing by the "unfit." What birth could be more dysgenic than this one of a child conceived out of wedlock, fathered by an "idiot," and mothered by a destitute orphan?

Chapter 3 focuses specifically on class, racial primitivism, and sexual radicalism in Warner's first two novels, the satirical fantasies *Lolly Willowes* and *Mr. Fortune's Maggot*. Chapter 4 discusses explorations of imperialism and the closet by Allatini (in *Despised and Rejected*, 1918), Woolf, and Warner: their narratives demonstrate the intersection of misogyny and homophobia with the class-bound, racist jingoism that justified the First World War. The final chapter contrasts Hall's courageous, primitivist, and utterly elitist plea for sexual tolerance in *The Well of Loneliness* (1928) with two novels that rewrite it—Price's *Not So Quiet . . . Stepdaughters of War* (1930) and Warner's open celebration of revolutionary lesbianism, *Summer Will Show*.

Modernist writers' and artists' representations of "primitive" sexuality have lately been much discussed.[8] Racial and class "primitives" figure in most of the narratives I shall consider, taking two opposing forms: they are either idealized in comparison to European "civilization" or recoiled from as "degenerate." Despite its invigorating satire, *Mr. Fortune's Maggot* idealizes the community that its innocent missionary sets out to convert on the island of Fanua; *The True Heart*'s allegory of class oppression both celebrates and simplifies the sexual and practical innocence of its destitute maid of all work, Sukey, and her beautiful "feeble-minded" lover. In *Mrs. Dalloway*, Woolf simultaneously mocks and participates in the primitivism of the time in her presentation of Clarissa's vision of Doris Kilman as a "prehistoric monster." Hall's identification of female masculinity with "primitive" sexuality makes Stephen Gordon "grotesque and splendid" as a child and "rather terrible" as a young woman perceived by Angela Crossby; finally, her inversion is identified with the "crude . . . primitive force" of the "Negro" singer Henry.[9]

Clemence Dane presents (re)productive eugenicist heterosexuality in opposition to a "vampirish" lesbian spinster: *Regiment of Women* is clearly an expression of lesbian panic. In Evadne Price's *Not So Quiet*, Georgina Toshington leads the persecution of the two lesbians in the ambulance unit, but her hugely maternal yet masculine, heroic yet cynical figure is the emotional and sexual center of the narrative. My concept of lesbian panic adapts Eve Kosofsky Sedgwick's theory of homosexual panic to the culture and communities of women; my readings of congenitalist sexologists, especially Havelock Ellis and Edward Carpenter, have drawn on the discussion of inversion in *The Well of Loneliness* by Esther Newton, Teresa de Lauretis, Jay Prosser, and Judith Halberstam. Terry Castle's theorization of the lesbian triangular plot and Thomas Foster's subsequent reading of *Summer Will Show* through Georg Lukàcs have deepened my delight in Sylvia Townsend Warner's masterpiece.[10]

All of these theorists and critics have influenced my choices of terminology. I use the words *lesbian* and *lesbianism* when I need umbrella terms; I prefer them to *sapphist* and *sapphism* because of the class implications of the latter: knowledge of Latin and Greek was a privilege of upper-middle-class men and a basic component of the system of exclusions that constituted the empire. While I try to avoid anachronisms when referring to romantic friends, passing women, inverts, butches, femmes, and lesbian feminists, I find I need an inclusive transhistorical term that can include both gender identification and sexual preference. Modernist lesbians themselves have used *lesbian, sapphist,* and *invert.* I use the word *lesbophobia*, which may seem cumbersome chiefly because it is unfamiliar, in order to avoid the elision of fear of lesbians with fear of gay men. I refer to the women writers I consider here as lesbian modernists even though most of them lived deep in the closet because they all foreground lesbian, gay, or other forbidden desire in their writing and because all of them, except for Evadne Price, have been identified as lesbian or bisexual at some point in their lives.[11] I enclose such words as "race," "primitive," and "civilization" in quotation marks to indicate my opinion that they lack nonexclusionary referents.

My main concern in writing this book has been with the narratives of history: I have aimed to historicize lesbian modernist writing and lives within and against—but never outside of—imperialism. While writers such as Warner and Woolf can be characterized as outsiders, and while marginalized communities can take refuge in separatism, modernists lived, as we do, at the mercy of history. My main guides, therefore, have been cultural historians. Lucy Bland's *Banishing the Beast: Sexuality and the Early Feminists* provided the background material to start me off on my first two chapters. John M. MacKenzie's *Propaganda and Empire: The Manipulation of British Public Opinion, 1880–1960* reminded me of the museums and radio programs of my childhood in 1950s London and of all the paraphernalia of empire: the coronation, the Trooping of the Colour, Trafalgar Square and Buckingham Palace, the uniforms of beefeaters and schoolchildren— the exhibitions and routines that taught us all our place. Peter Fryer's *Staying Power: The History of Black People in Britain* filled in some of the most glaring gaps in my schooling, while Modris Eksteins's *Rites of Spring: The Great War and the Birth of the Modern Age* made me reimagine the cataclysm that has influenced my thinking and politics ever since I recoiled from the war films of my childhood and bought Wilfred Owen's *Poems*. Claire M. Tylee's *The Great War and Women's Consciousness* has guided my research from the very beginning of this project

I am most indebted, however, to the books, articles, and conversation of Jane Marcus, who first introduced me to Sylvia Townsend Warner's writing and whose "Bluebeard's Daughters: Pretexts for Pre-Texts" inspired the development of my ideas about Warner's idiosyncratic crosswriting. I have found particularly thought provoking and informative the following articles and chapters by Marcus: "The Asylums of Antaeus" and "Corpus/Corps/Corpse" on women and the First World War; "Britannia Rules *The Waves*" and "Registering Objections" on modernism and colonialism; "Still Practice, A/Wrested

Alphabet" from *Art and Anger* on Woolf and Warner, reading and feminism, and that ur-text of lesbian criticism, "Sapphistry: Narration as Lesbian Seduction in *A Room of One's Own*" from *Virginia Woolf and the Languages of Patriarchy*. My insistent foregrounding of the narratives of history has been thoroughly fostered by Jane Marcus, but I take total responsibility for this book's socialist, pacifist, lesbian/gay/feminist slant.

1

LESBIAN HISTORIES

Imperialism and the Contexts of Silence

It is well known that the expansion and maintenance of the British Empire required a particular rigidity in its administrators; George Orwell, in "Shooting An Elephant," for instance, makes a very clear statement about the compulsory suppression of individual consciousness and will under the "hollow, posing dummy" of the imperialist: the individual "wears a mask, and his face grows to fit it."[1] He writes also about the impossibility of discussing with his fellow police officers in Burma the conflicts he feels about his role: "I had had to think out my problems in the utter silence that is imposed on every Englishman in the East."[2] It was not only abroad, however, and not only among men that the mask and the silence were obligatory. The British in Britain were also educated—by schools, newspapers, museums, music halls, and huge exhibitions and spectacles of "primitive" cultures such as Barnum and Bailey's Great Show at Olympia in 1897—into a sense of racial and national superiority that was essential to the maintenance of both the empire and the class system.[3] Imperialist capitalism relied on rigid codes of expression and behavior at home as well as abroad.

The barriers among the upper, middle, and working classes in Britain were still almost insurmountable in the first half of the twentieth century. Accounts of middle-class childhood like that of Rosemary Manning in *A Corridor of Mirrors* describe an education in the subtleties of class differences. As a doctor's child, Manning was never allowed to visit the home of her school friend Paul, whose father was a grocer, nor was Paul ever "invited home to tea" with her as was Eric, her middle-class playmate. Later, eleven years old during the 1920s in Sandhurst, a drab Surrey town that was also the site of a famous military academy, Manning found herself isolated between the working-class children and those of "the upper crust, moneyed and military rather than aristocratic."[4] The minuteness with which the rich and the officer class are here distinguished from the aristocracy reflects the British insistence on conformity within ranks, whether military or civilian; one was expected to associate with people whose appearance, possessions, education, speech patterns, and behavior were like one's own.

One also kept very quiet about individual differences or discomforts. We can be sure that Manning's middle-class parents did not explain to her exactly why little Paul was not invited to tea, for to speak about the nuances of the class system was to declass oneself. It was particularly bad form to remind an upper-class acquaintance of her superior status. Toward the end of Antonia White's *Frost in May*, Nanda Grey realizes that when she leaves school—the Convent of the Five Wounds where she has become fervently attached to three girls whose old Catholic families form part of the European aristocracy— she is unlikely to meet her friends again. " 'I shall probably be teaching a howling mob of children, and you'll be married to a duke,'" she tells Léonie, who stalks off in anger. Later, Nanda receives a note: "You're an idiot but you are my best friend. So kindly shut up now and always." It is signed: "Léonie Magdalena Hedwig de Wesseldorf."[5] It is because Léonie is only fourteen that she reveals so clearly the double message she is giving Nanda; it is because Nanda is only fourteen that she makes the mistake of mentioning their class difference at all. Those with less power or money are silently to make the best of their class oppression; to speak embarrasses the powerful because it endangers the status quo.

Virginia Woolf's writings repeatedly explore the connections between class silence and gendered silence in the lives of middle-class women. She devotes the second essay of *The Pargiters*, for example, to an analysis of the "principles underlying . . . and controlling" the family's day-to-day life in the 1880s: money and love. Neither preoccupation is spoken about; none of his children knows how much money Captain Pargiter has; his daughters feel unable to ask for money for education or for travel or amusement; their future security as wives and mothers depends on the bourgeois respectability that keeps them at home pouring tea for their father. Above all, anything to do with sexuality—"street love, common love . . . the kind of passion which . . . made it impossible for the Pargiter girls to walk in the West End alone"—is completely unmentionable. Milly and Delia feel ashamed of their interest in the young man in the street whom they watch from the curtained window; ten-year-old Rose cannot express her terror of the man who unbuttons his trousers by the pillar box because "she knew that she was able to feel what it was wrong to feel."[6] The myth of feminine innocence—that upper- and middle-class white women have no sexual desire—was basic to imperialist patriarchal hegemony.

Woolf is also persuasive in her representation of the kinds of silence that were both the product and the producer of continuing gender oppression. Twice within six pages of "A Sketch of the Past" she describes the devastating imbalance of power between the man who speaks or is silent at will and the woman who is only silent. After depicting the roars of outrage, the "extraordinary dramatization of self-pity, anger and despair" given by her father each week when Vanessa silently presented the account book, she turns to her own invariable response: "Never have I felt such rage and such frustration. For not a word of my feeling could be expressed."[7] Later, Woolf describes George Duckworth's reaction to a new dress made of unconventional material in which she came down to dinner one evening:

> He looked me up and down as if I were a horse turned into the ring. Then the sullen look came over him; a look in which one traced not only aesthetic disapproval; but something that went deeper; morally, socially, he scented some kind of insurrection; of defiance of social standards. I was condemned from many more points of view than I can analyze as I stood there, conscious of those criticisms; and conscious too of fear, of shame and of despair—"Go and tear it up," he said at last.[8]

Rage, frustration, fear, shame, and despair,[9] all these are experienced in a state of mute abjection that Woolf contrasts with the willed, sadistic silences of both men. After writing the weekly check, her father "sank into his chair and sat with his head on his breast" as the finale of his "extraordinary dramatization"; George's silence first dehumanizes his victim—she feels like a horse—and later, over dinner, tortures her.[10] To the powerful, silence can be a choice that further empowers the chooser; to the oppressed, it is an assault, a violent deprivation of speech.

It is within this context of multiple, compulsory self-censorships, within this society in which children and adults were rigorously educated as to the seemingly immutable differences of rank and power, that modernist women writers' breaking of silence about homosexuality and lesbianism must be considered. How was it possible for Clemence Dane, Rose Allatini, Virginia Woolf, Sylvia Townsend Warner, Radclyffe Hall, and Evadne Price to represent gay men and lesbians in fiction written between 1917 and 1930? Before examining their use of varying narrative strategies to explore and/or conceal same-sex desire—crosswriting, stream-of-consciousness, reconfiguring the accepted narrative of "history" and current events—I want to consider the knowledge about lesbianism available to them as young women starting to write. Regardless of whether they spoke or were silent, what could they actually have known from books or newspapers or from their own lives?

Inversion and Pollution

By the 1920s, sexuality was constantly discussed and written about by the experts: sexologists, ethnographers, and anthropologists formed an exclusive, almost entirely masculine club in which the interconnected discourses of sexual inversion and primitive sexuality were developed; it is no accident that Havelock Ellis wrote the preface to Bronislaw Malinowski's *The Sexual Life of Savages* (1929) as well as the introductory note, or commentary, that provided "scientific" credentials for Radclyffe Hall's *The Well of Loneliness*.[11] Ellis had been forming his ideas about sexuality since the 1880s when, along with Edward Carpenter, Edith Lees, and other critics of the Victorian sex-gender system he had belonged to the broadly socialist and sexually progressive Fellowship of the New Life.[12] The two sexological concepts that are most pertinent here are the merging of the ideas of same-sex desire and female masculinity in female inversion theory—that "actively inverted women" have "a more or less distinct trait of masculinity"[13]—and the insistence that inversion is congenital.

There has been considerable debate during the last twenty years about the impact on individual lives of the theory of congenital inversion. The most influential criticism is Michel Foucault's: he utterly condemns sexology along with eugenics and degeneration theory. Foucault includes Havelock Ellis in his list of the producers of the *scientia sexualis* and asserts that "The discourse on sex . . . combin[ed] . . . the great evolutionist myths with the recent institutions of public health . . . promised to eliminate defective individuals, degenerate and bastardized populations . . . [and] justified the racisms of the state."[14] I am not convinced, however, that the discourse of congenital inversion worked only to inhibit the sexual freedom of individuals.[15]

Biological explanations of homosexuality and lesbianism can certainly diminish guilt about same-sex desire as well as weakening arguments for criminalization, hospitalization, and subjection to "the talking cure." An 1896 editorial in *The Lancet* about Havelock Ellis's *Sexual Inversion* shows how dangerous congenital inversion theory was thought to be by the medical establishment on its first appearance in a book by a British writer a year after the Oscar Wilde trials: the editorialist asserts the prevailing view that homosexuality is "an acquired and depraved manifestation of the sexual passion"—a view that justified punishing and "curing" gay men and lesbians for much of the twentieth century.[16] Congenitalism was and is seen as justifying same-sex desire. Now, a century later, gay men and lesbians who wish to assimilate into the dominant culture are eagerly embracing the implications of the genetic research undertaken by Dean Hamer and others.[17]

Lucy Bland has argued that by the late 1920s sexology was enabling some women "to think about claiming a *sexual* identity."[18] I would set the date of *thinking about* it somewhat earlier: Lytton Strachey discussed a meeting of the British Society for the Study of Sex Psychology with Virginia Woolf in 1918, and Rose Allatini had certainly read some of Edward Carpenter's sociosexological writings by then; Dennis Blackwood in *Despised and Rejected* has clearly also been reading an expounder of "trapped soul" inversion theory such as Karl Heinrich Ulrichs or Richard von Krafft-Ebing. There was also considerable discussion of congenitalist theories in the *Freewoman* in 1912, though most of the writers on the topic were men.[19]

In "Acts of Female Indecency," Laura Doan examines the 1921

parliamentary records to show that only two of the British legislators who debated adding a clause criminalizing "any act of gross indecency between female[s]" to the Criminal Law Amendment Bill admitted knowledge of inversion theory. The air was thick with loud disclaimers of knowledge of this "disgusting and polluting subject," as such "acts" were described by Lord Malmesbury. Frederick A. Macquisten, Howard Gritten, and Sir Ernest Wild were three lawyers who had introduced the female indecency clause, not primarily to outlaw lesbianism (although doubtless they would have been glad to do so) but in order to scuttle the whole bill; it could pass only as agreed upon, without contentious additions.[20] The bill was mainly concerned with protecting young girls from prostitution by raising the legal age of consent and was strongly supported by feminists; such legislation was habitually opposed by men seeking to protect their age-old sexual prerogative.[21] Wild, the only speaker who alluded to sexologists by name, did so by reading a letter from an unnamed "nerve specialist" who referred him to the work of Krafft-Ebing and Ellis on forms of "malpractices between women." Wild named sexologists in order to impress his hearers with "the prestige of scientific knowledge"—cynically using the bogey of lesbianism, or active female sexuality, in order to preserve men's access to the bodies of young girls. He and his lawyer friends succeeded in their use of rhetoric and "evidence": the clause was added to the bill and thus ensured its defeat.

Macquisten and Wild might have learned from Noel Pemberton-Billing's performance at the Old Bailey in 1918 how to use the pollution of lesbianism and the prestige of sexology to distract their colleagues from their true purpose. Pemberton-Billing had provoked the dancer Maud Allan, who was billed to perform in Oscar Wilde's *Salome*, to sue him for libel; he had then turned the tables on her by conducting his own defense. His success in convincing the jury that she was not only a "moral pervert" but also a traitor in collusion with enemy aliens throws light on the uses to which sexological theories could be put by the radical right. His object was to foment unrest and anger at the conduct of the war and prevent the negotiation of peace. It is unsurprising that one of Pemberton-Billing's allies in the House of Commons was Sir William Joynson-Hicks, the power hungry, xenophobic, evangelical moralist who became home secretary in 1926 and unscrupulously manipulated the law in order to ban *The Well of Loneliness*.[22]

The Cult of the Clitoris and the Majesty of the Law

The story of Maud Allan's libel suit against Noel Pemberton-Billing is well known to readers of *The Eye in the Door*, the second volume of Pat Barker's *Regeneration Trilogy*. The trial's public production of "lesbianism" was infinitely more prominent than that of the sexologists' books or the debates of legislators. Press coverage of the trial, which took place from May 29 through June 4, 1918, was extensive and intense; it included many photographs, especially of the large crowd of supporters who cheered Pemberton-Billing as he emerged from the Old Bailey on June 4. The tabloid press celebrated Pemberton-Billing's acquittal as a victory for the common man, patriotism, and morality; the *Daily Mail* advocated the internment of enemy aliens; only the *Manchester Guardian*, the *Daily Chronicle*, and the *Herald* showed much dissatisfaction with the verdict. I cannot imagine that any of the writers whose work I have examined were unaware of that trial. It must have given them a disconcerting example of the dangers of being thought lesbian.

The trial is significant in lesbian history because of its sensationally negative representation of lesbianism, its attempt to prove that sexual knowledge—knowledge of the word *clitoris*—is an indicator of lesbianism, and its use of Krafft-Ebing's *Psychopathia Sexualis* as evidence for the defense. The trial was also significant in terms of national politics: both Krafft-Ebing's name and Allan's education in Germany encouraged jury members to conflate perversion with treachery, especially since Allan and Margot Asquith were rumored to be lovers and the Asquith family was thought to be involved in secret peace negotiations with Germany. Perhaps most significant, however, is the fact that Pemberton-Billing stage-managed the whole event as part of a right-wing conspiracy to topple Lloyd George's government and ensure the continuation of the war.[23]

Before the war, Maud Allan had been remarkably successful; she had danced *The Vision of Salome* in Europe, South Africa, India, Australia, and the United States. In England she became an icon of Edwardian decadence and primitivism, like Nijinsky in the Russian Ballet; she was especially popular among effete upper-class young men. Despite rumors that Allan was a lesbian, the image she offered to her audiences was assertively heterosexual. When she became the most notorious female "moral pervert" in England because of the trial, she certainly must have diminished the credibility of female sexual inversion theory, if anyone had been thinking about it. Both her appearance and her reputation thoroughly subverted the stereotype of the masculine, inverted woman.

Pemberton-Billing was a maverick politician and a talented self-publicist and demagogue; in 1916, he started his newspaper *The Imperialist*, which was "Published in the Interest of Purity in Public Life." When the Conservative Party proved unwilling to support his ambition to get into Parliament, he successfully fought the 1916 East Hertfordshire by-election as an independent. In the House of Commons he immediately allied himself with the radical Right, who sought victory without compromise. The following year he absorbed the aims of the new National Party, which advocated conscription up to the age of fifty, closure of all German-owned businesses, internment of enemy aliens, and conscription in Ireland; it opposed the honors system and the use of patronage. Pemberton-Billing took these ideas to the masses, along with proposals for Jewish ghettoes and yellow Star of David badges, by starting the Vigilante Society; his paper, renamed *The Vigilante* in February 1918, came to expound a conspiracy theory "against those of us who seek the salvation of this Empire, as distinct from the international subjugation of the world, as the outcome of this bloody struggle";[24] the conspirators were Jews, Germans, and Bolsheviks who already had the ear of the government and were busy profiteering from the war and inciting the British working men to strike.

Maud Allan's reputation as an icon of active female sexuality made her the perfect vehicle for Pemberton-Billing's attack on the decadent forces of liberalism, pacifism, perversion, and treachery that he maintained were betraying the empire; the traitors he most vilified were the German-Jewish members and advisers of the government. The discourses of primitivism and congenital sexuality were useful to him because they formed part of the racist, misogynist, and homophobic dominant ideology. Unlike the Marquess of Queensberry's libel of Oscar Wilde, there was nothing personal about Pemberton-Billing's selection of Allan as his victim; apart from his pleasure in performance—he had once been an actor—his motivation was political. Lesbophobia and homophobia were inextricable components of the xenophobic patriotic message he was promulgating as part of the radical Right's attempt to bring about the fall of Lloyd George's government.

On January 26, 1918, a front-page article in *The Imperialist,* "The First 47,000," maintained that the chief threat to the empire came from 47,000 homosexuals and lesbians listed in a mysterious German "Black Book"; they had been individually perverted and then black-mailed by German agents over the past twenty years. They ranged from sailors and "youths of the chorus" to "men and women in whose hands the destiny of this Empire rests. . . . wives of men in supreme position. . . . In Lesbian ecstacy [*sic*] the most sacred secrets of State were betrayed." Pemberton-Billing and his possibly insane assistant editor, Captain Harold Spencer, produced this salaciously alarmist fantasy to provoke homophobia and class hatred as well as rage against Germany.

Three weeks later, Marie Corelli sent Pemberton-Billing an advertisement of the forthcoming performance of *Salome,* and the following gnomic announcement appeared in *The Vigilante*:

The Cult of the Clitoris

To be a member of Maud Allen's private performances in Oscar Wilde's "Salome" one has to apply to a Miss Valetta, of 9, Duke Street, Adelphi, W.C. If Scotland Yard were to seize the list of these members, I have no doubt they would secure the names of several thousand of the first 47,000.[25]

It is probable that, as Pemberton-Billing later maintained, almost none of his readers knew what the word *clitoris* meant. But Maud Allan's career as a dancer was threatened by that word, besides the fact that her name was coupled with Oscar Wilde's and the names of the 47,000. Like Wilde in 1895, when the Marquess of Queensberry accused him of "posing as a somdomite [*sic*]," Allan sued. And like Wilde, she found that she herself was on trial; both of them lost their cases. Wilde's reason for suing was obvious: sodomy was punishable by life imprisonment. But there were no laws against lesbianism, and besides, the announcement in *The Vigilante* contains no explicit accusation of sexual perversion or vice. Maud Allan's reasons for suing Pemberton-Billing must be understood in terms of the cultural significance of the word *clitoris.*

Foucault's theory that sexual ideology in Europe during the nineteenth century was productive of titillating secrets and whispers rather than silence provides a useful way of thinking about the apparent paradox that middle-class women were supposedly childlike and innocent, incapable of active sexual desire, and yet lesbians (and nymphomaniacs and women of color) were believed to have a monstrously enlarged clitoris. This was the hidden sign of masculinity in outwardly feminine lesbians. Captain Spencer, who was the actual writer of "The Cult of the Clitoris," asserted in the witness box that he had been told by a medical "authority" that the clitoris is "what remains of the male organ in the female."[26] The enlarged clitoris was a sign of "primitive" sexuality—degeneration to an earlier stage of evolution when the sexes were less clearly differentiated.[27] Maud Allan's recognition of the word *clitoris* revealed her sexual perversion even before the trial began.

The word *perversion* was not usually part of legal proceedings about lesbianism: it was part of the medical language of sexology; lawyers and laymen preferred the high-sounding euphemisms of "morality." In 1920, Radclyffe Hall sued St. George Lane Fox-Pitt for slander because he had said that she was a *"grossly immoral woman"* who had lived with "a most objectionable person," Mabel Batten;[28] Hall's barrister charged that Fox-Pitt had made "as *horrible an accusation* as could be made against any woman in this country" and used words that "could only mean that the plaintiff was an *unchaste and immoral woman who was addicted to unnatural vice.*"[29] The following year, the chancellor, Lord Birkenhead, argued against criminalizing lesbianism because the knowledge of it would "taint" the innocence of the wives and daughters of the patriarchy: "I would be bold enough to say that of every thousand women, taken as a whole, 999 have never even heard a whisper of these practices. Among all these, in the homes of this country . . . the *taint of this noxious and horrible suspicion* is to be imparted."[30] Pemberton-Billing's introduction of the terminology of Krafft-Ebing's *Psychopathia Sexualis* into the Old Bailey made it clear that lesbianism was monstrously perverse as well as morally vicious.

After Spencer and Pemberton-Billing had used the word *clitoris* as a means of inducing Allan to incriminate herself by suing, they discredited her further by introducing congenitalist theory in conjunction with a shocking secret from her past. Her brother Theodore Durrant had been convicted and hanged in San Francisco in 1895 for the brutal murder in a church of two young women. Maud Allan was at school in Berlin at the time and was encouraged by her mother to stay in Europe to dissociate herself from Theodore, which she did.[31] Now Pemberton-Billing used her brother's crime to argue that her disposition to sadism and other forms of "moral perversion" was innate;

he then produced a medical witness who used Krafft-Ebing's categories of sexual perversions to label Allan's performances of *Salome* as sadistic.[32]

It didn't matter exactly what perversions Allan had practiced or that many congenitalist texts failed to condemn homosexuality or lesbianism. The jury found Pemberton-Billing innocent of libel because Maud Allan was associated with the decadent, pro-German, upper-class Asquiths as well as with Wilde; she performed perversion in *Salome*; her brother had committed a particularly perverted murder, and she was an independent, sexually knowledgeable woman. There was no need to examine her clitoris to prove that she was a lesbian. Maud Allan cannot have been a reassuring role model for women who suspected that they might be lesbians or for writers who wanted to explore the possibilities of portraying lesbians in their work. No wonder most representations of sexuality in women's narratives of the 1920s are oblique.

One lesbian, however, was old enough and comfortable enough about her sexuality to satirize the Maud Allan trial in a book that she was writing at the time: Vernon Lee (Violet Paget [1856–1935]) had been at work on *Satan the Waster* since 1915; she completed it in August 1919.[33] In the "Epilogue," Satan uses the latest technology to reveal to Clio, the muse and recorder of history, the "mystery . . . of what was passing behind the stage" during the "Ballet" of the First World War.[34] His cinema and gramophone portray a series of conversations among family members, journalists, political and military leaders, diplomats, and businessmen taking place in various parts of the world. The picture is one of unremitting greed, hypocrisy, deception and self-deception, callousness, cowardice, and pompous stupidity. Toward the end, the topic of peace is raised:

> *The gramophone wheezes. The cinema shows a council chamber full of statesmen.*
>
> *1st Voice*: Don't you think, my lords and gentlemen, that the time might be nearly approaching when it would . . . it might, possibly be just as well to be beginning just to cast an eye on any possible . . . I do not, mark, say *probable* . . . avenues—ahem!—leading to an eventual peace?
>
> *2nd Voice*: Avenues to peace! Almost the most dangerous things in the world! Let alone peace itself, which is, of course, the most dangerous thing of all!

3rd Voice: The name of peace must not be mentioned till they have restored Brobdingnag!

4th Voice: The name of peace must never be mentioned till they have given us back Lilliput!

5th Voice: The name of peace must not be mentioned until I have reannexed the seaboard of Bohemia, the flagstaffs of the sea-kings, the kingdoms of . . .

6th Voice: The name of peace must never be mentioned at all!
The gramophone wheezes. The cinema shows a Court of Law, packed with spectators.

A Voice: The name of peace must never be mentioned by any decent man or woman! Are any of you aware, I wonder, that at this present moment this country harbours in its bosom 47,000 aliens from Sodom and Gomorrah, all busily plotting peace? Does that seem too monstrous for belief? Well, their names and addresses are all registered in a printed book. This young lady, whom I have called as a witness, has actually *seen* the book!

Female Witness: I have. It was shown me by two gentlemen friends, since deceased, at a lunch-party at Greenwich. It was bound in American cloth.

Judicial Voice: Was it, indeed? And did you see the contents of the book?

1st Voice: The contents, my lord, comprised the name of everyone here present who dares to ask pacifist questions.[35]

Vernon Lee reproduces precisely the bullying tone in which Pemberton-Billing conducted his defense, the casual ineffectiveness of Justice Charles Darling, the charmingly feminine vagueness of Eileen Villiers-Stuart, and the absurdity of the invisible German "Black Book" of names.[36] But she also makes absolutely clear that Pemberton-Billing worked on the homophobia of his listeners and readers in order to further the political objective of much of the ruling class: to continue the war as long as possible.

It is conceivable that the negative lesbian stereotypes produced by sexological writings and the law were on the whole more valuable than damaging to lesbians: a negative image can be preferable to a blank when one is struggling with identity. There is plenty of evidence for a new prominence of lesbians during the war; Radclyffe Hall represents lesbians coming into their own in ambulance units behind the lines like the one led by her friend Toupie Lowther.[37]

Indeed, the increased visibility of lesbians may have contributed to the lesbophobic speed with which the jury in the Maud Allan trial produced their verdict; it took them only ninety minutes' deliberation to pronounce Pemberton-Billing innocent. Lord Desart might proclaim a fear that by criminalizing lesbianism one is "going to tell the whole world that there is such an offence, to bring it to the notice of women who have never heard of it, never thought of it, never dreamt of it,"[38] but by 1918 the discrepancy between the rhetoric of the patriarchy and the ways some women could choose to live their lives was considerable.

Tribades, Tommies, Sapphists, Inverts

> Our history includes teen-age crushes, romantic friendships, Boston marriages, theatrical cross-dressing, passing women, bulldykes and prostitutes, butches and femmes, and numerous other identifications which may—and may not—include genital sex.
>
> —Martha Vicinus, "They Wonder to Which Sex I Belong"

In this quotation, Martha Vicinus translates the language of the past—tribade, tommy, sapphist, invert—into familiar contemporary terminology in order to emphasize the multiplicity of lesbian relationships, then and now. We know that dildos were used in sixteenth- and seventeenth-century Europe; that from the 1720s until at least 1755 Charlotte Charke cross-dressed both in the theater and in her everyday life and that for many years she and her partner, living as "Mr. and Mrs. Brown," raised Charke's child together and attempted to eke out a living independently of men; that Anne Lister, unmarried and living with her respectable relatives in Yorkshire, managed between 1817 and 1826 to flirt, make love, and experience orgasm with several other upper-middle-class young women.[39] We have plenty of information, too, about the shared lives of romantic friends, from Eleanor Butler and Sarah Ponsonby, the "Ladies of Llangollen" who eloped in 1778, set up house together in rural Wales, and lived together openly and respectably for more than fifty years, to the nineteenth-century educational reformers Constance Maynard and Louisa Lumsden, who spoke of each other as wife and husband respectively.[40]

The Ladies' sex life has been the subject of speculation for two hundred years now and forms part of the continuing debate about what, if anything, romantic friends did in bed.[41] Anne Lister, who visited the Ladies in 1822, certainly had her suspicions. "I cannot help thinking surely it was not platonic," she wrote. "Heaven forgive me, but I look within myself & doubt. I feel the infirmity of our nature and hesitate to pronounce such attachments uncemented by something more tender still than friendship."[42]

To me it has always seemed likely that women who love each other and routinely share a bed, as women did in the eighteenth and nineteenth centuries, would embrace, and then explore, and then want to repeat the experience. I think that Anne Lister was exceptional not in her sexual activity but in the fact that her diaries show her creating a language to describe it; Terry Castle has argued persuasively that Lister used the word "kiss," for example, to denote orgasm.[43]

At the end of the nineteenth century, however, Constance Maynard supplied a complete contrast to Lister: she loved a number of women colleagues and students during her life but did not recognize her love as sexual because she thought desire was exclusively heterosexual. In her unpublished 1887 autobiography she wrote, "It is all very well to call my loneliness 'sex feeling,' but I can honestly say my thoughts never strayed to a man."[44] Maynard accepted unquestioningly the culture's conflation of women's desire not only with heterosexuality but with reproduction.

What had happened since the Ladies of Llangollen and Anne Lister was Darwinism and its progeny; the discourse of selective breeding was developing into eugenics; evolution had replaced Christianity as the ideology of empire. By the 1900s, evolutionists, eugenicists, most sexologists, and a disquietingly large number of feminists and socialists all believed that white middle-class women had a particular duty to reproduce efficiently because they were the "carriers of the race."[45]

So despite the lesbian multiplicity of earlier generations, their dildoes and disguises and private linguistic exuberance, the dominant ideology of motherhood was particularly repressive of British middle-class lesbians growing up between 1890 and 1920; most were further dissuaded from claiming their identity or acting, even silently, upon their desire by a mounting cacophony of conflicting popular beliefs. All women were considered sexually passive; active sexual desire in a woman was a mark of degeneracy. All lesbians were serpentine, vampirish predators like Miss Wade in *Little Dorrit* or Clare Hartill in Clemence Dane's *Regiment of Women*; all lesbians were barren because they were male souls trapped in women's bodies, which they had distorted into mythically mannish forms. Only aristocrats or prostitutes were lesbian; in either case, they were degenerate. It's a wonder that the writers I consider managed to represent lesbianism at all.

Edwardian Closets: Bloomsbury and Chelsea

> In her twenties, Virginia Stephen was sexually confused and uncertain. She could make private jokes in her own letters to Violet or Madge or Vanessa about feeling hot and ready for affection, but there was no acceptable outlet for her erotic feelings about women—as there were accredited ways of behaving for the apostolic Cambridge homosexuals. . . . Except as a joke, she did not define herself as a lesbian (or, as she would say, as a "Sapphist"): it was not a concept for her, or a group for her to join, or a political identity. Instead she was poised between incompatible identities and roles.
> —Hermione Lee, *Virginia Woolf* [46]

Virginia Stephen married Leonard Woolf when she was thirty, in 1912; ten years later she started writing *Mrs. Dalloway* and met Vita Sackville-West. By then, lesbianism was indeed a concept for her, although she never became a player in the lesbian subculture of the 1920s. I want to distinguish Virginia Woolf—along with Rose Allatini and Sylvia Townsend Warner, two other writers whose behavior was to some extent bisexual—from lesbians such as Valentine Ackland, Bryher, and Radclyffe Hall, whose female masculinity made conformity more difficult and encouraged earlier recognition of their desire for women. The latter identified themselves as lesbians even if they didn't use the word, and they acted on that identification comparatively early in their lives. (Vita Sackville-West belongs in both these groups—but then, she wasn't middle class; blessed with "all the supple ease of the aristocracy," she could afford to ignore, and perhaps enjoy, scandal.[47])

Woolf's 1922 memoir, "Old Bloomsbury," can be read as an account of her sexual education during the "Thursday Evenings" from 1905, when she joined her sister and brothers at 46 Gordon Square, to 1908. First, there is sheer delight in intellectual talk, in escaping the constant preoccupation with "love and marriage" in conversations at Hyde Park Gate,[48] followed by the hope that "things could go on like this, in abstract argument, without dressing for dinner."[49] But this illusion is quickly shattered by her sister Vanessa's contented prediction that they will all marry; Virginia feels "a horrible necessity impending over us . . . just as we had achieved freedom and happiness." Celibacy is freedom; marriage must be constraint.

After Vanessa's marriage in February 1907, the Thursday evenings continue at Fitzroy Square with more or less the same cast of characters, but Virginia finds that she is "intolerably bored." Celibacy is no longer enough. What she wants is a context in which she can "fizz up":

> The society of buggers . . . has this drawback—with buggers one cannot, as nurses say, show off. Something is always suppressed, held down. Yet this showing off, which is not copulating, necessarily, nor altogether being in love, is one of the great delights, one of the chief necessities of life. Only then does all effort cease; one ceases to be honest, one ceases to be clever. One fizzes up into some absurd delightful effervescence of soda water or champagne through which one sees the world tinged with all the colors of the rainbow.[50]

The memoir goes on to suggest that dining with Lady Ottoline Morrell at Bedford Square could provide the missing requisites for fizzing up. I've no doubt that Woolf could fizz up when she was speaking with both men and women, but she states in a famous 1930 letter to Ethel Smyth "I only want to show off to women. Women alone stir my imagination."[51] And her letter of October 1, 1905, to Violet Dickinson describes Virginia's boredom with "two Cambridge youths" (Sydney Saxon-Turner and R. G. Hawtrey) who are visiting the Stephens in Cornwall. "They sit silent, absolutely silent, all the time; occasionally they escape to a corner and chuckle over a Latin joke," she writes. "Oh women are my line and not these inanimate creatures."[52]

Fizzing up is what occurs throughout Woolf's life in her letters to women with whom she is "in love": Dickinson, Sackville-West, her sister Vanessa, or Smyth. There are examples in her letters to Sackville-West from 1925 right up to a rhapsody about butter on February 4, 1941. In a 1927 letter to Vita, who was spending three months with her husband Harold Nicolson in Persia, she writes,

> Do not buy me a coat. As you know I utterly refuse and abominate presents; and I dont want to spend a penny on clothes this summer. Last summer I spent £12.10: this summer 61/2d. . . . I'm that sick of making money I'd rather walk into Argyll House naked,

than earn another guinea. But if you have bought it, of course I'll joyfully flaunt in it, in the Haymarket, d'you remember, in the dusk. Sybils dropped me. Everybody's gone—no, there's Eddy coming to tea—We linger like ghosts in a world of incredible beauty—I take back any insult to England. I've just been buying cigarettes in the Tottenham Court road—rivers of silver, breasted by plumes of gold: omnibus and shops equally beautiful—Why go to Persia when the T. Ct. Rd. is like that? [53]

Another example is the letter Woolf wrote to Vanessa while she was anxiously awaiting her response to *To the Lighthouse*. It starts, "No letter from you—But I see how it is" and invents a fantastic, curiously matter-of-fact conversation between Vanessa and Duncan Grant about the impossibility of writing to Virginia about an unreadable book when the inkpot is full of dead insects.[54] The tone here is comically, absurdly affectionate in contrast to the flirtatious femme lyricism that pervades the letter to Vita.

Woolf's fizziest letters are to the women whose maternal permissiveness makes showing off possible: "Only then does all effort cease; one ceases to be honest, one ceases to be clever." Showing off is not sex—"not copulating, necessarily, nor altogether being in love"—but, like being in love, it can dissolve one's inhibitions in a kind of verbal orgasm. "The absurd delightful effervescence of soda water or champagne" is primarily an image of social interaction; it is about the erotic excitement of talk, not sex. In the 1922 memoir, Woolf's main theme is breaking the compulsory silence imposed on middle-class women: she celebrates her learning, through conversation with gay men, that she could speak about sexual desire. And soon after reading "Old Bloomsbury" to the Memoir Club, she started the writing of specifically lesbian desire in *Mrs. Dalloway*: its unhappy repression by the monstrous Miss Kilman, its sublimation by Lady Bruton, its willed suppression by Clarissa Dalloway despite her memory of its expression in a lost, interrupted moment of romance in her youth.

Speaking personally about lesbianism was not something Woolf wanted to do in 1922. So the memoir continues with the famous description of Lytton Strachey's dramatic entrance one evening, uttering the word "semen":

A flood of the sacred fluid seemed to overwhelm us. Sex permeated our conversation. The word bugger was never far from our lips. We discussed copulation with the same excitement and open-

ness that we had discussed the nature of good. . . . We had known
everything but we had never talked. Now we talked of nothing else.[55]

Woolf describes an education in speaking about buggery and copulation. There is no mention of sapphism. But I think we can assume
that she had "known everything" about that, too, before the war.
There is a 1909 letter to her from Vanessa teasing her about her
sapphist tendencies, and she had been studying Greek since 1897.[56]
So lesbianism was both a concept and a feeling for Virginia Woolf
before the war, but, as Hermione Lee says, it was not yet something
to be spoken about seriously.

There were, however, some women in London before the war
who were sufficiently out of the closet to talk seriously about lesbian
history; Radclyffe Hall was introduced to them by her lover, Mabel
Batten. Hall was twenty-seven when they met in 1907, and Batten
was fifty; she was a society lady and a singer and composer who had
had several known affairs—one of them reputedly with Edward VII
before he became king; her husband was a retired colonial adminis-
trator twenty-five years her senior. Batten had been to some extent a
(hetero)sexual outlaw as a young woman in India and London; she
now had a number of lesbian friends of her own generation, including Winnaretta Singer and Ethel Smyth.[57] For these women, lesbianism was certainly much more than a concept, but it was also fairly
safe; they were hedged around with the respectability of wealth, property, and middle age. Younger lesbians, too, visited the flat Hall and
Batten shared in Cadogan Square; Toupie Lowther was there at some
point before the war, when she formed a women's ambulance unit
and won the Croix de Guerre; Mabel Batten called her "Toupée."[58]
By 1912 Batten, Hall, and Singer were developing "a mutual interest
in ancient Greek culture, notably the works of Sappho."[59]

This prewar lesbian community forms a marked contrast to
Bloomsbury in average age, gender, political beliefs, and pursuits.
Apart from Ethel Smyth's feminism, in which she was particularly
activist during these years, serving a stint in prison alongside Emme-
line Pankhurst, this group was patriotic and conservative.

Hall was perhaps the most conventional member of this comfortably closeted circle. She was the least socially confident, despite
her wealth, and the most troubled by being a lesbian. Her outraged
conformity is much in evidence in a letter to the *Pall Mall Gazette*
on March 4, 1912, the day after the suffragettes' famous window-

breaking demonstration. Hall wrote, "Sir—Have the Suffragettes no spark of patriotism left, that they can spread revolt and hamper the Government in this moment of grave national danger? According to Mrs. Pankhurst, they are resorting to the methods of the miners! Since when have English ladies regulated their conduct by that of the working classes?"[60] Hall wrote anonymously, signing herself "A Former Suffragist," so I doubt that Ethel Smyth knew about this letter; prior to the demonstration, Smyth had instructed her friend Mrs. Pankhurst in the art of throwing stones, and she was one of the ninety-six women arrested on March 3.[61] The "grave national danger" Hall refers to was the miners' strike, which had started on February 29. The language of her letter, with its assumptions about patriotism and ruling-class loyalty and its distancing of the writer from the English ladies who had behaved so deplorably, seems so extremely patriarchal as to verge on caricature. In Hall's politics as in everything else, she was all too sincere.

Radclyffe Hall's espousal of imperialist, patriarchal values reflected her own interests—she had inherited a considerable fortune when she was twenty-one—but was also a reaction to the sense of rootlessness that made her long all her life for insider status. Growing up "foreign" in conformist England has always been sufficiently difficult to encourage swift assimilation. Hall's father, who had left her mother before his daughter was born, was a shadowy, romanticized figure who died when she was eighteen. Her American mother, who seems always to have resented the child, soon married Alberto Visetti, an Italian music professor. Beaten by her mother and probably sexually abused by her stepfather, Hall had a meaningful family connection only with her grandmother, Granny Diehl. I have no doubt that reaction against her childhood environment contributed to Hall's conformity and to the Colonel Blimpish persona she so often assumed, as in her repudiation of feminism in her letter to the *Pall Mall Gazette*.[62]

Apart from attachments to three young women, each of whom left her for a man, Hall's life in her twenties lacked purpose until she met Mabel Batten.[63] When George Batten and Granny Diehl died within days of one another in 1910, the two women had the money and the freedom to live together. They did so in Chelsea and in Worcestershire, among the Malvern Hills that surround Morton, the patriarchal Eden of *The Well of Loneliness*, until Mabel Batten's death six years later.

Batten encouraged Hall to take her writing seriously and gave her both pleasure and confidence as a lover and a lesbian. She also called her John, the name Hall was to use for the rest of her life. According to Michael Baker, Batten's love filled "the all-important emotional gap left by John's mother."[64] More specifically, Batten as the maternal beloved gave Hall "consent to [lesbian] activity," while as femme lover she validated and encouraged John's female masculinity.[65] An aspect of butch desire is for the desire of the femme: she wants to be loved for her masculinity, which is what the heterosexual culture most clearly rejects.[66]

Radclyffe Hall's appearance is so often confused with that of her protagonist, Stephen Gordon, that it is hard to keep in mind how comparatively cautious her butch performance really was. She did not cut her long, blond hair until 1920, when, as Laura Doan has demonstrated, short hair became fashionable.[67] She did not wear pants in public until the 1930s, although the long cape and boots she sometimes wore in the 1920s could disguise the fact that she was wearing a skirt. In a 1913 photograph of Hall and Batten on the veranda of their house in Malvern, Hall is sitting on a step at Batten's feet; their dog, Rufus, almost conceals her long skirt, and her hair is hidden by her hat.[68] Her hat, jacket, tie, and shoes make her look like a young man in this photograph, but it is important to remember that she did not look like one in life. She may have wished to present herself as a lesbian, but, at least until 1928, her appearance could be read as simply eccentric; the British tolerance of "eccentrics" has often been a convenient dismissal of what might otherwise prove embarrassing.

Hall evidently enjoyed her gender ambiguity in the photographs she posed for, but her masquerade, as long as she wore a skirt, was not necessarily intended as a challenge to patriarchal authority; she wanted to be accepted by the patriarchy, not to subvert it. It is clear, however, from her theatrical self-presentation that from the time of her relationship with Mabel Batten onward she wanted that acceptance on her own terms, and she was less and less willing to conceal her lesbian identity. The relation between her lesbian politics and her conservatism was to become clearer as she absorbed sexological theory during the twenties and thirties. In 1920, however, her need to belong to the ruling class (and gender) was strong enough to lead her to believe that because she was on the side of the establishment the establishment was on her side, too; she risked appealing for justification to its most patriarchal institution, the law. Despite the discouraging precedents set by Oscar Wilde in 1895 and Maud Allan in 1918, she defended her own reputation and that of her dead lover by bringing a slander suit against St. George Lane Fox-Pitt, who had implied that they were lesbians: Fox-Pitt had said to two of the officers of the Society for Psychical Research that Hall was a "thoroughly immoral woman" who had lived with "a most objectionable person," Mabel Batten. He had also said that Hall "has great influence over Lady Una Troubridge, and has come between her and her husband and wrecked the admiral's home"[69]

Lesbian Litigation: Spiritualism and Slander

Radclyffe Hall's 1920 slander suit provides a remarkable instance of the dominant culture's continuing determination that lesbianism remain invisible; it is also a painful example of the kind of public humiliation that being in the closet can entail even today. Hall sued Fox-Pitt to prove that his assertions about (lesbian) "immorality" were false. However successful Hall's masquerade as a woman of fashion and however imperative the conspiracy of silence about lesbianism may have been, in that context Hall must have been perceived as both lesbian and ashamed.

The intensity of Hall's need to identify with the patriarchy made her blind to the fact that she was the patriarchy's Other because she was a woman, and a sexually active woman, and a lesbian. Her lack of awareness involved her in an unnecessary lawsuit which put her in a humiliating false position: in defending Mabel Batten's honor, she was forced not only to deny her own lesbian sexuality but to acquiesce in her lawyer's characterization of lesbianism as "unnatural vice." The quixotic nature of her lawsuit becomes very clear when we compare her motivation with the reasons that induced Maud Allan to sue Pemberton-Billing in 1918 and those that impelled Marianne Woods and Jane Pirie to sue Dame Helen Cumming Gordon in 1811 in Edinburgh: they sued for libel because their livelihoods were threatened as well as their "reputations."

Following Mabel Batten's death in 1916, Hall became obsessed by grief and guilt. Her relationship with Una Troubridge had started nine months earlier; Batten certainly knew about it and was troubled by it just as she had known and felt upset about Hall's previous year-long affair with Phoebe Hoare. There was no indication while Batten was alive that Hall and Troubridge's relationship would be any more serious than the earlier one, but Hall's desire to be assured of her dead lover's forgiveness led her to consult a medium, Mrs. Osborne Leonard, who convinced Hall and Troubridge that they were in communication with Mabel Batten's spirit. This spiritual triangle became a central part of their lives and was to last for twenty years. It is the explanation of Hall's dedication of *The Well of Loneliness* to "Our Three Selves": Mabel Batten, Una Troubridge, and herself.

By 1920 Hall and Troubridge had become prominent members of the Society for Psychical Research (SPR) and had had an article about their findings in their séances with Mrs. Leonard published in the society's *Proceedings*. Hall had been proposed for election to the society's council. At this point Admiral Ernest Troubridge, who had finally signed the deed of separation from Una only the previous year, ran into Fox-Pitt, a member of the SPR council, at his club. Fox-Pitt gave Troubridge a copy of the paper Una Troubridge and Hall had written; it deeply disturbed the admiral, who convinced Fox-Pitt that "Miss Radclyffe Hall had somehow exploited the Society's authority to gain a pernicious influence over Una for her own purposes. He left little doubt in Fox-Pitt's mind as to what those purposes were and expressed his outrage that the Society should countenance such goings-on."[70]

So the source of Fox-Pitt's remarks about Hall's and Batten's immorality is a scene of patriarchal bonding; he is defending the honor of a "wronged" husband.[71] When his allegations were reported to Hall by the secretary of the SPR and the editor of the SPR *Proceedings*, she felt the need for action; her solicitor wrote Fox-Pitt a letter demanding an apology for his slander. Fox-Pitt refused, so Hall, according to Michael Baker, "had no alternative but to sue."[72] Hall trapped herself in a risky and humiliating lawsuit primarily because she was grieving and felt guilty but also because she adhered to upper-class male traditions about honor and chivalry—suing being the twentieth-century alternative to dueling—and because she cared very much what the patriarchy thought of her.[73]

During the trial Fox-Pitt defended himself with the absurd contention that his remarks had referred not to Hall and Batten's sexual behavior but to Hall's abilities as a psychical researcher. He also asserted under cross-examination that he had called Mabel Batten "objectionable" because her name "had been coupled with several men."[74] I wish this example of lesbian invisibility were more remarkable than it is; as Lucy Bland has pointed out, "in the early twentieth-century . . . what constituted the 'sexual' was still seen as essentially heterosexual."[75] And most lesbians, in most communities, continue to be invisible as sexually active women today.

Hall's slander case ended in a Pyrrhic victory. When Fox-Pitt appealed the verdict a new trial was ordered, but Hall's solicitor advised her to drop the case. All she had gotten out of it was five hundred pounds, some embarrassing publicity, and the knowledge that she had been perceived as a lesbian who was ashamed of being one. Her slander suit was certainly courageous, but it also reflects the naïveté of her identification with the patriarchy: she assumed that the law was on her side. I want next to contrast Hall's 1920 lawsuit with a later one involving two lesbians from the opposite end of the political spectrum, a 1935 libel case in which two of the defendants—significantly *not* the plaintiffs, since by that time neither of them had much faith in the majesty of the law—were Sylvia Townsend Warner and Valentine Ackland.

Love and Libel: "Literary Ladies"

Radclyffe Hall was forty when she sued Fox-Pitt in defense of Mabel Batten's honor in 1920. She was known mainly as a breeder of dogs and a writer of verse, several volumes of which had been printed by the publishers John and Edward Bumpus at her own expense; some of her poems had been set to music. She was working on her first novel, *The Unlit Lamp*, which would be published four years later. Her politics were still deeply conservative and would remain so for the rest of her life; they included "allegiance to the ruling class, inherited status, antipathy to communists and Jews."[76] Sylvia Townsend Warner was forty-one when she and her lover were summoned to appear at the Dorchester Assizes in 1935. They were being sued for libel by a neighbor who was renting the East Chaldon vicarage and abusing her young women servants. Unlike Hall, Warner was used to working for a living, as a musicologist until the success of *Lolly Willowes* in 1926 and subsequently as a writer. She had published three remarkable novels, two collections of short stories, and four books of poems in the career that was to delight, frustrate, and absorb her for the rest of her life. In the spring of 1935, she and Ackland joined the Communist Party of Great Britain.

Warner's early political and literary development can be traced from her sharp focus on the class system in her 1916 essay about her experiences as a munitions worker, through her early poems about Rosa Luxemburg and the lives of Dorset laborers, to the overtly political satire of imperialism and the class/sex/gender system that informs her three 1920s fantasy novels. Her politics, like her writing, were rooted in her lifelong consciousness of the manifold evils of the class system.

The poverty of the villagers of East Chaldon in Dorset is the subject of many of Warner's early short stories and sketches. But her most politically impassioned and memorable representation of East Chaldon or "Love Green" is in *Opus 7* (1931), a rhymed narrative satire in the manner of George Crabbe that celebrates a green-thumbed old woman who finances her addiction to gin through the sale of flowers from her mysteriously luxuriant garden. Warner depicts the rural gloom of the twenties following the cannibalistic prosperity of the war years "when Europe feasted well: bodies were munched in thousands." Now, in contrast, war babies are simply bastards, soldiers turned laborers can't tell whether their bones ache "for tillage or defence," and the rustics in the pub grumble about the tax on their drink; they "curse a government which could so fleece/on spirits under proof, and call it Peace."[77] *Opus 7* should be read alongside Valentine Ackland's 1936 book about farm laborers, *Country Conditions*, and Warner's evidence about the lives of village servant girls given in the "Vicarage Case" libel trial. Together, these three texts demonstrate the two women's certainty that the condition of working-class life in quaint old English country villages "was a grim and melancholy thing."[78] They were sued for acting on this certainty.

Opus 7 was completed in July 1930, two months before Warner and Ackland started sharing an East Chaldon cottage together. Much of both women's political writing during the thirties would contextualize the poverty and drudgery endured by farm laborers and their families within the increasingly oppressive conservative politics of the Depression and Appeasement years. Their shared political concerns were intensified after October 11, 1930, when they became lovers following an evening of village activism. It was at this point that Warner definitively ended her secret sexual relationship with

Percy C. Buck, the married man with whom she had been involved for seventeen years. For Warner and Ackland in the thirties, their political writing, local and international activism, and "deviant" sexuality were inextricably intertwined.

By 1930, Warner and Ackland had known each other for some years, and Valentine, who had come out as a lesbian several years earlier, knew that she was attracted to Sylvia,[79] but to Sylvia their first lovemaking came as a complete surprise. As her joyful diary entry on October 12, 1930 demonstrates, being a lesbian outsider came very naturally indeed to Warner: "It was a bridal of earth and sky, and we spent the morning lying in the hollowed tump of the Five Maries, listening to the wind blowing over our happiness, and talking about torpedoes, and starting up at footsteps. It is so natural to be hunted, and intuitive. Feeling safe and respectable is much more of a strain."[80] The Five Maries are the ancient tumuli that crown the ridge to the north of East Chaldon; the "tump" is just off the Drove, the lane that winds for a mile or two from the village to the main road. Everyone in East Chaldon knew the lovers, yet they immediately took their love into the open air, rejoicing in risk and freedom—the freedom-fighting lesbian politics that involved Sylvia and Valentine in the local activism that resulted in the 1935 "Vicarage Case."

In 1935 Sylvia Townsend Warner, Valentine Ackland, and Llewellyn Powys were sued for libel by Miss Joan Inez Drusilla Stevenson.[81] Joan Stevenson was a social worker—the "organising secretary for the Voluntary Association for Mental Welfare in Dorset"; she had rented the Chaldon vicarage and moved in, together with her mother Katherine Stevenson, in Easter of 1930.[82] Katherine Stevenson was paid one pound per week for each young woman she took in for domestic training; they were sent to her by various county councils; newspaper accounts of the libel trial describe her as keeping a "training home for girls of backward mental development."[83] By October, the village was seriously concerned about these young women's welfare. T. F. Powys described the situation to his brother Llewellyn on October 16: "The woman at the Vicarage Miss Stevenson has four mad girls to do her work out of an institution. One ran away—three times. I fear that Miss Stevenson is a very wicked woman, and her mother is worse. Efforts are being made to do something in the matter—Sylvia Warner is the person for that work."[84]

Warner and Ackland had indeed begun to take action on October 11. At tea with the Powyses they heard about Lily Roberts, the runaway, who had been brought back by the police; apparently Katherine Stevenson had been heard telling P. C. Wintle he had been too kind to her. Warner and Ackland immediately called at the vicarage. The next day, Warner described their visit in her diary:

> The dog bayed and padded, we saw it moving like water in the dusky house, then the old woman came, and tried to get our reason for calling from us, but we were firm and sinister, and would call again. . . . A rapid dinner, cooked with fury, and eaten with loins girded, and we were walking up for a third time, I telling Valentine what a comfort her pistol was. Miss Stevenson opened the door, and let us into an empty room. . . . She shook like a blancmange, and kept on trying to ingratiate herself into our assistance by laughter and uneasy cryings. She got little from me, and nothing from Valentine, who sat white and motionless like Justice, while this execrable woman gave herself away, saying the girl was sent her for special treatment (the whole housework), and had sex mania (and was left alone with Wallace in the cellar), and had the mentality of a child of six (and was shut up all day with the old hag and that dog), and had actually been comforted and called Miss by P. C. Wintle. But we frightened her, and kept her taken in, and so left her. As we walked from the door, speechless, Valentine shook her stick in the air like a squire. Righteous indignation is a beautiful thing, and lying exhausted on the rug I watched it flame in her with severe geometrical flames.
> And then we went to bed.[85]

The exuberant irony here—"we were firm and sinister," the melodramatic pistol, Valentine in the role of outraged country gentleman— is typical of Warner's style in the twenties and early thirties; the delight in the absurd pervades her early novels and stories. But her concern about Lily Roberts is serious; her book *The True Heart* is an attack on such concepts as "sex mania," especially as applied to the poor and the so-called feebleminded. Warner despised the stereotypes of "degeneracy" and eugenics, but presumably Joan Stevenson, exploitative employer and social worker, was an adherent of these key ingredients of the imperialist ideological stew.[86]

This narrative's sequel also needs to be read: after Sylvia and Valentine went up to their separate bedrooms, the conversation through the partition wall ended in Valentine's saying, as Warner records in her diary, "'I think I am utterly loveless.' The forsaken grave wail of her voice smote me, and had me up, and through the door, and at her bedside. There I stayed, till I got into her bed, and found love there." The euphoria of political activism meshes with that of desire; as the diary entry notes, "the Vicarage led to love."

It was also to lead to considerable anxiety and expense. The villagers' concern about the young women at the vicarage increased as the years passed. Betty Lucas, the postwoman, told Warner that "one of the girls had implored her to post a letter to her parents, but [she] had been forbidden by Mrs. Stevenson to deliver letters to the girls or take letters from them."[87] Another girl "escap[ed] by means of sheets from a bedroom."[88] Passers-by frequently heard the girls crying and saw them doing outdoor work that seemed too heavy for them. Mrs. Paine, a shepherd's wife who lived next door, told Warner that "cries of distress came from the vicarage on several occasions early in the morning and in the evening."[89] The girls were not allowed to mix with the villagers because of their "sexual mania," which, according to Katherine Stevenson, made it "impossible to let them go anywhere unattended."[90] Their lives must have been truly miserable. So in 1934, Llewellyn Powys circulated a petition that was signed by forty-two people and sent to the vicar, the Stevensons' landlord. It urged that their lease should not be renewed until there had been an investigation by the Dorset County Council. A copy was sent to the council, which was associated with the Dorset Voluntary Association for Mental Welfare, Joan Stevenson's employers; the Stevensons had quite a lot to lose.

Warner and Ackland, who were living in Norfolk then, wrote separately to the vicar and the council. In reply, they received a letter from Joan Stevenson's solicitors charging them, along with Powys and a West Chaldon farmer, James Cobb, with libel. An apology was demanded. At this point Warner and Ackland would have been willing to apologize; they were short of money, unlike Hall, and also unlike Hall, they were realists. But the document they were asked to sign still made them liable to pay the Stevensons for any "loss or damage [sustained] as a result of [their] statements."[91] So they refused to sign it and were consequently sued for libel. When the jury found all four petitioners guilty of acting with malice against the Stevensons, their financial penalties were considerable. Ackland and Warner had to pay fifty pounds each to the Stevensons, and their costs came to a "staggering" 733 pounds, 15 shillings, and threepence.[92]

Nonetheless, the villagers' petition had succeeded in getting the vicarage inspected by a doctor for the National Society for the Prevention of Cruelty to Children. He found some "borderline cases" and one "feeble-minded girl" at the vicarage and called upon Mrs. Stevenson to notify the board of her reception of this girl. He assumed Miss Stevenson would in the future "be very much under surveillance."[93] It is hard to say whether or not this was the case; the Stevensons left Chaldon in 1937; they may well have continued exploiting young women elsewhere, but the petitioners had at least been justified.

Warner's law case, then, arose from her concern about the abuse of the powerless: she wanted social, not personal, justice. It is significant that she was sued, rather than being the one to sue: she didn't believe that the majesty of the law would actually work for the oppressed. By 1935, she was starting to believe instead in the law of the people.

When Warner appeared in court, she had just completed *Summer Will Show*, a love story that takes place in Paris during the 1848 revolution. The narrative, like that of *The Well of Loneliness*, is a bildungsroman; here, Sophia Willoughby comes out first as a lesbian and then as a communist. At the novel's end, the revolution has failed: her beloved has died defending the barricades, and Sophia has been devastated by grief, but on the last page she is completely absorbed in reading *The Communist Manifesto*. The implication is that her life is far from over although she may never love again. Whereas Hall's Stephen Gordon dedicates her doomed, lonely future to writing novels that will make inversion acceptable, Warner's Sophia will fight the injustices of capitalism together with her communist comrades; she has transformed from an upper-class bigot into a revolutionary.

Warner's lesbian politics were both internationalist and intensely local. Her career as an activist started in 1930, with Valentine Ackland at the vicarage. But her three 1920s novels already reflect her deepening criticism of imperialism, war, and the class and sex/gender systems. I read them in the light of Arnold Rattenbury's uncompromising statement, "However bewitched her pen, however bewitching, she lived wholly in an unambiguous world where the only dignity lies in taking sides. The books, as well as the author, are always partisan."[94] Even before she became a communist or a lesbian, Warner had become a partisan of the disempowered, representing in her writing the lives of the barely visible; living in London in her thirties as a sexually active spinster, she gave agency and voice to those whom society silenced. Her first novel, *Lolly Willowes*, transforms a depressed spinster into a perversely independent witch; by her second and third novels, *Mr. Fortune's Maggot* and *The True Heart*, Warner has begun to explore lives much further away from her own, starting to experiment with her own daring forms of (lesbian-) feminist crosswriting.

2

IMPERIAL IDEOLOGY AND LESBIAN WRITING

Lesbian Crosswriting

Lesbian crosswriting is a literary practice that most often transposes the otherwise unrepresentable lives of invisible, silenced, or simply closeted lesbians into narratives about gay men. Gay men's crosswriting, in contrast, generally transforms homosexual into heterosexual romance. Between 1918 and 1929 Rose Allatini, Virginia Woolf, and Sylvia Townsend Warner chose to crosswrite representations of sexuality in *Despised and Rejected* (Allatini), *Mrs. Dalloway* (Woolf), and *The True Heart* and *Mr. Fortune's Maggot* (Warner). This choice reflected both their opposition to imperial ideology and their consciousness of deviance from the sexual roles that ideology prescribed for women. Their narratives contrast with those of their contemporaries Clemence Dane and Radclyffe Hall, whose ostensibly naturalistic representations of doomed or dangerous lesbians demonstrate the difficulty of combining adherence to the dominant ideology with acceptance of the lesbianism they so openly depict. Dane's *Regiment of Women* and Hall's *The Well of Loneliness* both end in a veritable welter of lesbian panic.

Both lesbian and gay crosswriting and the satirical fantasy of such sexual radicals as Oscar Wilde, Vernon Lee, Ronald Firbank, and Sylvia Townsend Warner are strategies of displacement and disguise for those who feel that they are sexual outlaws; such strategies are particularly apparent in gay men's writing following the trials of Oscar Wilde. The sensationalist press coverage of his conviction inhibited homosexual activity, including gay writing, for many decades.[1] Maud Allan's sensational and unsuccessful 1918 libel suit against Noel Pemberton-Billing made representations of lesbianism, too, both more easily recognizable and more dangerous than before. It is useful to contextualize the lesbian crosswriters of the 1920s within a homosexual narrative tradition of sexual radicalism that can be traced back to the 1885 Labouchère Amendment criminalizing acts of "gross indecency" between men.

Wilde's crosswriting of homosexuality in his 1890s comedies intensifies their camp absurdity; in *The Importance of Being Earnest*, for example, Algernon invents "an invaluable permanent invalid named Bunbury," ostensibly as an excuse for a gay young heterosexual bachelor's absences from home.[2] Bunburying, however, functions also as code for the masquerades and subterfuges of late Victorian homosexual life. E. M. Forster similarly transposes gay into heterosexual desire in his ebullient romance *A Room with a View* (1908).[3] Not all male crosswriting is "comic," however. George Moore's *A Drama in Muslin* (1886) was completed before the Labouchère Amendment became law and reflects its writer's sexual and political ambivalence. It contains a serious critique of colonial as well as sex/gender oppression.

Moore's transgender crosswriting is very clear indeed; his main focus is on a group of young women who endure the humiliating ordeal of the Dublin marriage market. This heterosexual plot includes both a lesbian subplot and a politically radical examination of the landlord/tenant conflict in County Mayo. The loving relationship between Moore's protagonist, Alice Barton, and Cecilia Cullen, her intellectual, hunchbacked schoolfriend, is doomed; Alice eventually marries a man of her own choice and escapes Cecilia's unhappiness and her own exploitation by her callous, greedy mother. On their way to England, Alice and her husband witness "one of those scenes for which Ireland is so infamously famous—an eviction";[4] they pay the evicted family's rent but can do nothing more to improve the lot of the Irish peasantry.

By 1880 the Irish Land League organized by Michael Davitt and Charles Stewart Parnell had two hundred thousand members, and George Moore had found himself unable to live on the rents that his uncle/agent could no longer collect from his angry, destitute tenants.

He gave up his carefree life in Paris and returned to Moore Hall in County Mayo. His depiction of the landlords' greed and the tenants' destitution in *A Drama of Muslin* reflects his ambivalence as a landlord just as Cecilia Cullen's lonely despair may reflect his homosexual panic.[5]

The most obvious examples of lesbian crosswriting are historical novels—adventure stories such as Bryher's *The Player's Boy* (1953) and *Roman Wall* (1954); romances such as Mary Renault's *The Last of the Wine* (1956), *The Mask of Apollo* (1966), *Fire from Heaven* (1969), and *The Praise Singer* (1972); or fictionalized cultural histories such as Marguerite Yourcenar's *Memoirs of Hadrian* (1951) and *The Abyss* (1968).[6] Other writers explore the connections between the class and sex/gender systems by contrasting middle-class with working-class gay men, as Sylvia Townsend Warner does in her representation of Crusoe, *The Flint Anchor*'s Victorian bisexual sailor. The desire of middle-class lesbians (and gay men such as Edward Carpenter and E. M. Forster) to escape the stifling middle-class silence about sexuality can lead such writers to idealize class or racial Others, reversing rather than calling into question the prevalent stereotypes of primitivism and degeneration theory. Some lesbian writers, also, were drawn beyond literary transgenderism to explore forbidden love in the form of sister/brother incest, distanced and romanticized by Marguerite Yourcenar in the sixteenth-century Naples of "Anna, Soror" but snugly domesticated by Warner in an English small-town setting between the two world wars in "A Love Match." These privileged, white, middle-class women crossed the boundaries of custom and taboo: their imagined worlds obliquely reflected both their lives in the sexual borderlands ("too limited, or else too secret" to be represented more directly) and their experience of the "cultural tyranny" that kept most lesbians in the closet.[7]

The lesbian crosswriters of the First World War and the twenties draw on an old tradition of crosswriting by women that simply transposes gender: (heterosexual) writers escape the limitations of their experience and power by crosswriting as men. Mary Shelley provides a clear example when she adopts the voice of heroic moderation as homosocial, heterosexual Lionel Verney in *The Last Man* (1826). This is in part a war novel, containing a female soldier, "lost, dying Evadne," who cross-dresses not primarily to fight but to search for her beloved on a battlefield in Greece.[8] Shelley represents national politics, revolutionary war, global plague, and solitary survival through her male narrator; the women in *The Last Man*, on the other hand, are concerned exclusively with romance or their husbands and children; even on a battlefield, a woman can be motivated only by love for a man and " seen only in relation to the other sex."[9]

This quotation from Woolf's *A Room of One's Own* is from the passage about the modernist novelist Mary Carmichael, who "breaks the sequence" by representing Chloe and Olivia working as scientists in affectionate relation to one another: "Chloe liked Olivia; they shared a ____. . . . laboratory." The blank in the text here is from *Women and Fiction*, the holograph draft that reveals how Woolf censored herself in the published version. The draft goes on to give the narrator's fantasy as she tries to turn the page immediately after "they shared a ____"; two pages are stuck together: she imagines Mary Carmichael being summoned by a policeman to a trial whose nightmare absurdity mirrors that of the recent trial of *The Well of Loneliness*; the book is then burned on Tower Hill. Woolf's draft continues, "Here the pages came apart. Heaven be praised! It was only a laboratory."[10] The blank signifies some unspeakable word that would explicitly reveal that the relationship between Chloe and Olivia is sexual; it is an apt representation of the invisibility, and hence the unrepresentability, of lesbian sex in most modernist women's writing. Yet in the published text of *A Room of One's Own*, the blank and the fantasy have been excised; the relationship may still be lesbian—Chloe likes Olivia, after all, and she watches as well as works with her—but if so, it is closeted: Olivia is going home to her children.[11] Mary Carmichael has "broken the sequence" of the heterosexual plot only implicitly.

Both living and writing openly as a lesbian required an exceptional courage right through the 1950s. Woolf recognizes and simultaneously ridicules the idea that writing about Chloe and Olivia could be a dangerous activity when she interrupts her account of Mary Carmichael's novel to alert her Girton audience to the possibility of male spies: Sir Chartres Biron, presiding magistrate at the trial of *The Well of Loneliness*, may be lurking behind the red curtain.[12] But she goes on to explore the dangers of writing about lesbianism in a series of underground images:

> For if Chloe likes Olivia and Mary Carmichael knows how to express it she will light a torch in that vast chamber where nobody has ever

been. It is all half lights and profound shadows like those serpentine caves where one goes with a candle peering up and down, not knowing where one is stepping. . . . She will need to hold her breath . . . for women are so . . . terribly accustomed to concealment and suppression, that they are off at the flicker of an eye turned observingly in their direction. The only way . . . would be to . . . note . . . in words that are hardly syllabled yet, what happens when Olivia—this organism that has been under the shadow of the rock these million years—feels the light fall on it, and sees coming her way a piece of strange food—knowledge, adventure, art.[13]

Woolf's imagery is subtly, resonantly ambivalent, for she is implicated in the ideology she condemns. Exploring that serpentine cave where women have lived secret intellectual and sexual lives is a creepy, anxious business, associated with disaster, with Eve and the Fall: one could step on something nasty, something so conscious of its nastiness that it would scurry away. In this cave of suppression and concealment Olivia reverts to a mere organism, a pregendered "it" that gains a different femaleness only when she recognizes the nourishment she requires. To write about lesbians is to write about primeval monsters, as Woolf does in the case of Doris Kilman, but it is also to nourish and nurture them into a capacity to live openly in the light: a capacity for "knowledge, adventure, art."

Woolf's ambivalence about sexuality is reflected by her crosswriting in her understated, elegiac representations of war during the twenties: in these novels' depictions of homoerotic loss, she distances both grief and desire. The most intense sexual desire in *Jacob's Room* is between men; Clara, Florinda, Laurette, and Fanny Elmer don't enter the room—or closet—where photographs of the Greeks preside over the visits of a succession of male friends; only on the novel's last page does Betty Flanders burst in, to find Bonamy, "who couldn't love a woman," mourning for her son.[14] Septimus Warren Smith in *Mrs. Dalloway* cannot grieve for Evans because he has suppressed his homosexual desire; in *To the Lighthouse*, Mr. Carmichael expresses his grief for Andrew Ramsay, blown up by a shell in France, by bringing out a volume of poems.[15]

Yet lesbian crosswriting is not only a strategy of disguise or ambivalence; it also reflects the identification with gay men that encouraged lesbians to acknowledge or act on their sexuality throughout the twentieth century. After all, gay literary men have been "out there" sexually ever since the example of Oscar Wilde. What is more, many of them, like Wilde, have publicly performed their homosexuality by means of clothes, codes, and camp. By the "liberated" 1920s, privileged lesbians such as Gluck and Radclyffe Hall were developing their own camp style alongside gay men with a freedom that would have been impossible ten years earlier.[16]

The sexually liberating influence of gay men on lesbians can be traced alongside women's impulses toward celibate separatism. Christabel Pankhurst is an extreme example of a widespread tendency toward celibacy among British feminists before and during the First World War. The celibates coexisted with some younger suffragists, such as Rebecca West, who openly discussed free unions with men. Lesbian suffragists certainly existed, too, but although the suffrage movement encouraged women to live independently of men, it was not an environment that supported coming out as a lesbian. In this, the movement resembled the start of the second wave of American feminism in the 1960s and early 1970s when lesbians were often excluded or harassed by heterosexual feminists; the lesbian presence was seen as compromising both movements' respectability. Kathlyn Oliver was a suffragist in 1912 when she wrote several times to the *Freewoman*; she argued in favor of "self-restraint in sex matters" and represented herself as celibate. Three years later, Oliver wrote to Edward Carpenter after reading *The Intermediate Sex*, asking him for help in meeting other "Uranians" and telling him her sexual history. She had loved a number of women but had not experienced sexual desire until 1913, when she was about thirty and passionately in love with a heterosexual woman who rejected her. So she had recognized lesbian desire before reading the sexologists, but she was unable to act on it, just as Allatini's Antoinette in *Despised and Rejected* is unable to act on her desire for heterosexual Hester. It is significant that Oliver turned to a gay man rather than to the (hetero)sexually radical writers and readers of the *Freewoman* to discuss her lesbian loneliness.[17]

Crosswriting about gay men was also a way for a lesbian writer to explore and imagine alternative sexuality while remaining in the closet.[18] We don't know when Rose Allatini first had a lesbian relationship, although Virginia Woolf speaks of her "illicit amour" in a 1919 letter to Vanessa Bell.[19] Sylvia Townsend Warner published *Mr. Fortune's Maggot* three years before beginning her thirty-nine-year lesbian relationship with Valentine Ackland; her secret affair with the married Percy Buck was still going on while she crosswrote about

Timothy Fortune's love for Lueli. Like Woolf, she had a number of close gay and bisexual male friends; for Warner, crosswriting about gay men may have served multiple purposes.

To understand Sylvia Townsend Warner's novels of the 1920s, the theory of crosswriting that I have outlined above needs to be expanded to include the crossing of cultural boundaries other than just those between genders: specifically, boundaries of sexuality, class, and "race." Warner experienced real joy when she crossed, in her actual life, the border between heterosexuality and lesbianism. She was able, in some of her novels and stories, to cross class boundaries successfully; racial stereotypes, however, were harder to deconstruct.[20] Warner's representations of racial difference, like those of other modernists, were contaminated by primitivism; even in *Mr. Fortune's Maggot*, where her touch is light, affectionate, and more consistently ironic than in any other novel, her depiction of Polynesian society is at moments almost as stereotypical as Robert Louis Stevenson's or Herman Melville's.[21] Warner's complicated, subtle crosswriting techniques, however, are generally more successful than those of her contemporaries in the 1920s because she combines the irresponsibility of fantasy with a meticulously accurate adherence to the minutiae of history.[22] She crosses cultural boundaries by mixing literary genres.

My theory of crosswriting draws to some extent on Julie Abraham's ideas in *Are Girls Necessary? Lesbian Writing and Modern Histories*. Abraham maintains that modern lesbian writers turned to history as a means of escaping the traditional heterosexual plot in which lesbians are doomed to unhappiness. Writing that used "the narrative of history" includes both historical novels about gay men, such as those by Mary Renault and Willa Cather, and narratives that "reconfigure" contemporary culture by such experimental writers as Woolf, Gertrude Stein, and Djuna Barnes. The historical novelists, according to Abraham, are conservative in politics and conventional in narrative technique; the experimental novelists are the only writers whom Abraham categorizes as modernist.[23]

I want to complicate both Abraham's notion of modernism and her characterization of lesbian crosswriters as politically conservative. I adhere to the broader definition of modernism proposed by Bonnie Kime Scott, who includes "nonexperimental . . . writers alongside the more traditional experimental canon, challeng[ing] language-centered interpretations of modernism favored in the canonization process" and focusing instead on "the marginalities of class, economics, exile," "race," and sexuality.[24] "Nonexperimental" (and much less known) modernist writers like Warner and Allatini call into question also Abraham's assertion that it was "historically conservative" lesbian writers who crosswrote: Allatini's homosexual romance *Despised and Rejected* reconfigures the history (or the actuality, when she was writing) of the First World War, both in its subject matter—her intense emphasis on conscientious objectors and her exceptionally frank representation of both homosexuality and lesbianism—and in its use of recurrent structural metaphors of mutilation and imprisonment. Her "narratively conservative" novel is "historically" and politically radical: Allatini, like Warner, attacks the ideology of empire, showing how misogyny and homophobia are entwined with the class-bound, racist jingoism that justified both worldwide economic exploitation and the slaughter of a generation of young men in the First World War.

Lesbian modernist writing reproduces contemporary ideology—degeneration theory, primitivism, eugenics, sexology—with varying degrees of detachment. When writers accept all or almost all the beliefs of the dominant ideology, as Clemence Dane and Radclyffe Hall appear to have done in *Regiment of Women* and *The Well of Loneliness* respectively, the result is, unsurprisingly, a negative and often cliché-ridden representation of lesbianism: the "lesbian novel" doomed to an unhappy ending, which Julie Abraham deplores.[25] Unlike Abraham, however, I think that unhappy endings for fictional lesbians are produced by ideology as much as by narrative techniques. Crosswriting certainly enables Rose Allatini to represent the harm of internalized homophobia—but not of internalized lesbophobia—in *Despised and Rejected*: Dennis Blackwood runs miserably away from his homosexuality because, it@Ppears, he has been reading the wrong sexologist—Krafft-Ebing, possibly, whom Stephen Gordon's father in *The Well of Loneliness* also reads, instead of Edward Carpenter. Finally, however, Dennis is permitted a happy ending, at least as far as his romance is concerned, but Antoinette, the lesbian, remains unacknowledged and lonely. Allatini herself seems to have accepted too uncritically Carpenter's male-centered gay primitivist idealism: more distance from his masculinist utopian sexology might have enabled her to provide some resolution for her invisible lesbian. Only by pay-ing careful attention to their relation to ideology can we understand the ways in which lesbian writers attempt to reconfigure history.

The True Heart, Sylvia Townsend Warner's third novel, is not, on the face of it, a lesbian narrative but an apparently simple retelling of the myth of Eros and Psyche as recounted by Apuleius in *The Golden Ass*. The subject matter clearly attracted Warner as a tale of forbidden love that runs as counter to imperial and family values as her story of incest, "A Love Match," or her cross-species cat fables, or the worldly, earthbound tales of the seemingly supernatural in her last book, *Kingdoms of Elfin*. Warner's estrangement from the dominant ideology is crystallized in these narratives' matter-of-fact crossings of borders that are generally assumed to be impassable: the incest taboo, the line between the human species and other animals, the distinction between the material and the supernatural. What all this crosswriting of borders does is to blur rather than cross the lines between genders, sexualities, and species: not just hierarchies but boundaries themselves are made ridiculous. In "Queering Narratology," Susan Lanser examines the way Jeanette Winterson's *Written on the Body* simultaneously emphasizes and decenters gender difference by refusing to establish the biological sex of its narrator: plot intensity is heightened by the reader's wish to know the answer, but the fact that there is no answer makes the wish ridiculous. Warner's decentering of human beings in *The Cat's Cradle Book* is even more uncompromising because no uncertainty is permitted: she reverses a hierarchy rather than destabilizing it. Jane Marcus has argued that in establishing cats as the first storytellers, and thereby deconstructing the assumptions of humanism and ethnography, this 1940 text is postmodern:

> Warner . . . attacks our cherished belief that storytelling is a uniquely human activity and that it differentiates us from the animals. . . . Both *The Cat's Cradle Book* and *Kingdoms of Elfin* are remarkably postmodern in their revolutionary unsettling of the reader's notions of reality and their upsetting of race, class, and gender issues by moving the site of action to interspecies interaction and attraction. . . . *The Cat's Cradle Book*, like Woolf's *A Room*, is *theory* disguised as fable, literary history cross-dressed as entertainment, a wonderful exposé of the politics of subject positions.[26]

It is clear that Sylvia Townsend Warner's cool, ironic, and outrageous theory-as-narrative blurs also the critical distinction between experimental modernist narratives and those nonexperimental "inferior" fictions that interest us so much as readers today.

The True Heart is a guide to the interlocking, destructive, ideological absurdities of empire—a guide book cross-dressed as a classical fable. The fable becomes an everyday love story, myth become mundane. Psyche is Sukey, an orphan servant girl, and Eric, a beautiful young man of irreproachably middle-class antecedents, is a neglected "idiot" Eros.[27] Because the mentally disabled were prototypical primitives, their "idiocy" was beyond question: obfuscation of their true mental state was basic to the maintenance of the empire. The destitute or "unemployable," the multitudinous "lower races," prostitutes and, often, all women as a class were regarded as mentally disabled or, at best, as innocent children in need of firm guidance from the white male ruling class. The rationale for the white man's burden was the convenient assumption that almost everyone else was an idiot.

"The True Secret of England's Greatness": Degeneracy, Primitivism, Eugenics

The protagonist of Warner's The True Heart (1929) is at the very base of the British class and gender systems: Sukey Bond graduates in 1873 from the Warburton Memorial Female Orphanage; aged sixteen, she goes "out to service" as maid of all work at New Easter Farm in the Essex marshes; her place has been found for her by Mrs. Seaborn, a "lady patroness" of the orphanage.[28] The True Heart was published a year before the Stevensons moved into the vicarage at East Chaldon and started their reign of terror over their adolescent maids, some of whom may well have come from orphanages.[29] Apart from the beguiling notion that Warner's life had begun to imitate her art— the novel being a kind of rehearsal for her encounter with Joan Stevenson—it seems probable that the year of living with Sukey while she was writing her book intensified the outrage that she later felt about the treatment of Lily Roberts.[30]

There is another eerie similarity between The True Heart and the situation at the vicarage, where the doctor from the National Society for the Prevention of Cruelty to Children certainly found one "feeble-minded" young woman, although Katherine Stevenson wasn't training "four mad girls" as Theodore Powys had asserted. Sukey falls deeply in love with a young man whose position at the farm appears somewhat anomalous; he returns her love affectionately but seems strangely detached; only when he falls twitching to the ground at the sight of a slaughtered rooster is Sukey told that her Eric is "an idiot in a fit."[31] The young man has been farmed out to New Easter by his mother, the lady patroness who found Sukey her place there. Sukey is in love with the idiot scion of a most respectable family: his father is the rector of Southend. And his mother, Mrs. Seaborn, is Warner's version of the Venus in Apuleius's *The Golden Ass*.

The True Heart retells the story of Cupid and Psyche to produce an allegory of class oppression. Its plot, from Eric's fit, when his mother takes him away from New Easter, right up to the marriage of the lovers through the intervention of a kindly Victorian Jupiter, consists of Sukey's apparently impossible quest for her lover. She knows pretty clearly what her culture thinks of such a match:

> People could . . . send a policeman to take her to prison, a warder to carry Eric to the madhouse. Not only could they: she knew only too well that there was a great likelihood that they would; for people have strong views on such matters as hers: they disapprove when a servant-girl marries a gentleman, and they might further—for all she knew—disapprove when an idiot marries a servant-girl.[32]

Sukey was right. In the 1870s, "idiots" were considered degenerate, or retrogressive, as were immodest or fallen women. To lose one's modesty, which was an unconscious quality since women were thought to have no willpower and an altogether more limited conscious mind than men's, was inevitably to fall. Sukey, on the quest for her upper-middle-class lover, was certainly not behaving as a modest, mid-Victorian young working woman should. And once modesty was lost, "a woman became transformed: she crossed the boundary on which the entire female sex already hovered and entered a state of pathology and/or vice."[33] There was no middle way between modesty and prostitution, and the prostitute was always atavistic, in a state of moral (and physical) idiocy.[34]

The idea of degeneracy as a reversion to earlier stages of evolution had been current since the eighteenth century, based on the Lamarckian theory that acquired characteristics could alter heredity for better and for worse. It had been used alongside Christianity to justify the oppression of women, the poor, and "the lower races."[35]

As mid-Victorian intellectuals became freethinkers, evolutionary theory gradually replaced Christianity as the main source of the ideology of empire. The ideas of progress and retrogression became essential to maintaining the patriarchal status quo. This appeared somewhat precarious in the 1850s and 1860s when threats from the colonized in both hemispheres—the mutiny in India and the Morant Bay rebellion in Jamaica—were followed by the beginnings of the British women's movement;[36] there was concern also about the question of extending the franchise to the working classes.[37] But it was hard to read Charles Darwin's *The Origin of Species* as supporting the rigid gender, class, and racial hierarchies that were essential to imperialism; natural selection was more or less random and did not imply progress or degeneracy. As Adam Kuper points out, "those untrained in biology were very likely to prefer a Lamarckian to a Darwinian view of evolution," at least until the publication in 1871 of Darwin's *The Descent of Man*.[38] Kuper argues further that Henry Maine's *Ancient Law* (1861), which he sees as the foundation text for "the invention of primitive society," was based largely on the work of Jean Baptiste Lamarck.

Lucy Bland explains late-Victorian stereotypes about primitive sexuality as follows:

> To most evolutionists . . . "savages" or "primitives" were thought to be "living fossils"—relics of an earlier evolutionary stage. In examining the sexual and moral behavior of contemporary "savages," anthropologists claimed to have access to the behaviour of the "savage" ancestors of whites. There was much talk of "primitive promiscuity." Although the term was used by anthropologists to refer to an early stage of human development, it was also used as a description of contemporary "primitives."[39]

The contemporary "primitives" included the prostitute in London as well as the "savage" in Africa. And even if they were not promiscuous, both women and the "lower races" were considered childlike, necessitating protection by white, Western man.[40] Sukey Bond in 1873 is a mid-Victorian "primitive" on account of her childlike innocence—she thinks a kiss has made her pregnant—as well as her immodest forwardness in searching for her lover. In 1873 as in 1929, people would certainly disapprove if "a servant-girl marrie[d] a gentleman" or "an idiot marrie[d]" at all.

As soon as Eric is brought home to Southend by his mother, the gossip about primitive sexuality and degeneracy starts. Here is a conversation in the rectory kitchen; the speakers at this point believe that Sukey is pregnant:

> "Fancy an idiot getting a girl that way," remarked the housemaid, filling her mouth with currants. "I shouldn't have thought it hardly possible."
>
> "Oh, they're wonderful at it. Like the blacks. If you must wolf all the currants, all I say is, wolf those you've picked over yourself."
>
> "Well, I call it disgusting. Do you suppose the child will be wanting too?"[41]

Both Sukey and Eric are in danger of institutionalization. And Sukey is determined to keep Eric out of an asylum, for she has memories of being driven past the local madhouse each year on the way to the orphans' annual picnic. It was a solitary house, "surrounded by a high wall, built of stone and topped with iron spikes. Beneath that wall, under that roof, were the lunatics, creatures so different from their fellows that at the thought of them congregated there, the mind quickened with a peculiar excitement, almost as if they were gas and might explode."[42] The "peculiar excitement" here is erotic; the lunatics are the ultimate Other, and, as Bland notes, "the very separateness of the Other promotes curiosity and desire."[43] Warner had examined another aspect of that desire in *Mr. Fortune's Maggot*.[44]

Throughout her writing life, Sylvia Townsend Warner was a learned and reliable historian; in *The True Heart*, the first of her five historical novels, she satirizes the dominant ideology of her own time together with that of 1873. I agree with Warner's friend and comrade Arnold Rattenbury that Warner's historical novels are all about the time of their writing; as Rattenbury has noted, "Sylvia is deeply concerned with her *own* times, is only and always political, and *that* is why whatever the ostensible period, setting and concerns may *seem* to be, however carefully researched for detail, and then however accurately described, the actuality is *now*."[45] In fact, the ideological requirements of empire had hardly changed between 1873 and 1929. The main difference was the growth of the science of eugenics, which was enormously influential from the beginning of the twentieth century until World War II, when it was taken to its logical conclusion in Nazism's "final solution." The word *eugenics* was coined by Francis Galton in 1883; he defined it as "the science of improving stock."[46] By 1900 his followers were increasingly emphasizing the dangers of

breeding by the "dysgenic," as well as the importance of encouraging eugenic marriages among the "fit": white middle-class or respectable working-class couples. It should be clear that eugenics, like the older ideas of primitivism and degeneracy, strongly encouraged racial, class, and gender discrimination.

In 1929, the feebleminded were definitely considered dysgenic—unfit breeders—as were the undeserving poor.[47] Feeblemindedness was thought to be hereditary, and the feebleminded were believed more prolific than others. The definition of *feeblemindedness*—the term that had replaced *idiocy*—was very broad indeed: alcoholics, vagrants, criminals, prostitutes, and other undesirables, such as unmarried, pregnant young women without visible means of support, could all be considered feebleminded and open to incarceration in mental-defective establishments. As Lucy Bland notes in her *Banishing the Beast: Sexuality and the Early Feminists*, "To the eugenicist, the feeble-minded person became the archetypal representation of a deteriorat-ing, degenerate race."[48]

In the course of her quest for Eric, Sukey Bond finds a second farming family, the Mulleins, to employ her. Theirs is not a clean farm—neither outdoors, because Mr. Mullein is lazy and has a rov-ing eye, nor indoors, where Mrs. Mullein is entirely occupied with her seven indistinguishable and constantly ailing children, who form an ironic allusion both to the joys of motherhood and to the heap of small seeds that Psyche is required to sort. Sukey, who enjoys clean-ing, is delighted to unveil from a thick coating of grime an engrav-ing entitled *The True Secret of England's Greatness*. We are told that

> [t]he story was simple, but at the same time magnificent. Queen Victoria stood on the steps of her throne, as upright as a pillar-box. Round her, at a lower level and in a suitable shading of per-spective, were grouped statesmen, courtiers, field-marshalls, bishops, pages, and ladies-in-waiting. At the foot of the throne knelt a negro . . . [and] with her gloved hand she was extending to him the gift of a Bible. Sukey would stand in front of this picture and sigh. She wanted to marry Eric beyond all things, but she had also a natural wish to go to court.[49]

It is well known that pictures of the Royal Family were the equiva-lent of religious icons for the British working class: the national ob-session with royalty functioned to some extent as the opium of the people. This particular celebration of imperial largesse was probably

1. *Queen Victoria Opens the Imperial Institute*; engraving by G. Durand. *Illustrated London News*, 1893.

on the walls of many Essex farmhouses. A similar example is an engraving by G. Durand, *Queen Victoria Opens the Imperial Institute*, which accompanied an account of this long-awaited event in *The Illustrated London News* in 1893. The Imperial Institute in South Kensington was a propagandist institution that had been planned since the 1870s as "a permanent exhibition, 'The Empire under One Roof,' to which the populace could flock to wonder at the benefits colonial rule afforded them."[50] Durand's engraving shows Queen Victoria and assorted members of the ruling class standing on the steps of this florid example of Victorian baroque architecture, facing a crowd of imperial subjects who stand or kneel with their backs to the viewer. Predominantly African and Asian, these subjects appear in "national" dress or undress and are accompanied by some characteristically colonial animals; a muscular young man in a loincloth is paired with a kangaroo and so presumably hails from Australia. Writing forty years after Warner, Paul Scott uses a similar picture as a central symbol to satirize imperialist propaganda in *The Raj Quartet*, his series of historical novels depicting the British in India during the years before 1947;[51] a passage in *The Towers of Silence* recalls how Edwina Crane had used the painting as an instructional text in 1914 at the mission school in Muzzafirabad:

> Here is the Queen. The Queen is sitting on her throne. The uniform of the Sahib is scarlet. The sky here is blue. Who are these people in the sky? They are angels. They blow on golden trumpets. They protect the Queen. The Queen protects the people. The people bring presents to the Queen. The Prince carries a jewel on a velvet cushion. The Jewel is India. She will place the Jewel in her Crown.[52]

No doubt the charges of the Warburton Memorial Female Orphanage were thoroughly enough indoctrinated with the romance and respectability of the court for Sukey to feel a "natural" wish to participate in this most unnatural, most posed and calculated of settings.

When Sukey hears that Mrs. Seaborn is "carrying on something frantic" because she has been snubbed by a royal princess who has heard the gossip about Eric, she looks at the engraving and is inspired:

> There was Queen Victoria, and there behind her were the statesmen and the courtiers, the field-marshalls, bishops, pages, and ladies-in-waiting. The Bible was still in the royal hand. Only the negro was not there; in his place, kneeling at the foot of the throne, was

Sukey Bond. She had always wanted to go to court. Now she was going.[53]

In her vision of disempowered empowerment, Sukey is delighted to imagine herself as literally interchangeable with the "negro." Class, gender, and racial oppression have become identical in the fantasy world of this novel. In terms of the Cupid and Psyche story, Queen Victoria takes the place of Proserpine, and London becomes identified with Hades. Just as Psyche is miraculously guided through Hades to Proserpine's throne, where the queen of the underworld graciously fills Venus's empty box with her magic beauty, so Sukey is miraculously lucky on her way to her audience with Queen Victoria, who kindly bestows on her the Bible for Mrs. Seaborn—a sign of royal favor bound, as Sukey thinks, to ensure her acceptance as a daughter-in-law. In this absurdly topsy-turvy, ebulliently satirical representation of empire, *The True Heart* expresses the political concerns that were to preoccupy Warner throughout her writing life.

The novel ends with marriage and the birth of Sukey and Eric's child—an event as appropriate to myth and fairy tale as it would have been horrifying to a eugenicist. In the 1890s and 1900s, the growing influence of eugenics, with its focus on selective breeding as a vital component of "national efficiency," coincided with the increasing challenges to the British Empire from Germany, the United States, and Japan. "The race" came to mean "the nation" as well as "whiteness"; nationalism and imperialism became synonymous; the "sexual instinct" was often called the "racial instinct." Eugenics was accepted by a number of people who otherwise saw themselves as opposed to ruling-class politics. H. G. Wells, speaking to the Sociological Society, publicly advocated sterilization, saying, "It is in the sterilisation of failures, and not in the selection of successes for breeding, that the possibility of an improvement of the human stock lies."[54] The poor, and especially the "casual poor" or, to use the Fabians' term, the "unemployable," were still seen as degenerate: due to the violation of natural selection by philanthropy, medicine, and indiscriminate state aid, they had reverted to earlier stages of evolution. They were also considered dangerously prolific, as were immigrants; Sidney Webb lamented in 1907 that, while the English birth rate was falling, "children are being freely born to the Irish Catholics and the Polish, Russian and German Jews on the one hand, and to the thriftless and irresponsible . . . on the other."[55]

Even before eugenics became dominant, late-Victorian feminists read Lamarck and Darwin, especially the latter's *Descent of Man*, to support the notion that biology was transformable by means of morally conscious sexual selection; mothers were therefore of vital importance in preventing degeneracy and safeguarding the "purity of the race." By the prewar years only a few feminists, such as Dora Marsden and Stella Browne in *The Freewoman* and Christabel Pankhurst, who blamed men for venereal disease and "race suicide" in *The Great Scourge and How to End It*, opposed eugenics. There were still few roles besides motherhood open to middle-class women, so the eugenicist focus on mothers as sexual selectors and educators of their children made the notion of racialized motherhood seem empowering.[56] Even Edith Lees Ellis, a childless lesbian, argued in a lecture she delivered to the Eugenics Education Society in 1911 that the inverted had "special powers of work in the eugenic fields of spiritual parenthood": they could create spiritual children, works of art.[57]

Lesbian Panic: Regiment of Women

It is hardly surprising that all this emphasis on patriotic motherhood resulted in the demonization of lesbians along with the contempt for spinsters that Warner satirizes in *Lolly Willowes*; but lesbian writing all too often reflects and even actively preaches those aspects of the dominant ideology that condemn lesbianism. Such writing may have a veneer of irony, but its representation of the world purports to be "realistic," as in Hall's *The Well of Loneliness*, which is in many ways a "condition of England" novel like those of John Galsworthy or Arnold Bennett. Its naturalism is aesthetically as well as politically the opposite of *The True Heart*, which purports to be fantasy.

A typical victory of imperialist marriage over barren inversion is portrayed in the final pages of *The Well*, where Mary is tricked by Stephen's heroic self-sacrifice into the arms of Martin Hallam and, presumably, a prolific motherhood in Canada, populating the colony with the "master race." Stephen Gordon is the prototypical doomed lesbian hero of British and American literature. Clare Hartill of *Regiment of Women* (1917), Clemence Dane's eugenicist bestseller, is, as far as I know, the prototypical lesbian vampire or demon lover in women's writing, although she is preceded by such figures of male fantasy as Samuel Taylor Coleridge's Geraldine and Sheridan LeFanu's

Carmilla.[58] *Regiment* had a great deal of influence on the development of the novel of lesbian panic during the 1920s.

In her introduction to the Virago edition, Alison Hennegan finds several of *Regiment*'s characters prototypical:

> *Regiment of Women* established a pattern and a cast of characters which would exert a powerful influence over lesbian fiction for the next half-century. Versions of Clare the Vampire, Alwynne the Innocent, Elsbeth the Guardian Angel and Roger the Redeemer appear in various permutations in novels such as Naomi Royde-Smith's *The Tortoise-Shell Cat* (1925), Rosamond Lehmann's *Dusty Answer* (1927), Radclyffe Hall's *The Well of Loneliness* (1928), Molly Keane's *Devoted Ladies* (1934), and Dorothy Baker's *Trio* (1943).[59]

Hennegan goes on to argue that Christa Winsloe's *The Child Manuela* was also influenced by Dane's novel.

With the exception of *The Well of Loneliness*, these are narratives of lesbian panic.[60] I would add to Hennegan's list Dorothy Sayers's exceptionally misogynist mystery, *Unnatural Death* (1927), which combines lesbian crosswriting with lesbian panic: Lord Peter Wimsey—whose aristocratic lineage makes all the more acceptable his obvious, closeted homosexuality—pins a series of murders on a lesbian nurse.[61] Naomi Royde-Smith provides a particularly interesting example of 1920s class primitivism in *The Tortoiseshell Cat*. After briefly introducing a benign lesbian schoolteacher in her first chapter, Royde-Smith goes on to depict the seduction of her naive protagonist, Gillian, by the sexually ambiguous, lower-middle-class V. V., who was long ago so "maimed . . . warped and stunted by some influence . . . that nothing that happened to her now would make much difference."[62] The sensibly heterosexual Jane Bird comforts Gillian with the observation, "It's no use being intimate out of your own class."[63] All of these novels are either uncritical of the imperialist class system or else downright elitist.

Radclyffe Hall—herself quite an expert in classism—maintained that *The Well* was unique, but nevertheless recognized *Regiment* as a precursor.[64] Claire M. Tylee also sees the misogyny and lesbophobia of *Regiment of Women* as an influence on *The Well of Loneliness*.[65] I agree, but since Dane's novel was a bestseller during the last years of World War I, I historicize it also as a reflection of prevalent home front attitudes: the national obsession with marriages and war babies to replace the dead and dying young men; uneasiness about the new prominence of women in traditionally male jobs, and nostalgia for a prewar, idyllic, pastoral England.[66]

Unlike *The Well of Loneliness*, which confronts the puzzled or outraged lesbian reader with the heterosexual climax only in the last few pages, *Regiment of Women* is divided neatly in half. First we have the claustrophobic world of the Utterbridge boarding school for girls, reigned over by Clare Hartill, "vampirish" lesbian schoolteacher: she discards one of her adoring students, Louise Denny, so ruthlessly that the child kills herself, and she wins the love of Alwynne Durand, junior teacher, so successfully that it looks as if an exemplarily wholesome young woman may ignore her duty to bear children. In the second half of the book, however, Alwynne is sent to the country to ward off an incipient, Clare-induced nervous breakdown; there she meets Roger Lumsden, market gardener. Shocked by Alwynne's narrative of events at Utterbridge, Roger is quick to "sow a seed of distrust" of Clare in her mind and ends up "uprooting all the weeds that were choking her and planting good seed in their stead."[67]

This is eugenicist seed, of course; we are to believe that Roger and Alwynne will produce good stock once she has been rescued from the sinister intensities of her life with Clare Hartill. Indeed, Roger is "horrified at the idea of such a woman, such a type of woman, in undisputed authority, moulding the mothers of the next generation."[68] What we have here is an allusion to an ongoing debate about the object of girls' education.[69] Schools like Utterbridge prepared women to live as professionals, like Claire Hartill, independently of men; Dane is contrasting such "unnatural" girls' boarding schools with "healthy" new coeducational schools like Bedales. Such schools—represented in *Regiment of Women* by the fictional Compton Dene, which is located on Roger Lumsden's family property—focused on teaching girls to be responsible mothers and educators of their children. Where Utterbridge prepares girls to take demanding scholarship examinations, the teachers at Compton Dene are "quite content if they produce gentlewomen."[70] Both types of school, of course, have their conventional selling points: the rigid rules about manners and dress at Utterbridge and the more modern eugenicist emphasis on practical, maternal skills at Compton Dene, where discipline is relaxed, students live in informal "houses," and classes are coeducational apart from the ones the girls take in needlework and housewifery. Above all, there is an emphasis on space and fresh air.

Roger Lumsden's extended gardening metaphor emphasizes the claustrophobic atmosphere at Utterbridge:

> He detected an hysterical tendency in the emulations and enthusiasms to which [Alwynne] referred. The gardener in him revolted at the thought of such congestion of minds and bodies. He felt as indignant as if he had discovered a tray of unthinned seedlings. Alwynne conveyed to him an idea of the forcing-house atmosphere that she, and those still younger than she, had been breathing.[71]

Roger will fight against " 'this—this unpleasant school-marm,' " as he calls Clare, and champion the natural world of marriage and procreation.[72] And naturally, the spring countryside, as idyllic as the pastoral lyrics of the Georgian poets, is on his side, for "[Alwynne] was in her own country again. She loved the country . . . Kent and Hampshire and the Sussex Weald. But Clare would never hear of a country holiday. Alwynne took deep breaths of the clean, kindly air. . . . this good air made one feel alive again."[73] She divides her time between breathing the coeducational fresh air on her constant visits to Compton Dene, picking wildflowers in the mossy spring woods, and writing delighted letters to Clare and her aunt Elsbeth about violets and cuckoopint, primroses and budding larch trees. Dane's use of flower imagery harks back to the literary glorification of the English countryside by poets such as Gordon Bottomley, Rupert Brooke, and Walter de la Mare during the years of imperialist conflict leading up to the First World War. Clare's lack of enthusiasm for country walks is as unpatriotic as her lesbianism.[74]

In conventional British girls' boarding schools from the beginning of the twentieth century until at least the end of the 1960s, the rigid hierarchy of teachers, head girls, prefects, games captains, and form monitors was based on a belief that reverence for and emulation of seniority are educational. And so, intense female bonding was to some extent compulsory. That it might be lesbian desire was unrecognized by Constance Maynard in 1887, but twenty years later Sara Burstall, headmistress of Manchester Grammar School for Girls, was starting to feel uneasy.[75] Burstall believed that

> hero-worship, adoration, or *schwärmerei*—there is no exact English word for it—. . . . [could be] a really true and not ignoble emotion, a natural product of the age and circumstances of the girl, which should be recognized, allowed for, regulated, controlled, and made a help and not a hindrance to moral development. . . . A woman's

life is, moreover, largely concerned with emotion; to suppress this will be injurious, to allow it to develop slowly and harmlessly, in respect and even reverence for someone who is older and presumably wiser than the girl herself, is not injurious and may be helpful.[76]

Burstall's anxiety is reflected both in her inability to find the appropriate word in the English language to denote the attachment—how hard it is to find a name for the love that dares not speak it, if indeed it exists in England at all—and in the list of verbs following that admonitory "should": the emotion, whatever it is, must be rigorously controlled. She goes on to recommend lots of fresh air and exercise—and silence about feelings.[77] More consistent, though still inexplicit, attempts to prohibit lesbianism and encourage lesbophobia are recorded by Bryher in her account of Queenwood, the boarding school she attended from 1910 to 1912: the headmistress, Miss Chudleigh, lectured the girls twice a term about "unhealthy friendships."[78]

Bryher was sent to Queenwood when she was fourteen, after an informal, stimulating early education while traveling with her parents. She was miserably alienated and bored at a school even more conventional than the fictional Utterbridge, where students certainly received a far better education from Clare Hartill and Alwynne. Bryher writes that intellectually—in preparation, of course, for marriage—they were given a "diet of crumbs. [W]e were girls and so sacrificed to the prevalent spirit of the age; knowledge might make us discontented."[79]

Bryher might well have enjoyed being taught by the inspiring, if controlling, Clare Hartill. Early on in *Regiment of Women* Dane writes, "There are women today . . . who owe Clare Hartill the best things of their lives, their wide knowledge, their original ideals, their hopeful futures and happy memories: to whom she was inspiration incarnate."[80] We can see the qualities that make Clare an inspiring teacher in the class on Robert Browning's "The Dark Tower," in which she rewards the precocious Louise Denny for her industry and imagination and punishes Agatha for bullying.[81] The punishment is public humiliation, but it ends with Clare's intensifying Agatha's devotion to herself by praising her work. From the moment that Clare enters the classroom unseen, "in her usual noiseless fashion," we witness her manipulative pedagogy: she is witty, dry, unpredictable; she appears to take her students seriously; she rewards originality and intelligence with her interest. But it quickly becomes apparent that her motivating force is her love of power. An ambivalent attitude to lesbianism as well as to lesbian schoolteachers is apparent in Dane's depiction of Clare. Hence the novel's representation of lesbian panic.

One never doubts, reading this novel, that Clemence Dane knows how boarding schools like Utterbridge work. The economical, authoritative delineation of the school secretary, Henrietta Vigers, exemplifies this knowledge. Miss Vigers is both self-important and ineffective, delighting in petty rules and rigid uniformity; threatened by Alwynne's popularity, she does her best to make the junior teacher's life a misery. Later, however, we pity her. After Louise Denny's "fall" from an upstairs window to her death, Miss Vigers is afraid that she may be held responsible, and her anxiety makes her easily manipulable: Clare is able to make her believe that Louise was overly attached to Alwynne rather than herself. Later, it suits Clare to feel outraged at Vigers' bullying of Alwynne and to manipulate the aging headmistress, Miss Marsham, into suggesting that Vigers' responsibilities be considerably decreased. When the secretary offers her resignation in a huff, she is amazed to find it accepted. Dane makes absolutely clear that Clare's interference has ruined this woman's life:

> Henrietta Vigers was forty-seven when she left. She had spent youth and prime at the school and. . . . had neither certificates nor recommendations behind her. She was hampered by her aggressive gentility. Out of a £50 salary she had scraped together £500. Invested daringly it yielded her £25 a year. She had no friends outside the school. She left none within it. Miss Marsham presented her with a gold watch, decorously inscribed; the school with a handsomely bound edition of Shakespeare.[82]

Clemence Dane can write with economy and wit, but the then current debate about spinster teachers and students was on her mind as she wrote her first novel. It is in this context that her narrative's descent into melodramatic lesbian panic must be considered.

Lesbianism in this novel is monstrous, not military. The title alludes to John Knox's *The First Blast of the Trumpet against the Monstrous Regiment of Women*, a misogynist tract aimed at Mary Tudor in 1558. Dane's epigraph, which refers to "the monstruous empire of cruell woman," is also a quotation from Knox. "Monstrous regiment" in this context should be glossed as "unnatural government." The queen of Utterbridge School is not the aging headmistress (although she too has a lesbian roving eye),[83] but the ruthlessly unnatural usurper, Clare.

Elsbeth, Alwynne's loving maiden aunt—"the childless woman"[84]—cares for her niece with her "motherly soul,"[85] in contrast to Clare *Hart-ill* who is "unmaternal to the core,"[86] and whose insatiable demands drain Alwynne's vitality until she "flag[s] like a transplanted tree."[87] At the end of the novel Elsbeth confronts Clare in outrage and panic at the "abnormal, spiritually perverse" behavior of a fellow spinster.[88] It is a familiar syndrome—the fear of guilt by association: some gay men and lesbians still don't want the drag queens and S/M dykes in the Gay Pride parade. When Clare has the temerity to suggest that " '[t]here are better things in life than marriage,'" Elsbeth responds with the eugenicist stereotype, " '[W]hen her youth is over, what is the average single woman? A derelict, drifting aimlessly on the high seas of life. . . . We both know that an unmated woman—she's a failure—she's unfulfilled.'"[89] Clare refuses to acknowledge this sad spinsterly plight, fighting back with the suggestion that Alwynne move in with her full-time. Now Elsbeth feels sufficiently threatened to invoke the myth of the lesbian vampire, responding, " 'Do you think I don't know your effect on the children at the school? Oh, you are a good teacher! You force them successfully; but all the while you eat up their souls. . . . I tell you, it's vampirism. . . . You grow greedier as you grow older. . . . One day you'll be old. What will you do when your glamour's gone? I tell you, Clare Hartill, you'll die of hunger.'"[90] Elsbeth is presented throughout the novel as unwaveringly heterosexual: her love for Alwynne is maternal; the disappointment of her life was Roger's father's transferral of his affections to Another; her fluttering happiness at Roger's interest in Alwynne is a patronizing stereotype of harmless, middle-aged spinsterhood. Yet spinsters are vulnerable to the lesbian panic expressed in Elsbeth's vampire metaphor: she needs to distance Clare as a monster.

In both *Between Men* and *Epistemology of the Closet* Eve Kosofsky Sedgwick discusses the double bind of male friendship: her thesis—that homosocial bonding is virtually compulsory for male success in the world while at the same time a homophobic culture ensures that all bonding between men is a source of homosexual panic—has been exceptionally illuminating. Still, I want to distinguish here between *lesbian panic* and *homosexual panic*: they reflect differences between lesbophobia and homophobia as well as differences in social bonding. I think that Sedgwick emphasizes the physical violence of homophobia without sufficiently connecting it to routine male violence against women.[91] Gay men get bashed or raped by (homosexually panicking) men predominantly because they are seen as behaving like women; lesbians get bashed or raped by men primarily because they *are* women, and *also* because they are seen as behaving like men, especially in their desire for women instead of, and/or in competition with, men. And lesbians also encounter lesbophobia from other women, who tend to use psychological rather than physical violence: their lesbophobia can take the form of ostracism, for example, or derision, or—in cases of such gothic intensity as Elsbeth's attack on Clare—accusations of cannibalism or vampirism.

Sedgwick has observed that in "the paranoid Gothic . . . intense male homosocial desire [is] at once the most compulsory and the most prohibited of social bonds."[92] In contrast, both in fiction and in life, gynosocial or lesbosocial bonding is generally far from compulsory; in the workplace and in the home, women are encouraged to bond with men, in competition with one another. The equivalent for women of Sedgwick's double bind manifests itself mainly in lesbian vampire stories, which are usually Gothic, or in novels set in female communities such as convents or boarding schools or all-women ambulance units.[93] It is in these contexts, at least before 1960, that literary lesbian panic is most likely to occur, as it does in *Regiment of Women*.

Clare Hartill's fatal flaws are her unscrupulousness, her possessiveness, and above all her love of power. Cynthia Griffiths, a visiting American student, is quick to grasp that she is a swiftly bored Niccolò Machiavelli rather than the goddess that students like Louise Denny imagine her to be. But she realizes also that Clare's wicked lust for power is as seductive as her intelligence. She tries to disabuse her friend Louise:

> "Why, she simply lives for effect! She's the most gorgeous hypocrite. . . . I admire her heaps! But I understand her. You don't. She likes to be top dog. She'll do anything for that. She likes to know every woman and child in the school is a bit of putty, to knead into shape. I know! I've met her sort before—only generally it was men they were after."[94]

And so the stereotype of the "man-eating" woman is neatly replaced in this novel by the cannibalistic lesbian vampire. Both figures are the product of sexual fear. The man-eater castrates her victim by means of the vagina dentata; the vampire drains innocent blood by means of the lesbian kiss.[95]

As it is to vampires, "Love of some sort was vital to [Clare Hartill]."[96] Both of the lesbian kisses depicted in predictably panicky detail reveal Clare's sinister sexuality. Neither is remotely seductive. After Alwynne's repellently coy love scene with Roger—another product of lesbian panic—she compares his "comforting peck" to Clare's kisses: "She remembered . . . the thin fingers that gripped her shoulders; the long, fierce pressure, mouth to mouth; the rough gesture that released her, flung her aside."[97] This suddenness, violence, and total lack of both sensuous and emotional pleasure sets Clare worlds away from the seductive lesbian vampires of nineteenth-century male-authored English narratives. Nina Auerbach has written brilliantly about the interfusion and entwining of vampire and victim in Samuel Taylor Coleridge's "Christabel" and Sheridan LeFanu's "Carmilla."[98] Carmilla's seductive languor—"I live in your warm life, and you shall die—die, sweetly die—into mine"—evokes a response in Laura that makes being a vampire's victim sound like an adolescent sexual awakening: "I experienced a strange tumultuous excitement that was pleasurable, ever and anon, mingled with a vague sense of fear and disgust. . . . I was conscious of a love growing into adoration, and also of abhorrence."[99] In contrast, Clare, gripping Alwynne, pressing her, roughly flinging her aside when sated, behaves more like an everynight hungry vampire, as described by one of LeFanu's tedious experts at the end of Laura's story: "[I]t goes direct to its object, overpowers with violence, and strangles and exhausts often at a single feast."[100] Lesbophobia really destroys the second half of this novel, imprisoning Clare Hartill in melodrama and Alwynne in an insipidly clichéd romance.

Alison Hennegan suggests that, rather than condemning Clare to "a hell of loneliness," the final chapter of *Regiment of Women* is open-ended.[101] I wish I found that easier to believe. At the beginning of the chapter Clare is waiting for Alwynne, unaware that she has humiliated and teased her for the last time. Night falls outside the window as, to the accompaniment of a thunderstorm, Clare's feelings change from impatience to hysteria to a moment of sadism followed by repentance and plans for a new start. Then the telegram from Alwynne arrives, telling Clare that she has gone to Roger. Rage is followed by disbelief; then a momentary hallucination of blood-stains reminds Clare of her part in Louise's death. The rain outside sobs until finally Clare is able to feel her loss and weep. And she starts to recall the others, from Louise Denny back to her childhood nurse, whose love she has abused. The novel's final sentence is, "When the dawn came, she was still sitting there, thinking—thinking."[102]

Dane asks us to imagine that Clare Hartill may be capable of change. But what growth is possible in this overwritten setting of thunder and hallucinations, sobbing rain and faces from the past that rise about Clare, whispering? The lesbian panic that led Clemence Dane to abandon the naturalism and intermittent wit and irony of the first half of her novel has robbed her characters of credibility as inhabitants of an everyday world in which psychological growth or change might be imaginable.

Intermediate Types among Imperialist Folk: Sexology and Primitivism

Regiment of Women can function as a kind of cultural mirror of the stereotypes of gender and sexuality prevalent during the years immediately preceding the First World War.[103] Clemence Dane is up to date in both eugenicist and sexological theory. Her novel includes, for example, an appropriately mannish suffragist, Miss Hamilton, the music teacher at Utterbridge, who "dressed tweedily and carried her hands in her pockets, slouching a little. It was her harmless vanity to have none. Teaching music was her business; her recreations, hockey, and the more law-abiding forms of suffrage agitation."[104] The stereotyping of feminists as mannish, and therefore as either lesbian or lacking in the "sexual instinct," was a commonplace of sexological writing. It is well known that Havelock Ellis, in his theorizing of female inversion, was able to conceive of lesbians only as trans-genderists, equating lesbianism with gender inversion rather than sexual object choice even though he denied that gay men were necessarily effeminate.[105] To conceive of lesbianism in terms of object choice rather than gender inversion would entail admitting that "normal" women, as well as the "mannish," experience active sexual desire—a threat that the patriarchy managed to stave off fairly successfully until the 1960s.[106]

Even Edward Carpenter reproduced the prevalent negative stereotype of feminists, conceptualizing them as "not-women" in his extremely popular collection of his pamphlets about heterosexual "sex-questions," *Love's Coming-of-Age* (1896):[107]

> The women of the new movement are naturally largely drawn from those in whom the maternal instinct is not especially strong; also from those in whom the sexual instinct is not preponderant. Such women do not altogether represent their sex; some are rather mannish in temperament; some are "homogenic," that is, inclined to attachments to their own, rather than to the opposite, sex.[108]

Yet Carpenter blames men for "the long historic serfdom of woman" in Britain,[109] and as early as this he finds "something more deep-lying fundamental and primitive in the woman nature than in that of the man" that he associates with "the Greek goddesses . . . far America, Australasia, Africa, Norway, Russia."[110] This is the idealization of the "primitive" that we find in the writing about gay men that he cannot yet publish for general circulation. I suspect that the ambivalence about "mannish" women that Ellis expressed in 1896 arose as much from caution in publicizing his ideas about "intermediates" as from misogyny. That his caution was justified is demonstrated by the fate of Ellis's *Sexual Inversion*, which was labeled "lewd and obscene" in a court of law in 1897. As a result, *Studies in the Psychology of Sex*, of which *Sexual Inversion* formed the first volume, was published in the United States; Ellis refused to bring it out in Britain until the 1930s.[111]

According to Lucy Bland, Ellis's work did not become widely known in England until the 1920s,[112] but Elazar Barkan maintains that "his impact on contemporaries was radical—sexology was ripe to lead a reform."[113] Ellis certainly argued that the 1885 Labouchère Amendment criminalizing homosexuality should be changed. Furthermore, however problematic his representation of women's sexuality may seem to us today, he was a good friend to many sexually radical women during his long life; they included his wife, Edith Lees Ellis; Olive Schreiner; Bryher; H.D.; Nancy Cunard; and Radclyffe Hall.

In *Sexual Inversion*, much of Ellis's theory, as well as his case studies, is dependent on the writings of his gay forerunners and acquaintances, especially Karl Heinrich Ulrichs, John Addington Symonds, and Edward Carpenter. Ulrichs introduced in 1864 the ideas of the "third sex" and the "Urning"—derived from "Uranos" or "heaven" in Plato's *Symposium*—as well as those sad stereotypes, "a woman's soul in a man's body" and vice versa. *Sexual Inversion* was actually Symonds's brainchild: he suggested to Ellis that they collaborate on the book, wrote more than a third of it before he died in 1893, and contributed about half of the homosexual "cases."[114] Other "cases" came from Edward Carpenter, whose 1895 pamphlet *Homogenic Love* Ellis acknowledges;[115] Edith Lees Ellis, the author's lesbian wife, contributed her own "case" and provided Ellis with access to her friends, whose narratives he used for his "cases" of female inversion. All of these gay sexual theorists aimed to gain the sympathy, or at least the toleration, of the "normal" majority; more specifically, they wanted to change the German and British laws criminalizing homosexuality.

Both Havelock Ellis and the gay Victorian theorists allude to ancient Greece to provide respectable, and romantic, precedents for same-sex male desire. John Addington Symonds was a classical scholar; his defense in *A Problem in Greek Ethics* of "Greek" love (or "paederastia") was a groundbreaking endeavor in England; ten copies were privately printed in 1883, and in 1897 the entire text formed appendix A in *Sexual Inversion*. Carpenter certainly made use in *Homogenic Love* and *An Unknown People* of the copy Symonds sent him in 1892.[116] But Ellis and Carpenter, like the anthropologist James Frazer, cite contemporary "primitives" as well as the ancients as exemplars of homosexuality: Ellis's list of exemplars includes ancient Mexicans, Peruvians, Persians, Chinese, Hebrews, and Mohammedans; warlike peoples such as Carthaginians, Normans, Dorians, Scythians, Tartars, Kelts, and contemporary New Caledonians; and modern "primitives" in Albania, Greece, China, Brazil, and among American Indians.[117] Elazar Barkan sees these allusions as a "strategy for addressing the 'unspeakable' . . . through the Other. . . . The attraction of primitives was that they were viewed as closer to nature than Victorians—not quite brutes, but close enough, which gave writers licence to speculate about the 'nature' of sexuality."[118] The "racial distance" of Polynesians and American Indians made speculation about their sexuality safe. In *Gone Primitive*, Marianna Torgovnick also emphasizes distance as an important aspect of both the speculations of Freud the sexologist and the observations of Bronislaw Malinowski the ethnographer. As Torgovnick has noted, "[Ethnographers] must document the intimate life of primitive peoples so that we can learn the truth about us—safely, as observers."[119]

It is useful to set alongside Barkan's apparently apolitical approach to primitivism an article about Carpenter by Parminder Kaur Bakshi. In "Homosexuality and Orientalism: Edward Carpenter's Journey to the East," Bakshi reads Carpenter's *From Adam's Peak to Elephanta* (1892) as an example of sexual colonialism. He draws on the account in Edward Said's *Orientalism* of the overlap in the Victorian imagination between Hellenism and orientalism; this overlap is visible in Carpenter's treatment, in both *The Intermediate Sex* and *Intermediate Types among Primitive Folk*, of sexuality among the Dorian Greeks, the Japanese Samurai, and "primitive folk" such as American Indians, West Africans, Polynesians, and Indians. Bakshi claims that Carpenter saw sex in everything during his travels in the East.

Carpenter believed that intermediates would lead humankind toward a more spiritual, natural life in which the divisions of sex and gender would be transcended.[120] His allusions to contemporary "primitives" became more extensive and enthusiastic as he felt progressively freer from self-censorship in writing about sex. By 1914 his "primitives" function as ideals as well as exemplars: *Intermediate Types among Primitive Folk: A Study in Social Evolution* gives a distinctly idealized vision of the distant past, the "primitive" present, and the possible future development of the intermediate sex.

The book is divided into two parts; part 2, "The Intermediate as Warrior," develops Symonds's celebration of "paederastia" in the relationship between older and younger men among Dorian Greeks, emphasizing the nobility and educational value of such love and extending Symonds's range to examine relationships among early Greek women and among the Samurai in Japan. Part 1, "The Intermediate in the Service of Religion," is particularly Carpenterian in its combination of the rational and the spiritual: after surveying the evidence for cross-dressed, homosexual, and hermaphrodite priests, prophets, wizards, and witches in history, mythology, and among contemporary "primitive" peoples, Carpenter attributes social development beyond the gender-specific activities of war making, hunting, growing crops, keeping house, and rearing children to the contributions of intermediate types. These "became the initiators of new activities" because they didn't want to fight or hunt or farm or do housework or raise children. They were bored:

> Non-warlike men and the non-domestic women, in short, sought new outlets for their energies. . . . They became students of life and nature, inventors and teachers of arts and crafts, or wizards . . . and sorcerers; they became diviners and seers, or revealers of the gods and religion; they became medicine-men and healers, prophets and prophetesses; and so ultimately laid the foundation of the priesthood, and of science, literature, and art.[121]

Carpenter justifies this theory with characteristic clarity and simplicity: those intermediate men or women who combined "the emotionality of the feminine with the practicality of the masculine, and many other qualities and powers of both sexes, as well as much of their experience, would undoubtedly be greatly superior in ability to the rest of their tribe, and making forward progress in the world of thought and imagination, would become inventors, teachers, musicians, medicine men and priests."[122] Here he applies to anthropology the theories about the special abilities of the "intermediate sex" in Europe and elsewhere that he has already developed. Yet what gives his theorizing its particular appeal is the transparency with which his "primitives" mirror his own development as a gay man, a socialist, and a writer:

> Finding himself *different* from the great majority, sought after by some and despised by others, now an object of contumely and now an object of love and admiration, [the intermediate] would be forced to *think*. His mind turned inwards on himself would be forced to tackle the problem of his own nature, and afterwards the problem of the world and of outer nature. He would become one of the first thinkers, dreamers, discoverers.[123]

Few of Carpenter's ideas are original; he tends to function as the popularizer of other writers' "facts" and theories. His tone, however, differs from the ponderous urbanity of other armchair anthropologists: his primitivism is transfused with the urgent idealism of a mid-Victorian socialist's belief in the "simple life." Writing about American Indians at the end of *Intermediate Types among Primitive Folk*, Carpenter expresses both a hope and a plea for the future: "There was a religion of the body, and a belief in the essential sacredness of all its processes, which we somehow have lost, and which we shall not probably socially regain until we once more adopt the free life of the open air and restore the healing and gracious sense of human community and solidarity."[124]

The narrative that Edward Carpenter wrote for Havelock Ellis during the early 1880s, when both men belonged to the broadly socialist and sexually progressive Fellowship of the New Life, forms the sixth of the "cases" in *Sexual Inversion*. In it, Carpenter declares, "Now—at the age of 37—my ideal of love is a powerful strongly built man . . . preferably of the working class."[125] George Hukin, who was Carpenter's comrade in socialist activism in Sheffield and intermittently his lover during the 1880s, was such a man; so was George Merrill, whom Carpenter met in a train in 1891; they lived together openly from 1898 until Merrill's death in 1928. According to Sheila Rowbotham, Merrill had formed part of "the late Victorian homosexual underground," so familiar to us now from the trials of Oscar Wilde. Before he and Carpenter met, he worked as a bartender and waiter, traveled around on the railway, and had sexual encounters with a priest, an Italian count, and "a young man in the retinue of the Prince of Wales," among others.[126] Carpenter and Merrill's home at Millthorpe formed a liberating center of "the English homosexual system whereby bourgeois men had sexual contacts only with virile working class youths."[127]

It was easy during his lifetime and it is still a temptation now to dismiss or deride Carpenter's socialism, his interest in "primitive" peoples, his idealization of the "intermediate sex." First, there's the combination of his upper-middle-class privilege with his choice of working-class lovers: he can be seen as practicing a kind of class-primitivism. Second, Carpenter's was a moral rather than Marxist kind of socialism, emphasizing comradeship and withdrawal from the consumer culture; those who lived the "simple life," as Carpenter did, were objects of derision in Britain; when Alwynne in *Regiment of Women* first hears of the school at Dene Compton she says, " 'It's all cranks and simple lifers and socialists though, isn't it?'"[128] Third, there is the disquieting orientalism discernible both in Carpenter's writings about India and in the idealization of both "primitive folk" and gay men that underlies his glowing vision of intermediate types as the leaders of the future. So how was Carpenter credible to his socialist comrades and helpful even to some lesbians as well as gay men?

Carpenter's political activism—like his writing—sprang from his own needs and preoccupations. The brief anonymous account of himself that he gave Havelock Ellis emphasizes his misery as a boy, when he thought he was a "hopeless monstrosity."[129] In *My Days and Dreams* he writes at length about the repression and vacuity of Victorian family life, as it oppressed his sisters as well as himself.[130] Throughout his life his radical politics were personal, from his decision in 1874 to give up his career in the church and become a university extension lecturer, through his socialist activism all over England in the 1880s, to his foundation, with Laurence Housman, of the British Society for the Study of Sex Psychology and his support of the No-Conscription Fellowship during World War I.

There is plenty of evidence of the liberating effects on young men of Carpenter's writings about homosexuality: Dilip Barua gives an engaging account of Carpenter's influence on Siegfried Sassoon and Robert Graves.[131] Sassoon wrote to Carpenter in 1911 about the painful self-suppression of his sexuality prior to reading *The Intermediate Sex*; he and Carpenter remained friends for many years.[132] Graves wrote as a schoolboy in 1914 about the "immense elation" with which he had devoured *Ioläus* and *The Intermediate Sex*; he claimed that mutual attractions between boys were the purest and most inspiring factors of school life. Graves was a student at Charterhouse, a boys' public school rather like Harrow, where Sylvia Townsend Warner grew up among her father's students. Many of those students were killed in the war, but Warner remained friendly with several of the probably bisexual survivors during the 1920s.

Carpenter's influence on women is less well documented, but it was considerable. Although both his personal commitments and his writing focused mainly on men, his friends included feminists such as Edith Lees Ellis, Olive Schreiner, Isabella Ford, and Charlotte Despard; he writes rather persuasively that "Uranian" men "chiefly support the women's movement" whereas, although heterosexual men may love women, "it is generally with a proprietary sort of love."[133] Carpenter's freedom from patriarchal proprietorship made him a welcome participant in at least some feminist actions: when Despard formed the Women's Freedom League, he marched alongside her to Alexandra Park, where he gave a speech on prison reform.[134] I want to focus here, however, on the reflection of Carpenter's ideas in lesbian writing rather than on his personal friendships and political actions.

Among the novels that I consider, Rose Allatini's *Despised and Rejected* (1918), which provides a groundbreaking representation of gay and lesbian pacifists during the First World War, demonstrates most clearly the importance of Carpenter's sociosexological and utopian primitivist ideas to lesbian as well as gay writers who were dissidents from the dominant ideology. One of these was Sylvia Townsend Warner; Carpenter's influence on her writing is particularly apparent in the representation of class, imperialism, and the sex/gender system in her 1920s novels.

It seems to me likely, for example, that Warner read Carpenter's 1923 translation of Apuleius's story of Cupid and Psyche; she reproduces both his use of Greek instead of Latin names—as in Eric for Eros—and his naming of one of Aphrodite's servants Grief rather than most translators' Sorrow. Carpenter's absurdities of character and action may also have contributed to the exuberant satire in *The True Heart*. And while Warner was herself independent and sexually experienced by the time she started writing fiction in the 1920s, she chose to represent desire in working-class rather than middle-class women in her early novels and stories. Sukey's love for Eric in *The True Heart*; the lustful antics of Emily in *Lolly Willowes* (1926); even the momentary vision of beauty vouchsafed to Minnie Parr, the respectably married middle-aged bedmaker in a brothel in "Some World Far from Ours" (1929): the sexual desire of all these working-class women is at once simplified and idealized with a class primitivism reminiscent of Carpenter. Both writers naturalize desire, freeing it from the repressive middle-class conformity that they had rejected in their private lives.

Yet it is in her apparently idyllic representation of oceanic sexuality in *Mr. Fortune's Maggot* (1927) that Warner most explicitly draws upon (and satirizes) the utopian evolutionist sexology of *The Intermediate Sex* and *Intermediate Types among Primitive Folk*. Her critique of imperialism is far more explicit and complex than Carpenter's; she is, after all, two generations younger than he, a modernist rather than a Victorian. Nonetheless, despite the invigorating comedy in her depiction of the belated sexual awakening of her missionary protagonist, her idealized representation of the islanders of Fanua and, above all, of the beautiful adolescent boy, Lueli, is imbued with a definitely Carpenterian primitivism.

3

CROSSWRITING THE "PRIMITIVE"

Political Fantasies

The main focus of this chapter is Sylvia Townsend Warner's *Mr. Fortune's Maggot*, now an almost unknown romance about an innocent, devout missionary who falls in love with a beautiful young boy on a Polynesian island. I consider it a masterpiece: a resonant response to primitivist predecessors such as Joseph Conrad and Robert Louis Stevenson, a brilliantly satirical examination of the workings of Christian imperialism, and an important contribution to the 1920s literature of sexual radicalism. What makes it beloved by those who read it in the past and the few who read it now is its mixture of escapism and moral/political rigor. We share with Mr. Fortune, whose anxious innocence resembles that of Fyodor Dostoyevsky's Alyosha or Prince Myshkin, an idyllic fantasy world of tolerance, peace, leisure, and natural beauty that is flawed only by the missionary's Christian work ethic and sexual repression. Yet as the lyrical, comic, and always ironic narrative proceeds, revealing to Mr. Fortune both his sexual desire and his implication in the evils of imperialism, both he and the similarly implicated Western reader are forced to leave the island and face the beginning of the First World War. The elegiac, political end of the novel—its representation of the realities of violent change and loss—is essential to its artistic success.

Warner wrote about transvestism, pederasty, lesbianism, homo-

2. *Sylvia Townsend Warner in the 1920s.* Photograph courtesy of Susanna Pinney and the Dorset County Museum.

sexuality, and incest as a comedian and as a moralist. Her early novels in particular combine a delight in absurdity with the moral certainty of satire. They are often very funny indeed; it is unsurprising that Warner sometimes laughed out loud as she wrote.[1] Nevertheless, as she herself sardonically asserted, all her writing is imbued with "moral tone."[2] During the thirties and forties she often chose to write moral fables to drive home her political message as a member of the Communist Party.[3] Her 1920s plots are fantastic: Laura Willowes escapes her lot as a middle-class old maid by transforming into a witch; Mr. Fortune loses his missionary faith during a volcanic eruption; true-hearted, destitute Sukey (Psyche) Bond is personally empowered by Queen Victoria (Persephone) to marry her middle-class "idiot" Eric (Eros); but these novels are narrated with the materially specific detail of feminist and Marxist realism.[4]

Warner's sexual radicalism had its roots in the enforced secrecy of her long affair with Percy C. Buck, a married man old enough to be her father; their relationship started when she was nineteen, and she was thirty-six when she ended it. Her celebration of forbidden love in her 1920s novels is the expression of what she had to hide; only after 1930, when she and Valentine Ackland discovered their love and began to live openly as lesbians, did she focus on explicitly lesbian romance in *Summer Will Show* (1936). Lesbianism is just one of the sexually radical themes she explored throughout her writing life, from the 1923–24 poem about Nelly Trim, who lives alone on a Dorset hillside and will comfort any man who passes by to such late stories as "Elphenor and Weasel" (1974); here, the noise of church bells literally deafens and dismembers a pair of supernatural, cross-species, cross-class, cross-color lovers who are trapped in the clamor of a bell tower. Weasel is a small green fairy who lives under a Suffolk hill, while Elphenor is the white nephew of the master of ceremonies at the Elfin Court at Zuy.[5] It is because Warner creates her narratives in a socially and economically complex world that sexually radical romance so rarely triumphs in them any more than it does for Mr. Fortune. Fantasy turns to elegy when he leaves the island at the start of the First World War; lesbian romance and exuberant political satire turn to tragedy in 1848 Paris at the end of *Summer Will Show* with the deaths of Minna and Caspar and the painfully historical mass executions of the working class; the love of the bisexual fisherman Crusoe, whose freedom and pride illuminate for a moment the evangelical repressions of *The Flint Anchor* (1954), fails to rescue Thomas Kettle from the prison of Victorian hypocrisy. Shifts of genre and tone are central to Warner's literary achievement as a leftist sexual radical: unlike the merrily escapist creations of Ronald Firbank or Elinor Wylie, the joys of her pederasts, lesbians, and homosexuals are severely limited by history. Even Crusoe dies prematurely, in a storm at sea, laboring at his daily, dangerous craft.[6] Warner's writing was rooted in her lifelong consciousness of the manifold evils of the class system.

The Powys Circle: *Class Politics and Primitivism*

At the end of 1915, Warner joined the Women Relief Munition Workers' Organisation, established by Lady Moir and Lady Cowan to enable women factory workers to take weekends off without interrupting production.[7] The Vickers' factory at Erith trained women volunteers for three weeks, after which they were used as weekend workers. In her 1939 article "The Way by Which I Have Come," Warner recognizes the political implications of her work there. "I now see that this was a 'dilution' scheme, devised to avoid the payment of overtime

rates to the regular workers," she writes. "I am ashamed of an ignorance that made me a blackleg: on the other hand, I am glad to have
worked, even for a little time, in a factory."[8]

Yet however ignorant the twenty-two-year-old Warner may have
been of socialism and unionism, the article "Behind the Firing Line:
Some Experiences in a Munitions Factory," written for *Blackwoods
Edinburgh Magazine* in 1916, is surprisingly free from snobbery. Noting that the "lady workers . . . are called the Miaows . . . among the
regular hands,"[9] and that they sit during their breaks in their own
wooden shed, separate from the shed for the "workgirls," she comments dryly, "I never noticed any difference in the smell": sweat
knows no class distinctions.[10] She is appreciative of the teaching
methods of the young woman who shows her how to shape a shell
case on the lathe and of the skill and stamina of "my friend the larg-
est mechanic," one of the men who tend the machines at which the
women work.[11] The machinists depend on these men's skills; Warner
dissociates herself from her fellow Miaows in her account of them:

> Unswerving from the most exacting of standards . . . going from one
> machine to another, always watching, always setting to rights, they
> flirt with all the workgirls—flirtations that are algebraic in their de-
> tachment and universality. It is said . . . that the Miaows took coun-
> sel together as to the terms that they would be on with these men:
> and in the end they agreed to treat them with 'distant politeness.'[12]

Warner's distancing of the Miaows rather than the mechanics
indicates her increasing detachment from the values of the class she
grew up in: in 1917, a year after the death of her father when she
was twenty-two, she took advantage of the increased freedom that
the war offered young women to establish herself in a flat above a
furrier's shop in London.[13] Her father's will left her dependent on
her mother, who gave her an annual allowance of £100, while her
work for the Tudor Church Music Committee paid £150 a year.[14] I
have no doubt that Warner's poverty contributed to her keen sense
of economic realities; such details as the wartime price of butter and
her public altercation with a grocer who had sold her a bad egg are
recalled in her 1970 story "Being a Lily."

Warner's insights into the class system are central to all her work;
in the early writing they complicate the primitivist influence of such
popular novelists of rural life as T. F. Powys and Mary Webb. In 1921,
the sculptor Stephen Tomlin introduced Warner to the Dorset village

of East Chaldon and to Powys, who welcomed her immediately into his imaginative and actual world and dedicated *The Left Leg* to her in 1923. Warner writes that Powys "knows the countryside like an old dog fox,"[15] and recounts how, on her first visit to his house, she "felt a little like a cat that has been let out of a hamper but knows it has come to a good home."[16] By 1923, the Powys clan had become her surrogate family and East Chaldon the focus of her imaginative life.

East Chaldon under various names—Shelton, Madder, Little Dodder, Folly Down—forms the setting for most of Powys's fables and allegories of rural life. They are remarkable for their evocation of the greed of the rich, the brutal abjection of the poor, the malice of elderly women, and the mad rush to ruin of lissome, white-limbed young girls. Apart from some of the poems in *The Espalier* (1925) and some early stories in *The Salutation* (1932), Warner's writing seems remarkably free of Powys's influence: her tone and fictional worlds very quickly became quite unmistakably her own. Of her novels, *The True Heart* reflects Powys the most, but Warner's nuanced representation of imperialist ideology is totally unlike Powys's more obvious attacks on hypocrisy, folly, and vice.

T. F. Powys's class primitivism can be usefully contrasted to Warner's. His sexist, primitivist violence is often quite disturbing. Warner herself was troubled by the draft of *Mr. Tasker's Gods* that Powys sent her in 1921: she "found it hard to stomach the ruthless hatred with which he pursued the peasant characters."[17] Marianna Torgovnick's account of the binary tropes of primitivist discourse is quite apposite here; as she notes, "Primitives are our untamed selves, our id forces—libidinous, irrational, violent, dangerous"—like the tramp who fathered Mr. Tasker. But "primitives" also "are mystics, in tune with nature, part of its harmonies"—like Eric in *The True Heart*, or the muscular young fisherman Crusoe in *The Flint Anchor*.[18] Class primitivism, in the British novel anyway, is very similar to, and just as important as, the racial primitivism that is currently so prominent a concern in North American academic discourse.

Mr. Tasker's father receives payment for murdering the blameless Henry; he is promised a bottle of whiskey by Farmer Dane, who sees Henry as an "agitator" inciting his laborers to demand higher wages. Even in this essentially primitivist book, Powys shows a leftist grasp of economics. This is why Warner includes him along with William Langland, William Cobbett, and George Crabbe in her 1939 list of writers who were "witnesses towards the likelihood that the English Pastoral was a grim and melancholy thing."[19] Like Langland, Powys foregrounds both the social evils and the spiritual mysteries of Christianity.

Powys's attack on clerical self-importance and hypocrisy is particularly extreme in *Mr. Tasker's Gods*, but even his most innocent and caring clergymen can do little to change or help the oppressed and ignorant peasantry. It takes Christ's return on Judgment Day in the allegorical *Mr. Weston's Good Wine* (1927) to effect meaningful—if drastic—change. Warner dedicated *Mr. Fortune's Maggot*, in which a missionary's sexual awakening coincides with his political disillusionment, "To Theo" in 1927.[20] Nonetheless, her rejection of Christianity is total; she does not share Powys's ambivalence.

From her early poems to her delineation of Victorian evangelicism in *The Flint Anchor*, Warner conducts an increasingly subtle analysis of Christian power relations. In her eighties, she asserted blithely, "I've never had any temptations to be a Christian."[21] Yet she visited churches constantly, both in her work for the Tudor Church Music Committee and for pleasure. For Warner, Christianity produced evil, but it had also produced beauty; in contemporary British culture, it was an everyday affair. Its deadly tedium is crystallized in a creepily banal moment of her first novel, *Lolly Willowes* (1926).

Lolly Willowes—or, more properly, Laura, since Lolly is what she is called only by her patronizing relatives—is commodified and belittled as a maiden aunt for nineteen years at her brother's house in London. Each Sunday morning, her brother Henry winds up the grandfather clock, whose leaden weights descend for the rest of the week. The sister-in-law, Caroline, who is a model wife to the stupid and self-important Henry, "was a religious woman. . . . Once only did she speak her spiritual mind to Laura."

> Laura was nursing her when she had influenza; Caroline wished to put on a clean nightdress, and Laura, opening the third drawer of the large mahogany wardrobe, had commented upon the beautiful orderliness with which Caroline's body linen was arranged therein. "We have our example," said Caroline. "The graveclothes were folded in the tomb."[22]

A critique of Christianity, capitalism, and the bourgeois family intersects in *Lolly Willowes* with Warner's representation of spinsterhood, perverse sexuality, and a coven of rural witches. Laura moved to London after her father died, when she lost her home in the country where she had happily spent her days ignoring pressures to marry, reading John Locke on the understanding and Joseph Glanvil on witches, and discovering the properties of herbs and simples. At the age of forty-seven, she finally demands the use of her patrimony, but it has been halved by her brother's greed and mismanagement; he explains that he has "transferred the greater part of it to the Ethiopian Development Syndicate, a perfectly sound investment which will in time be as good as ever, if not better."[23] Refusing to be deterred by this attempt to capture two birds—Ethiopia and his sister—with one colonizing stone, Laura insists that Henry reinvest the remaining money in "something . . . like War Loan, that will pay a proper dividend."[24] She then moves into rented rooms in Great Mop, a village near London in the unromantic Chilterns, acquires a familiar, and becomes a witch.

Her first spring at Great Mop, Laura experiences an epiphany in a cowslip field: her release from the leaden weights of servitude is accompanied by a recognition of the collusion among church, state, and the family in the oppression of women:

> There was no question of forgiving them. . . . the injury they had done her was not done by them. If she were to start forgiving she must needs forgive Society, the Law, the Church, the History of Europe, the Old Testament . . . the Bank of England, Prostitution . . . and half a dozen other useful props of civilization.[25]

Like Virginia Woolf, Warner represents sexism as inseparable from the other oppressions that buttress imperialism; her depiction of sexuality is similarly inclusive. Particularly in *Lolly Willowes*, freedom from gender oppression leads to freedom of desire. The novel presents a kind of continuum of sexualities, from Henry and Caroline's unappealing heterosexuality through perverse hints of lesbianism and transgender masquerade to a contented enjoyment of solitude. The fact that it ends with a celebration of celibacy—Laura asleep in the open air, "a hind couched in the Devil's coverts"—perhaps reflects Warner's own dissatisfaction as her seventeen-year-long affair with Percy C. Buck was drawing to its close.[26]

Once Laura realizes that "she [is] a witch by vocation,"[27] she is introduced to the flourishing local coven by her working-class landlady, Mrs. Leak, who has spent the winter evenings with her in front

of the fire, gossiping about or "call[ing] up" their neighbors.[28] Most
of the villagers have assembled for the Witches' Sabbath; they are
dancing in the dark at the top of a hill. It is characteristic of Warner
that this event at first seems dispiritingly familiar; Laura watches the
dancers and recollects past social failures until she is rescued from
her gloom:

> These depressing thoughts were interrupted by red-haired Emily,
> who came spinning from her partner's arms, seized hold of Laura
> and carried her back into the dance. Laura liked dancing with
> Emily. . . .They whirled faster and faster, fused together like two suns
> that whirl and blaze in a single destruction. A strand of the red
> hair came undone and brushed across Laura's face. The contact
> made her tingle from head to foot.[29]

Later, Laura notes that the always respectable Mrs. Leak "danced very
well. Her feet flickered to and fro as nimbly as a tongue."[30]

In "Encoding Bi-Location," Jane Garrity reads *Lolly Willowes* as a
"destabilizing" text in which she sees lesbianism as "a kind of con-
spiratorial inscription," with the witch signifying the lesbian.[31] Much
as I'd like to believe this, and despite Mrs. Leak's tonguelike feet and
the polymorphously perverse Emily, I remain unconvinced. *Lolly
Willowes* celebrates the perverse in salutary opposition to the "normal," and there is certainly a lesboerotic element in Laura's cowslip—
or elderberry-wine-tippling evenings with Mrs. Leak; but the novel
starts and ends with celibate contentment. Satan's "satisfied but profoundly indifferent ownership" replaces the loving, respectful protection
of Laura's father: under either guardian her freedom is guaranteed.[32]

I find particularly useful, however, Garrity's emphasis on the
sexological and eugenicist classification of spinsters as deviant.[33] It
is as if Warner, a thirty-one-year-old sexually active spinster, were defying the "expert" establishment with her sexual freedom and radicalism: "You say I'm deviant; I'll give you deviance" is what I imagine
her saying as she created the antics of Emily and the effeminate young
man at the Sabbath. Laura takes him to be a "Chinaman" until she
realizes he is wearing a mask.[34] "Mincing like a girl," Warner writes,
"the masked young man approached her. . . . With secretive and un-
dulating movements he came to her side. . . . Suddenly she felt upon
her cheeks a cold darting touch. With a fine tongue like a serpent's
he had licked her right cheek, close to the ear."[35] No wonder that

Laura turns her back, even though she believes that this young man may be Satan; in fact, he is just a young exhibitionist who has sold his soul to the devil "on the condition that once a week he should be without doubt the most important person at a party."[36] Once again, the social life of the coven proves all too similar to that of "society"; of course Laura prefers solitude.

When Satan eventually does appear to claim Laura as his own, he masquerades first as a gamekeeper and later as the gardener of Maulgrave Folly, a gothic burial ground built by Sir Ralph Maulgrave, Wickendon's Satanic Baronet. Again, Warner is unable to resist an ironic allusion to the Resurrection. Laura at first does not recognize Satan, like Mary Magdalene who, when Jesus appears to her by the sepulchre, "suppos[es] him to be the gardener."[37] Laura soon understands Satan's joke, pities dead, mocked, unsatanic Sir Ralph, and says, "'How can you?'"[38] I like to think that this is what Warner might have said when she read the end of Rudyard Kipling's story "The Gardener," which was first published in *McCall's* magazine in April 1926—three months after *Lolly Willowes*. It provides an oddly coincidental intertextual moment.[39] In "The Gardener," the spinster Helen Turrell is guided to a grave in a war cemetery in Flanders by a man who is "firming a young plant in the soft earth." Helen is mourning the son whom she has raised as her nephew—a sin of which Kipling absolves her with characteristic mawkishness: "When Helen left the Cemetery she turned for a last look. In the distance she saw the man bending over his young plants; and she went away, supposing him to be the gardener."[40] One of the pleasures of *Lolly Willowes* is that it mocks heavy symbolism; Warner's Satan, whatever his disguises, is quite literally *there*.

Satan's appearance as a gamekeeper is one of several similar apparitions in British modernist narratives of sexual liberation. It is unlikely that Warner knew about E. M. Forster's homosexual gamekeeper in *Maurice*; even though Forster wrote his famous gay romance in 1913, it wasn't published until 1971. It was, however, passed around some members of the homosexual community in manuscript; maybe Stephen Tomlin or David Garnett, both of whom had Bloomsbury connections, read it and spoke about it or even lent it to Warner. It is possible, also, that D. H. Lawrence's aggressively heterosexual gamekeeper in *Lady Chatterley's Lover* (1928) might owe something to Warner's Satan. But in *Lolly Willowes* Warner avoids the idealization of rural working-class masculinity that pervades Forster's and Lawrence's narratives. The Great Mop coven includes the upper-class Misses Larpent as well as the down-to-earth Mrs. Leak; Emily may be a rustic "slattern," but the masked effeminate "Chinaman" is a young writer known by Laura's nephew Titus. Even in the 1920s Warner's writing deconstructs the class system far more often than colluding in it through class primitivism.

Warner can lapse, however, into a problematic appropriation of the oppression of racial Others.[41] The narrative neither distances nor ironizes Laura's comparison of her first "triumph over her tyrants" to the joy of an escaped slave: "The amusement she had drawn from their disapproval was a slavish remnant, a derisive dance on the north bank of the Ohio."[42] This is the kind of stereotype that Warner might have seen represented in one of the early film versions of *Uncle Tom's Cabin*.[43]

Several white women writers have likened the oppression of women to slavery. Woolf's famous passage in *A Room of One's Own* about G. M. Trevelyan's representation of the history of women culminates as follows: "[Woman] was locked up, beaten, and flung about the room. . . . she was the slave of any boy whose parents forced a ring upon her finger. . . . she could hardly read, could scarcely spell, and was the property of her husband."[44] In Christina Stead's *The Man Who Loved Children* (1940), Henny, wife of the monstrous Sam Pollitt, "found it sweet to sit there and think of her boys' future. . . . About the girls she only thought of marriage, and about marriage she thought as an ignorant, dissatisfied, but helpless slave did of slavery."[45] Like Henny, whose absurd diminutive reflects her abjection, the spinster "Lolly" has internalized the contempt of her relatives and of her eugenicist culture. Shortly after rejoicing in her escape, she regresses into servitude, succumbing to her nephew Titus's will. She suffers intensely from her loss of the freedom that she now values so much.[46] Yet Warner's lighthearted reference to that derisive dance on the northern bank of the Ohio remains disturbing.

Such cultural appropriations are troubling in a different way from the equally colonialist racial primitivism that is characteristic of modernism. Warner started writing *Mr. Fortune's Maggot* shortly after reading *The Sailor's Return*, a primitivist novel by David Garnett, another member of the Powys circle and a close friend of Warner's in the twenties.[47] He took the name of the East Chaldon pub as the title of

The Sailor's Return (1925), a historical novel set in the 1850s. On the surface, this book is an attack on British racism.[48]

William Targett, a British sailor, is stranded in Whydah (Ouidah), Dahomey, in the 1850s. He is happy there and marries the king's daughter, whom he loves but nevertheless calls Tulip instead of her given name, Gundemey. They have a dark-skinned son, whom William calls Sambo. Tulip is beautiful and brave; when William marries her she is in training to become one of the women warriors of the Dahomey army.[49] She brings William a large dowry, so that after her father dies he is able to bring Tulip and Sambo home to Dorset and set up as the publican of Maiden Newbarrow (East Chaldon).

William's farming relatives and the villagers distrust and dislike Tulip because she is black and a stranger, and because she is fearless and wears fine clothes. The men of the village, however, are eager to drink and play games in the newly refurbished pub—and William is a strong, intimidating man. Yet when he is absent, his scheming relatives and neighbors persecute Tulip: they try to burn down the pub, and they loose a bull at Tulip and Sambo in the village street. On his return, William is manipulated into fighting an out-of-work pugilist; none of the onlookers tries to prevent the foul play that kills him. Tulip sends Sambo back to Dahomey but cannot get a passage for herself; she returns to the pub, which is now leased by a new publican, and is still there ten years later, "working all day long as the drudge of everyone about the place."[50]

Garnett wrote in *Great Friends* that *The Sailor's Return* is "a tale of racial intolerance";[51] the persecution of Tulip certainly proceeds relentlessly until her final degradation. The villagers are "primitives": in their apathy, malice, and cruelty they resemble Powys's rustics, although Garnett's more matter-of-fact fictional world lacks the nightmare aspect of *Mr. Tasker's Gods*. Even William's loving younger brother, Harry, who appears to be fond of Tulip, tells him, "[Y]ou ought not to mix the two breeds."[52] The novel presents Tulip as far more likeable than the country people. She raises Sambo better than they do their children, and her views about their work, eating, and social habits are a witty reversal of current stereotypes about the "lower races":

> It seemed to her that the white people here did not know how to live; that their lives were like the lives of animals and not like those of human beings. They went out all day into the fields like the cows

going out to graze; when they came back at night they chewed the cud like cows, and if they talked at all they talked slowly and awkwardly.[53]

Yet Tulip is stereotyped also; she is overly simple. Too much is made of her misunderstandings about Christianity. When the parson wants to christen Sambo, she takes literally his promise that after the child is christened he will "be as white as snow."[54] She refuses to attend the ceremony and is so transformed by her fear of it that on Sambo's return "it was a wonder her own child knew her, for he had never seen her like that before, with her skin grey, her eyes rolling, her lips thrust out, and her whole face working and twitching as if she had lost her reason."[55] The racist/misogynist emphasis on her physiognomy intensifies when Tulip is reduced to a drudge at the end of the novel: "In the village they were used to her, and now that she was always dressed in the poorest cast-off clothes . . . nobody shouted at her or jeered as she went by. But by degrees her name changed from Mrs. Tulip to Mrs. Two Lips, because as Tulip grew older and uglier her lips grew broader and more blubbery."[56]

The "jarringly racist anti-racism" in *The Sailor's Return* must have been less clear to Sylvia Townsend Warner in 1925 than it is to a 1990s reader.[57] She plainly had reservations about Garnett's two early novellas;[58] nonetheless, Warner wrote to him enthusiastically about *The Sailor's Return*, "I think it is extremely good. . . . [I]t gives me the impression of something round, close-grained, and resilient with the kind of interior unapproachable life of a very good india-rubber ball."[59] She was already developing the isolated, primitivist, and resiliently complete fictional world of her second novel, *Mr. Fortune's Maggot.*

"Fatally Sodomitic": Pederasty and Primitivism in Mr. Fortune's Maggot

A month after reading *The Sailor Returns*, Warner wrote to Garnett about her new novel,

> You would laugh if you could see the story I am writing now. It is a lovely subject, there is nothing original about it, for it takes place on a Pacific island (like Defoe and H. de Vere Stacpoole), and the hero is a clergyman (like Mrs. Humphry Ward and Oliver Goldsmith),

and it is written in alternate layers of Powys and Garnett, both imitated to the life.[60]

After four months' more work on *Mr. Fortune's Maggot*, however, she adopted a very different tone: "Yet in spite of these gaieties it is not a gay story, and perhaps you will not like it, for it is not like *Lolly*, it has none of her pretty ways."[61] There is a shift of genre and tone toward the end of the narrative that is fundamental to the resonance of Warner's mature novels. Unlike Laura Willowes and Sukey Bond, Mr. Fortune is not permitted a happy ending: he returns to reality rather than escaping it. Warner's crosswriting of this homosexual romance may have been a way of recreating and distancing her intense experience of loss in the First World War.

In a note Warner wrote in the 1960s for William Maxwell about the composition of her novels, she described Mr. Fortune's birth in a dream:

> [O]ne early morning I woke up remembering an extremely vivid dream. A man stood alone on an ocean beach, wringing his hands in an intensity of despair; as I saw him in my dream I knew something about him. He was a missionary, he was middle-aged and a deprived character . . . he was on an island where he had made only one convert and at the moment I saw him he had realised that the convert was no convert at all. I jumped out of bed and began to write this down and even as I wrote a great deal that I knew from the dream began to scatter; but the main facts and the man's loneliness, simplicity and despair and the look of the island all remained as actual as something I had really experienced.[62]

I read Warner's crosswriting in *Mr. Fortune's Maggot* as connected with her father and her affair with Percy Buck rather than as an expression of suppressed lesbian desire. Writing the novel may have offered her some respite from the constraints of her secret heterosexual life: the interracial pederasty in *Mr. Fortune's Maggot*—like the escape into Satanic celibacy in *Lolly Willowes*—may have freed her imagination not only from the multiple inhibitions of secrecy but also from the everyday irritation of seeming to be an "old maid." What these first two novels have in common with the heterosexual primitivist fantasy of *The True Heart* is that all three 1920s narratives explore and celebrate desire that is explicitly forbidden: self-loving spinsterhood in *Lolly Willowes*; same-sex desire in *Mr. Fortune's Maggot*; a young woman's active pursuit not only of a lover but of her culture's ulti-mate "primitive," the "idiot," in *The True Heart*. Writing the two ro-mances, in particular, may have provided relief from the unromantic silence of Warner's own romance.

I don't think that actually practicing forbidden love posed much of a problem for Warner when she started writing *Mr. Fortune's Mag-got* in 1925: she had been a sexual outlaw since the age of nineteen, when her secret affair with the married, middle-aged Percy Buck started. But speaking about this most important aspect of her sexual and emotional life was personally forbidden to her between 1913 and 1930—that is, throughout her entire youth. Warner crosswrote in the 1920s in order to represent forbidden love in forms that would not threaten Percy Buck's secret. The spinster, the pederast, the danger-ously desirous young working-class woman—all these were recogniz-able alternative figures of deviant sexuality. A pederast on a Pacific island was an inviting subject for the sexually radical writer as well as the critic of colonialism.

The Reverend Timothy Fortune, is, in 1911, an innocent abroad; his "maggot"—the word is glossed by Warner as "a whimsical or per-verse fancy; a crotchet"—is to persuade the British Protestant mission at St. Fabien in the Raratongan Archipelago to send him to convert the people of the nearby island of Fanua. The islanders welcome him hospitably, and he immediately settles down happily with a Fanuan boy, Lueli, whom he regards as his one and only convert. The novel, however, is an account of Mr. Fortune's own conversion experiences during the three years that he spends on the island: his love for Lueli, his loss of his God, and his increasingly critical consciousness of the meanings of militant Christianity and imperialism.

Warner's crosswriting in *Mr. Fortune's Maggot* is remarkably con-sistent; there is only the one romance—no heterosexual relationships, no lesbian subplot—and women are only minimally present in the novel. In so far as they do appear, however, they are strikingly com-petent. A bevy of young girls rescue Lueli from his attempt at sui-cide by drowning; their subsequent attentions distract him from his despair. Then there are the nameless old women: Ori, the Fanuan chief, dispatches one of them up the volcano to ascertain which way the lava is flowing; she returns swiftly with news that the commu-nity is safe. A celebrated great-grandmother storyteller makes a crony out of Mr. Fortune; they engage in comparative ethnography, swapping such folktales as the story of Joseph and his brethren. And when Mr. Fortune feels more than usually ineffectual, he is apt to recall the fearless resolution of certain women missionaries: they are Chinese or Hawaiian, not British. None of these women has an ounce of romance in her; they are this novel's artists and adventurers. And a narrative by a woman like them was part of the genesis of the novel.

I attribute the satisfying completeness of *Mr. Fortune's Maggot*— its "interior unapproachable life"—to Warner's insistence on materially specific details within the "primitive" freedom of Fanua. Her description to Maxwell of the novel's genesis emphasizes this fusion of the naturalistic with the fantastic:

> When I first went to live in London, in 1917, in a flat over a furrier's at 127 Queens Road, Bayswater, I was poor and could not afford a lending library subscription. I had the British Museum by day but I wanted something to read in the evenings. Then I found the Westbourne Grove branch of the Paddington Public Library. . . . One of the books I took out was a volume of letters by a woman missionary in Polynesia. . . . It had only the minimum of religion, only elementary scenery and a mass of details of every-day life. The woman wrote out of her own heart—for instance, describing an earthquake she said that the ground trembled like the lid of a boiling kettle.[63]

The woman missionary's influence is especially evident near the end of the novel, during Mr. Fortune's expedition to the crater of the volcano: the crags surmounting the crater "reminded him of a group of ruined gas-vats with the paint scaling off them, standing in the middle of a brick-field. It smelt of brick-fields too; and . . . new sounds came to his ear, ugly to match the landscape, and of a kind of baleful insignificance like the landscape—far-off crashes and rumblings, the hiss and spurt of escaping steam: the noise of a flustered kitchen."[64] This solitary exploration occurs after the eruption and earthquake that precipitate the ex-missionary's crisis of conscience: he no longer has access to the comfortably primitivizing imperialist gaze.

Some of Warner's British Museum reading must have been connected to her work as a musicologist, but it seems to me likely that she also encountered the primitivist anthropological theory that was then being published, even though she doesn't mention it in the account she wrote for Maxwell when she was in her seventies.[65] *How*

Natives Think (1925), the translation of Lucien Lévy-Bruhl's *Les Fonctions Mentales dans les Sociétés Inférieures*, would have been acquired by the British Museum just when Warner was working on the question of how to represent the Fanuans' thoughts and language in *Mr. Fortune's Maggot*. She might well have been attracted to the book by the arrogant absurdity of Lévy-Bruhl's title. Modernist representations of "primitive" speech are often problematic to postmodern readers: pidgin English further characterizes the colonized as inferior to the colonizers, who are blessed with the King's/Queen's English.

In his famous essay on Conrad's *Heart of Darkness*, Chinua Achebe claims that the most significant difference between the "savage and superb" African woman on the bank of the river and the spectral, mourning figure of Kurtz's Intended is the fact that the latter is permitted to speak. On the two occasions when Africans do speak in this primitivist textbook, the first announces—in absurdly ferocious pidgin—cannibal starvation, and the second, as quoted by T. S. Eliot, laconically announces the death of Mr. Kurtz, modernism's most hollow man.[66] Conrad's *Victory* (1915), set on a fictional island in Indonesia, clearly delineates some of the complex ranking of imperialist ideology: we have the protagonist, Axel Heyst, heroically antiheroic "disarmed man," the villainously decadent homosexual Mr. Jones, and their two class Others: the sexually ambiguous Ricardo, Mr. Jones's "secretary," and Lena, the "English girl" whom Heyst chivalrously rescued in Sourabaya from Zangiacomo's Ladies' Orchestra. The racial Others range from Heyst's cowardly servant, Wang the "Chinaman," who speaks pidgin, through Wang's silent and invisible mistress, a member of the indigenous people who lurk behind a barricade of felled trees and spears (we see only her shadow), to Pedro, Mr. Jones's servant: this hairy, black "creature" has "enormous brown paws [and] a wide mouth full of fangs."[67] Pedro speaks a pidgin Spanish comprehensible only to Ricardo.

Warner's sensible decision to avoid pidgin may well have been influenced by a writer with whom she had long been deeply familiar: Robert Louis Stevenson.[68] I want to set him beside Conrad as an early modernist primitivist "master" who in fact knew rather more than Conrad about the lives of Pacific Islanders. Stevenson's representation of the speech of "primitive" peoples is often problematic, but it is far more thoughtful and various than that of most of his British contemporaries. In "The Beach of Falesá" the first-person narrator, Wiltshire, is a copra trader in Polynesia whose ambition is to make enough money to go home to England and buy a nice pub. He tells his story in the language of adventurers' yarns—a literary dialect in which Stevenson was skilled—but Wiltshire's wife Uma and the other Polynesians all speak pidgin; this is reproduced as Wiltshire hears it. When Wiltshire is talking to the Polynesians he speaks pidgin too at first, but as his love and knowledge of Uma grow, his language becomes more English. The dialogue in "The Isle of Voices" and "The Bottle Imp" is simple and grammatically "correct." These are "Hawaiian" folk- or fairy tales with omniscient narrators and Hawaiian protagonists; they read rather like English translations of Hans Christian Andersen or the Brothers Grimm. They work well, although the question of which "folk" these tales by a British traveler actually represent and what readers they were written for remains a vexed one; both stories contain primitivist stereotypes. And neither story represents dialogue between Hawaiians and Europeans.

The ungendered omniscient narrator of *Mr. Fortune's Maggot* assumes a shared culture, almost a friendship, with the reader: allusions to William Wordsworth, Oscar Wilde, and Arnold Schoenberg require an educated reader, while the novel's success depends on one familiar with the minutiae of British imperialism and the class and sex-gender systems. Such a reader would probably expect Lueli, Ori the hospitable chief, and all the other Fanuans to speak to Mr. Fortune in pidgin. Warner, of course, surprises us. She evades the problem at first, before Mr. Fortune and the reader have accustomed themselves to the island, by avoiding the necessity for direct Fanuan speech—but she cannot silence her "primitives" for long. By page 50 of the book, Lueli is miraculously able to convey shades of mood and emotion in perfectly "correct" English. Mr. Fortune gets properly scolded on his return from a very British walk in the rain: "'How very wet! How very silly! Come in at once! Why do you go out when it rains?'"[69] On a similar occasion three years later, after Lueli's attempt at suicide following the loss of his god, he speaks with greater formality: "'I was growing very anxious, I assure you.'"[70] And except when he is expounding Christianity or Euclid, Mr. Fortune's syntax is similarly unpretentious. Although he is British, he is not a self-important man.

Warner respected Stevenson both as a writer and as a man and alluded to him at several important moments in her life.[71] She must have read Stevenson's "children's books" as a child, including *Treasure Island* (1883), in which the island scenery is strikingly drab—like the upper slopes of Fanua's mountain, which "rise up in crags or steep tracts of scrub and clinker to the . . . curious cactus-shaped pinnacles of rock [around] . . . the old crater."[72] Her earliest literary allusion to Stevenson occurs in her first published work, "Behind the Firing Line: Some Experiences in a Munitions Factory." Her job in the factory was to operate a lathe that shaved twelve-pound shell cases to the requisite shape and size—monotonous, heavy work that became increasingly exhausting. She describes the thoughts with which she whiled away her shift—at least at the beginning of her time there "while the dirt could still be washed off and the aches slept off without much difficulty, and while the idea of the extreme picturesqueness and daring of such an adventure as ours still upheld one. . . . Like Stevenson combating the sensitive plant at Vailima, standing at my lathe I talked wittily and at length with my friends that were not there."[73] The sensitive plant is a voracious Samoan weed; this is an allusion to the comparatively obscure *Vailima Letters*, a posthumously published collection of the monthly letters about Stevenson's life in Samoa that he wrote to his friend Sidney Colvin.[74]

Stevenson left San Francisco on his South Pacific travels in June 1888 and arrived in December 1889 at the Samoan island of Upolu, where he was to settle for the remaining five years of his life. He built a house called Vailima on the mountain above Apia and lived there with his wife, a continually shifting band of their relatives—mother, stepson, stepdaughter and husband, stepgrandson, cousin—and a number of Samoan servants and laborers. He spent his time writing (often driven by the need to pay their considerable bills), clearing and weeding his land, playing his flageolet, and taking an active interest in Samoan politics.

Stevenson's influence is more clearly discernible in *Mr. Fortune's Maggot* than that of any other writer except perhaps Daniel Defoe. Most obviously, Stevenson gave Warner the name of her island, Fanua. His story "The Beach of Falesá" was originally titled "The High Woods of Ulufanua." Delighted with this title, Stevenson defined it for Colvin: "Ulufanua is an imaginary island; the name is a beautiful Samoan word for the *top* of a forest; ulu—leaves or hair; fanua = land. The ground or country of the leaves. 'Ulufanua the isle of the sea,' read that verse dactylically and you get the beat; the u's are like our double oo; did you ever hear a prettier word?"[75]

Warner's Fanua is remarkable for the variety of its scenery: the calm solitude of the dell among the woods, where Mr. Fortune makes his home in a forsaken hut; the loud Pacific surf and the sheltered tidal pool where he and Lueli swim; the dense forest traversed by the islanders' paths, and the gentle stream that emerges from a gorge where "the noise of the cataract echoes from cliff to cliff."[76] A source for these tropical details can be found in Stevenson: the stream, the cataract, the extraordinary fecundity and the sudden surprising sounds of the forest come up repeatedly in his *Vailima Letters*. He even experiences a minor earthquake. But Warner's matter-of-factness, her lyricism, her moments of understated horror—these are all her own.

During a lull in the earthquake, Lueli fears there will be a tidal wave, so he hurries Mr. Fortune up the mountain. As the shocks start again, they sit "side by side, holding on to one another . . . upon a little grassy platform, overlooking the ravine." Mr. Fortune begins to look about him:

> They were close to the cataract. Tonight, instead of the usual steady roar of falling water, the noise was coming in curious gusts of sound, now loud, now almost nothing. He turned his eyes and saw the slender column of falling water all distorted and flapping like a piece of muslin in a draught. For some reason this sight was overwhelmingly piteous and a sort of throe hollowed him as if he were going to cry.[77]

Stevenson compares his earthquake to "a huge mill-wheel . . . not going steadily but with a *schottische* movement";[78] this is interesting, but how much more immediate and uncanny is Warner's waterfall, flapping like a piece of muslin cloth. The *heimlich* is doubly defamiliarized here, for the muslin recalls window curtains or washing lines in the suburbs of Mr. Fortune's youth, while the stream has been the companion of his daily walks in this island that he loves. That he wants to cry for the waterfall's transformation and not for his own plight is a product of shock as well as of his habitual estrangement from himself.

Missionaries were all the rage among British writers in the twenties and thirties; usually, as in Evelyn Waugh's colonialist satires, they appear as figures of derision and/or homophobia.[79] Stevenson's

fictional missionaries of the 1890s are neither mocked nor stereotyped, perhaps because he knew so many missionaries himself; one
of his closest friends in Samoa was the Reverend W. E. Clarke. The
English missionary whom Keola and Lehua consult at the end of "The
Isle of Voices" is both greedy and treacherous (or racist—which comes
to the same thing in this context): he advises them to give some of
their magically coined money to the lepers and the missionary fund
and to keep their story to themselves; but he also tells the police at
Honolulu to keep an eye on the couple because they've been coin-
ing false money.[80] Then there's the good, peripatetic Mr. Tarleton,
who comes and goes in "The Beach at Falesá"; he is honest and courageous, and his attitude to the Hawaiians closely resembles the pa-
ternalism we find in Stevenson's own dealings with his Samoan
servants.

Stevenson's life in Samoa was essentially patriarchal: he was the
head of a family in which the Samoans were his children. Like the
Romans, he believed in building character and roads.[81] And after all,
he built a property. But it is characteristic of Mr. Fortune to live in a
forsaken hut, a choice of residence that prepares us for his rejection
of Christian imperialism. Marianna Torgovnick writes memorably
about this age-old collaboration in the amassing and development
of property; she quotes from Stanley's *How I Found Livingstone*:

> To find Livingstone, Stanley must pass through African lands rarely
> seen by Western eyes. . . .
>> At a place called Sigunga, we put in for lunch. An island at the
>> mouth of the bay suggested to our minds that this was a beau-
>> tiful spot for a mission station. . . . The island, capable of con-
>> taining quite a large village, and perfectly defensible, might, for
>> prudence' sake, contain the mission and its congregation; the
>> landlocked bay would protect their fishery and trade vessels.
> Now there is a bare island; after the West's arrival there will be a
> mission station, with fishery and trade vessels, on a site easy to
> defend from hostile Africans and foreign powers. What will be there
> after Western intervention always impinges on Stanley's view of what
> is there now.[82]

To a certain extent, Stevenson must have seen Samoa with the similarly colonizing eyes of a property developer.

Stevenson treats his servants as childlike dependents without
showing much awareness that he depends on the Samoans, as a colo-

nist living off the labor and skills of the colonized. Mr. Fortune, in contrast, does not affect the Fanuans at all, although they look after him kindly. He realizes in the end that he has been their guest; he has been the oddity, not they. As the story tells us,

> They had been on easy terms with him . . . they had accepted his odd ways without demur. . . . And at all times they had continued to supply him with food and to perform any service he had required of them. They had grown accustomed to him, but they had not assimilated him; and his odd ways they had taken as something quite natural since he himself was an oddity.[83]

To require a service is to assume a superior position, but I am sure that Mr. Fortune must have done his requiring with the utmost diffidence. His ineffectualness, his innocence, and his humility are the qualities that save him. The fact is that, whatever the future depredations of imperialism may be—and Mr. Fortune himself foresees them—he leaves both Lueli and Fanua unharmed by his three years' stay.

Yet I don't want to demonize Stevenson; his colonialism was comparatively innocuous; his narratives are far more readable and their racism and sexism less offensive than, for example, Conrad's. And I have no doubt about the intertextuality of his and Warner's writing. *Vailima Letters* may also be a source for her remarkable evocation of the music Lueli plays on his "wooden pipe, rather like a flageolet."

The most incongruous item in Mr. Fortune's equipment is his "second-hand harmonium (rather cumbrous and wheezy but certainly a bargain)"; he is able to play "many classical larghettos and loud marches" on it "quite nicely."[84] During their shared musical evenings Mr. Fortune "obliges" first, and then Lueli provides quite a contrast:

> Lueli's tunes were very long tunes, though the phrases composing them were short; the music seemed to waver to and fro, alighting unexpectedly and then taking another small flight, and listening to it was like watching a bird flitting about in a bush; the music ends, the bird flies away; and one is equally at a loss to explain why the bird stayed so long and seemed so busy or why it suddenly made up its mind that the time had come for a longer flight, for a flight that dismisses it from our vision.
>
> To tell the truth, Mr. Fortune was not as much impressed by Lueli's music as Lueli was by his.[85]

Both Stevenson and Warner loved music; Stevenson played his flageolet; Warner played the piano and composed; she had plans before the First World War to go to Vienna to study composition with Schoenberg. It was probably around that time that she first read *Vailima Letters*, so I expect she paid some attention to this remarkable passage:

> About four in the morning I was awakened by the sound of a whistle pipe blown outside . . . very softly and to a pleasing, simple air. . . . It sounded very peaceful, sweet and strange in the dark; and I found this was a part of the routine of my rebel's night, and it was done (he said) to give good dreams.[86]

Stevenson transcribes the first phrase he hears, giving the tempo and mood as "Andante tranquillo." How different from poor Mr. Fortune's "loud marches" on the harmonium!

Throughout this novel, Warner presents the colonialist discourse of the "primitive" ironically, introducing and then immediately undercutting stereotypes of class and "race" upon which imperialist power depends. Soon after Lueli's first appearance, seemingly as a gift from God—Mr. Fortune finds Lueli kneeling beside him as he completes his prayers on his first Sunday on the island—the missionary takes a good look at his convert:

> Broad-minded persons with no colour prejudices might have described [Lueli] as aristocratic-looking. This definition did not occur to Mr. Fortune, who had had no dealings with aristocrats and was consequently unaware of any marked difference between them and other people; but he reflected with satisfaction that the boy looked very refined for one who had been so recently a heathen.[87]

Here the broad-minded persons' superior judgment is immediately undercut by their class assumptions; Mr. Fortune is free from this particular form of snobbery, but he replaces it with the equally absurd supposition that Lueli's facial expression—possibly even his bone structure—reflects his newfound spirituality. The new Christian looks "very refined."

The description continues, "Though when he talked he pulled very charming faces, in repose his expression was slightly satirical." Those charming faces are troubling; there certainly is an objectification of the Other. But a little further into the novel, when the two friends have set up house together and fallen into a contented routine, we learn what keeps Lueli with his mentor: Mr. Fortune pulls fascinating faces too:

> What [Lueli] loved beyond anything was novelty, and for this he worshipped Mr. Fortune, whose every action might reveal some new and august entertainment. The faces he made in shaving, the patches of hair on his chest, his ceremonious method of spitting out pips into his hand, the way in which his boot-laces went round the little hooks, his watch, his pockets and the things he kept in them—Lueli might grow accustomed to these daily delights, but he did not tire of them any more than Wordsworth tired of the Lesser Celandine.[88]

It is arguable that although Lueli is amused by Mr. Fortune he is nonetheless objectified in this passage and in the novel as a whole. Certainly the emphasis on his love of novelty is a primitivist cliché. And Warner rarely permits us to know his thoughts and feelings; the narrative point of view is usually limited to what is experienced, thought, and felt by Mr. Fortune.[89] Yet Lueli's intent contemplation of Mr. Fortune is no more nor less primitivizing than Mr. Fortune's contemplation of him; both gazes are simultaneously objectifying and absurd, and perhaps as harmless to their object as Wordsworth's is to the celandine. Furthermore, Lueli wears his hair "gathered up in a tuft over either ear, in much the same manner as was fashionable at the French Court in the year 1671."[90] The satiric tone undercuts the racist "Otherings" of imperialism, the pretensions of the world of fashion, be it Parisian or Fanuan, and the homophobic stereotypes of effeminacy.

The use of irony in this novel airily rewrites a number of the binaries of that Other: civilized versus primitive, male versus female, hetero- versus homosexual. The male/female binary is constantly mocked. We are told that Mr. Fortune has a "housewifely mind," and among the many essential supplies he takes with him to Fanua—they include a harmonium, a silver teapot, and a sewing machine—is a "gentleman's housewife."[91] This article, generally pronounced "huzzif," is a sewing kit; Mr. Fortune will need it to make white garments for his converts. His equipment should be compared with the copious (and manly) supplies so laboriously amassed by Robinson Crusoe: planks, food, liquor, tools, guns and ammunition, a grindstone, a hammock, bedding, ropes, sails, razors, scissors, and money.[92] As Mr. Fortune sits on the rocks watching Lueli swim before cumbrously addressing himself to their shared daily bathing, he often thinks gratefully how much happier he is than Crusoe was with "his man Friday" on that other island: "But poor Crusoe had no such contented mind. . . . 'I see numbers of goats. Melancholy reflections.'"[93]

The heterosexual/homosexual binary is persistently called into question, too, partly because Mr. Fortune's prudishness and innocence prevent him from either recognizing or acting on his own sexual desire. He is horrified when Ori, the Fanuan chief, asks him if he would like a girl as well as a boy to live with him, and he purposely schedules his daily walks during the siesta period to avoid meeting the "bevies" of young girls who "gather round him . . . naked from the sea . . . begging and cajoling him to go bathing with them" or "entrap . . . him in the centre of a dance, wanton enough to inflame a maypole."[94] His prudishness can be read as both homosexual and misogynist.

Mr. Fortune's sense of his own identity as a respectable British missionary depends on such routines as taking long walks in the midday sun; this identity is threatened by the insidious possibility of which Fanua and the Fanuans persist in reminding him: the possibility of bodily pleasure. Take, for example, the matter of oiling. Mr. Fortune has no objection to the islanders' custom of oiling themselves, but he categorically rejects Lueli's offers to oil him. Oiling, he thinks, is effeminate, unbecoming, un-British. Eventually, however, he has to succumb in order to avoid hurting Lueli's feelings: Lueli is permitted, after their daily swim, to oil, first, Mr. Fortune's sprained knee; then his rheumatic back; and finally the whole of his long, bony, goosefleshy body, which, needless to say, improves considerably in appearance.[95] Nevertheless, rejection of the physical continues to impoverish Mr. Fortune's life throughout the novel.

The turning point of this narrative, as in so many South Sea–island fantasies, is the eruption of Fanua's volcano; it should make a very happy missionary out of Mr. Fortune, for fire descends from the heavens and burns up Lueli's idol. But the irony becomes bitter as Mr. Fortune sees ever more clearly the complicity of Christian proselytizing with imperialism: he finally begins to understand his own unconscious hypocrisy. He sees that possessive love rather than religious faith is the source of his rage when he discovers that Lueli, throughout the three years of their relationship, has secretly continued to worship his idol—for each Fanuan worships his or her own god. Mr. Fortune demands that Lueli burn the idol; Lueli refuses to do so; the volcano erupts. Lueli saves his friend from burning, and leaves his idol to the flames. But when the excitement is over, on their return to the ashes of their home, Lueli is overwhelmed by grief and despair, and Mr. Fortune realizes that the consolations of Christianity are worse than useless:

> He should say something of this sort: "Your god, Lueli, was only made of wood. . . . Now will you not see that my God is a better God than yours?" . . . Yes, that was the sort of thing to say, but he felt a deep reluctance to saying it. It seemed ungentlemanly to have such a superior invulnerable God, part of the European conspiracy which opposes gunboats to canoes and rifles to bows and arrows, which showers death from the mountains upon Indian villages, which rounds up the negro in an empire and tricks him of his patrimony.[96]

It is unsurprising that this vision of the church's collaboration in imperialism is swiftly followed by the Reverend Timothy Fortune's loss of his faith.

In a 1926 letter to David Garnett, written when she was completing the novel, Warner described her missionary as "fatally sodomitic."[97] She exaggerates the fatality, or danger of censorship, of course: it is well known that during the twenties and thirties the interpretive powers of the censorious were limited by the fact that they were entirely literal minded.[98] But the words "perverse fancy" in the *New English Dictionary* definition of *maggot* that Warner quotes as her epigraph are surely a pointer to the crucial importance of Mr. Fortune's deviant desire. The maggot also symbolizes Mr. Fortune's penis—that habitually quiescent member that so embarrasses him by its maypole-like tendency during the Fanuan dances.[99] A maypole or a maggot: male sexuality is rendered doubly absurd. No wonder Mr. Fortune attempts to sublimate his desire, first in his painstaking efforts to seal his conversion of Lueli with a rigorous Christian education and later in his absurd but desperate attempt to shore up "rational" Western discourse by teaching Lueli Euclidean geometry.

The narrative makes clear that Mr. Fortune and Lueli never consummate their love; indeed, the missionary does not even recognize his emotion as sexual desire until near the end of the novel, when Lueli has tried to kill himself in despair over the loss of his god.

Mr. Fortune, thinking him drowned, now can realize that he "set his desire on him" with a possessive interfering love that seeks to change the beloved.[100] It is at this point that Mr. Fortune decides to leave the island, for he sees that although his love for Lueli is not "what is accounted a criminal love"—there's certainly been no "gross indecency," let alone sodomy, in their relationship—it has been as bound up with the will to power as his Christianity; both his love and his presence on the island are irrevocably contaminated by imperialism.

In her 1960s note for William Maxwell, Warner wrote that toward the end of the narrative "things kept working out right" and gave as an example the fact that Mr. Fortune's watch stops during the volcanic eruption.[101] When he realizes it is not running he makes futile, anxious efforts to guess how much time has elapsed, but he finally has to reset the watch arbitrarily. Thus, for the rest of his stay on Fanua he is out of sync with that center of "civilization," Greenwich. Briefly, he can live outside time. Here Warner is literalizing the idea that "primitive" people live outside time and are therefore without history—a notion that has been shown by such writers as Marianna Torgovnick and David Theo Goldberg to be central to colonialism: if people have no history, then they are essentially lesser than their more "advanced" oppressors, who are thereby licensed to destroy their environment, steal their resources, exploit their labor, abuse their women (or young boys), and appropriate or erase their culture.

Torgovnick offers a clear exposition of the idea that the "natural" lives of "primitive" peoples represent human origins, and she delineates some of primitivism's uses to the West:

> The belief that primitive societies reveal origins or natural order depends on an ethnocentric sense of existing primitive societies as outside of linear time, and on a corresponding assumption that primitive societies exist in an eternal present which mirrors the past of Western civilization. . . . Explorations of the primitive could thus potentially make us change our ideas about ourselves. . . . Or they could support traditional values and arrest changes found threatening in contemporary culture. Through the power invested in original, "natural" systems, definitions of the primitive could comment on and affect social change.[102]

Edward Carpenter, for example, alluded to such "primitives" as American Indians, West Africans, and Polynesians in his endeavors to establish same-sex desire as natural and his "intermediates" as possessing the special creative and nurturing powers of priests and healers. Warner ironizes this kind of idealism, and yet I believe that the appeal of *Mr. Fortune's Maggot* resides at least partly in Western readers' wishes to imagine that their past resembled the Fanuans' present. I am sure that David Theo Goldberg, whose *Racist Culture* critiques Torgovnick for lapsing into collusion with the primitivism that she describes, would condemn *Mr. Fortune's Maggot* despite the clarity of Warner's critique of colonialism.[103]

Aware of the nature of both his love and his Christianity, Mr. Fortune knows that he must leave the island. Finally, he is able to act with an uninhibited generosity and tolerance that he has learned from the Fanuans. He carves Lueli a new idol, places it on the rock that once served as a Christian altar, weaves a garland of red flowers for it, and leaves it for Lueli to find. After making this love gift he can tell Lueli that he is going to leave Fanua. "'I must, my dear,'" he says. "'It is time.'"[104] But reentering time and resetting his watch in the archdeacon's launch on the way back to St. Fabien, Mr. Fortune watches the island diminish into the ocean and feels desolate, pillaged: "Everything that was real, everything that was significant, had gone down with the island of Fanua and was lost for ever."[105]

The ending of this novel finally reveals that the fantasy has been an elegy all along. No sooner does Mr. Fortune set foot in the launch than the secretary of the mission erupts into nationalistic bombast about the Great War that has just started. The Germans, he says, have crucified Belgian children and should be crucified themselves; he inveighs against the French, the Turks, the Italians; he boasts that there is now a gunboat at St. Fabien. Meanwhile, Mr. Fortune watches the island of Fanua "sinking back into the sea." The First World War started when Warner was twenty; during it, she lost her beloved father and many of his ex-pupils at Harrow who were her friends. This novel is both a product of these losses and a kind of monument or memorial to her prewar happiness. The sadness at the end of the novel may well also express the cultural myth that "the Great War was the loss of innocence."[106]

Mr. Fortune's desolation represents mourning and loss as well as primitivist nostalgia for a prewar paradise on a tropical island. After his decision to leave Fanua, a number of lapses occur in the narrator's ironic detachment from Mr. Fortune's perceptions of the Fanuans.

And without that detachment, the primitivism in the novel's representation of Polynesians becomes increasingly evident. How can Lueli's discovery of the newly carved idol restore his happiness so quickly and completely that Mr. Fortune hears "a murmur, a wandering wreath of sound [that] was Lueli talking softly to his god"?[107] Isn't this instant consolation rather too childlike—as if Mr. Fortune had substituted one toy for another? Despite such tonic moments as the description of Mr. Fortune "flushed with praise and wearing as many garlands as a May Queen or a coffin" at the islanders' farewell feast in his honor, and despite its wit, courage, and originality, I read *Mr. Fortune's Maggot* as a primitivist romance, after all.[108] Of course, Warner was a product of ideology; she problematized but also participated in the primitivism of her culture (and ours).

Reading *Mr. Fortune's Maggot* alongside Stevenson, however, makes even more apparent the subtlety of Warner's representation of difference in her particular version of race primitivism. Mr. Fortune may be unheroic, but he is not to be patronized: he has had his day and his dance. The 1908 edition of the *New English Dictionary*—cited by Warner as the source for her definition of *maggot*—offers a pertinent illustration of that capacious word: it was "used in the names of many dance-tunes." Examples from the sixteenth edition of the *Dancing Master* (1716) include "Betty's Maggot," "Mr. Beveridge's Maggot," and—a perversely anachronistic touch—"My Lord Byron's Maggot."[109] Warner must have come across these dances during her musicological researches, however churchy they were meant to be; indeed, she directs the reader toward music in the last word of her definition: "A nonsensical or perverse fancy; a crotchet." When she imagined Mr. Fortune's incongruous Fanuan romance, she may also have envisioned a page of old-fashioned musical notation. In his formal, angular, out-of-date way, he had his three years of anxious, inhibited joy.

In her 1960s account for Maxwell of her writing of the novel, Warner describes her anxiety as she completed the book: "I was so intensely conscious that the shape and balance of the narrative must be exactly right—or the whole thing would fall and break to smithereens and I could never pick it up again. I remember saying . . . that I felt as if I were in an advanced pregnancy with a Venetian glass child."[110] She alludes here to *The Venetian Glass Nephew* (1924) by Elinor Wylie, a baroquely inventive, crisply ridiculous fantasy set in eighteenth-century Venice. It depicts the literal materialization, through the intervention of Casanova and a Murano glassblower, of a saintly old cleric's innocent desire. A beautiful young man is created in lifesize Venetian glass—a form in which sexual activity would indeed be fatal. It is because *Mr. Fortune's Maggot* succeeds in holding politics and perverse desire, primitivism and satire, material specificity, fantasy, and elegy in a fragile, fleeting equilibrium that its representation of innocent interracial pederasty can continue to delight.

The foregrounding in this novel of romance rather than gay liberation becomes very clear when one compares *Mr. Fortune's Maggot* to Radclyffe Hall's *The Well of Loneliness* or E. M. Forster's *Maurice*: the gay bildungsroman set amid the constraints of Edwardian England is a very different genre from the primitivist romance. Both Stephen Gordon and Maurice try to escape from society's rules: Stephen can't make good her escape because compulsory heterosexuality is an essential component of the imperialist race and class system whose rules she still wants to live by, but Maurice—however unconvincingly—takes a deep breath and breaks out. It is perhaps indicative of Forster's own entrapment in the closet that he envisaged an epilogue for his lovers in which they are encountered several years later as woodcutters in the forest—the primitivist Robin Hood fantasy, with Maid Marian displaced. One of the reasons Forster gives for his rejection of this ending is that "the novel's action-date is about 1912, and 'some years later' would plunge it into the transformed England of the First World War." Yet such an ending might have been preferable to the idealized ending he finally chose, representing a middle-class lover united with his working-class beloved within an apparently unchanged class/sex/gender system.[111] The primitivist idyll in Fanua is less idealistic than the more "real" world represented by Forster, for Fanua offers neither an escape nor a solution—only a period of respite for both Mr. Fortune and the (primitivizing) reader. At the end, the reader, too, is exiled from paradise into the First World War.

Grief and Rage: Warner's War

Mr. Fortune's Maggot is the only work by Warner to end with an "envoy": "My poor Timothy, Goodbye! I do not know what will become of you."[112] It is also the only work of hers, as far as I know, to have a sequel.[113] Warner's novella, "The Salutation" (1932), is perhaps evidence that her attachment to her missionary and his loss was too intense for her to abandon him. We meet him on the Argentinian pampas a few years after his leaving Fanua; he has come there seeking "a place where there would be elbow-room for sorrow."[114] The novella's plot is driven by the energies of Angustias, widow of an Englishman and owner of the House of the Salutation. She welcomes the aging wanderer, whom she hears coughing an unmistakably English cough on the bench outside her house, and she cures his fever but proves unable to cure the homesickness for Fanua that enshrouds Mr. Fortune in unremitting depression. The ending of this narrative, like that of *Mr. Fortune's Maggot*, is both inconclusive and hopeless; "The Salutation" is relentlessly sad to read. Warner attributed its weakness to an excess of attachment that made her "more interested in the story than in the telling."[115] I do not believe that authorial attachment seriously flaws *Mr. Fortune's Maggot*, but it certainly contributes to its elegiac ending.

George Townsend Warner, Sylvia's father, died suddenly in 1916, when she was twenty-two; the following year Warner escaped from Devon and her unloving, demanding mother and found her first London flat. The effect of the loss of her father on her life as a young woman can be gauged from letters she wrote more than fifty years later out of the loneliness that followed Valentine Ackland's death; the devastation they express appears whenever she writes of the First World War. In 1971 Warner wrote to William Maxwell, "My father died when I was twenty-two, and I was mutilated. He was fifty-one, and we were making plans of what we would do together when he retired. It was as though I had been crippled and at the same moment realized I must make my journey alone."[116] The language of amputation and exile connotes both the war wounded in the streets and the solitude of Warner's first years in London. Its sadness pervades "The Salutation" and reverberates especially at the end of *Mr. Fortune's Maggot* in the missionary's desolation on the launch. Nothing has significance for him anymore.

The note of mourning occurs also in *Lolly Willowes* following Laura's father's death, but the war is evoked in that novel with bitter rage rather than sorrow. We see this rage in another late letter of Warner's, written with apparent casualness to Ben Hellman in August 1974:

> It rains & rains, and is as cold as winter, and I am haunted by thoughts of our good harvest being destroyed—an exceptionally good harvest, so exceptionally liable to be destroyed. And this leads me back to 1916 when so many exceptionally good pupils of my father's were being killed in France. He died, mainly of grief, that autumn; so . . . he was mercifully spared the casualty lists of 1917 & 1918.[117]

The keynote here is the bitterness of waste. Sylvia was friendly with many of those exceptionally good pupils; she wrote to them when they were in the trenches, and she read, one by one, of their deaths.

Some insight into the father's grief and the daughter's rage is provided by a 1915 letter to George Townsend Warner from a pupil. Eric Milner-White was an army chaplain in France and wrote on behalf of a school friend, Geoffrey Hopley. Hopley had been in Harrow recently enough to know about Sylvia's work there with Belgian refugees;[118] now he was wounded in the thigh and suffered from a recurrent nightmare about "legs that he had to order this way and that." As Milner-White explains,

> Whenever he moved in his sleep, he knew really that that slight movement of an arm or leg was a platoon marching off right or left with twinkling legs in motion. . . . Finally he would wake up having given the horrifying order to one of his own legs to march off with the squad, in a cold sweat first because the ordered leg made such painful difficulties about separating from the unordered, and secondly because the mental agony was so great from the ordered leg being unwilling or unable to obey orders.

Milner-White gives Warner Hopley's address and then his own, saying he can wait for his letter, "or put Sylvia on to me": it is clear that George Townsend Warner shared with his daughter his friendships with his ex-students. Hopley died three months later, following an amputation.[119]

In *Lolly Willowes*, a sense of the bitterness of waste and the hollow sham of patriotism dominates Laura's war. She spends it packing up parcels in an office decorated with gradually fading recruiting posters that depict women scrificing their sons to the war: "The ruddy young man and his Spartan mother grew pale, as if with fear, and Britannia's scarlet cloak trailing on the waters bleached to a cocoa-ish pink. Laura watched them discolor with a muffled heart. . . . until the eleventh day of November 1918. Then, when she heard the noise of cheering and the sounding of hooters, she left her work and went home."[120] A muffled heart will have its revenge: "She felt cold and sick, she trembled from head to foot as once she had done after witnessing a dog-fight. All the hooters . . . seemed to domineer with sarcastic emphasis." Laura hears the hooters' message about the futile violence of the past four years. In her empty room, she faints. Later, she discovers that she cannot be entirely remuffled in her relatives' "resumption of peace. . . . [T]hey, she thought, had done with the war, whereas she had only shelved it."[121]

Laura's abiding knowledge that war is waste and destruction is crucial to her resumption both of the heart she had started to muffle after the death of her father and of her early passion for herbs, simples, and witchcraft. Exploring distant parts of London, she daydreams "that she was in the country, at dusk, and alone, and strangely at peace. . . . [H]er mind walked by lonely sea-bords, in marshes and fens, or came at nightfall to the edge of a wood."[122] Within that wood she will find the Witches' Sabbath and an alternative, eternal father: Satan.

Lolly Willowes, or The Loving Huntsman is the complete title of this novel. Satan is loving in that he shows a naturalist's care: he collects Laura with a butterfly net rather than a gun as part of his recreation after his exertions during the war. But he is menacing, too: "And Satan, who has hunted from eternity, *a little jaded moreover by the success of his latest organized Flanders battue,* might well feel that his interest in a Solitary Snipe like Laura was but sooner or later to measure the length of her nose."[123] The echo of Vernon Lee's *Satan the Waster* is unmistakable: the mannered, euphemistic irony is just the tone that Satan adopts to explicate the war to Clio, the sycophantic muse of history who records his ballet of the nations. For Lee, the First World War had been "a daily and hourly exhibition of the Waster."[124] Warner's experience of it marks each of her novels except for *The True Heart*: the devastation of war reverberates through her work and life.

4

WAR STORIES
Crosswriting the Closet

Men and Women Together

The First World War and its aftermath are particularly central to the 1920s narratives of two of "the women of 1928," Sylvia Townsend Warner and Virginia Woolf.[1] Both writers' representations of war and sexuality reverberate with a sense of loss; they wrote and rewrote into their novels of the twenties the traumatic deaths in their lives. Both also continued to explore the intersections of war and perverse sexuality in their later fiction—Woolf in *The Years* and *Between the Acts*, and Warner in such stories as "My Shirt Is in Mexico," set during the Second World War, and "A Love Match," a tale of shell shock, incest, and the closet. In this chapter, I consider Woolf's *Mrs. Dalloway* and Warner's "My Shirt Is in Mexico" and "A Love Match" alongside Rose Allatini's banned 1918 novel, *Despised and Rejected*, which explores closeted homosexuality and lesbianism within the brutal absurdities of militarism on the home front; Allatini dramatizes Edward Carpenter's idea that, since violence is endemic to masculinity, humankind should evolve toward an androgynous future.[2] Like the primitivist fantasies discussed in chapter 3, and in marked contrast to Radclyffe Hall's *The Well of Loneliness*, the war narratives that I discuss here attack the ideology of empire, showing how misogyny and homophobia intersect with the class-bound, racist jingoism that justified both worldwide economic exploitation and the slaughter of a generation of young men in World War I. Crosswriting is used to represent deviant sexuality, "madness," and the aspects of war outside women's experience, but these narratives are only partially crosswritten: they depict women's experiences of war and sexuality alongside those of men.

Women's work in the First World War was almost without exception limited to the home front or to hazardous, undervalued labor behind the lines. Crosswriting was thus nearly as essential to modernist women's depictions of life and death in the trenches as it had been to Mary Shelley nearly one hundred years earlier in the battlefield scenes of *The Last Man* (1826).[3] Nevertheless, women's war work led not only to women's right to vote (for those over the age of thirty—younger women were still classified as children); it also made possible a more open depiction of sexuality. The demands and losses of wartime temporarily freed women from the imperial ideology that insisted on their childlike sexual passivity; besides, the nation "needed" war babies.[4] Extramarital sex—including homosexuality and lesbianism—became more common in all classes, although it was generally still closeted. Representations of lesbianism as well as homosexuality were beginning to be recognizable to at least some readers of narratives of the closet.

Rose Allatini's fourth novel, *Despised and Rejected*, was published under the pseudonym A. T. Fitzroy in 1918 and immediately banned under the Defence of the Realm Act. It is set on the home front among a group of conscientious objectors; its protagonists are a gay man in the process of coming out of the closet and a young woman for whom lesbianism offers so shadowy a future that she abandons it for unrequited heterosexual love and celibacy. Allatini's critique of militarism and her representation of homosexual romance are informed and courageous, but her 1918 lesbian is doomed to invisibility. Her neglected novel is an essential document of lesbian literary history.

In *Mrs. Dalloway* (1925), Virginia Woolf explores the theme of same-sex desire not only in the shell-shocked hallucinations and epiphanies of Septimus Warren Smith but also in the closeted lives of five or six suppressed or repressed lesbians: Clarissa Dalloway, Sally Seton, Doris Kilman, Millicent Bruton, Milly Brush, and perhaps even Ellie Henderson, the dowdy spinster cousin whom Clarissa sees as a blot on the glamorous surface of her party. None of the rich, however, seem to be scarred by the war; they have succeeded in distracting themselves from its memory. Only Doris Kilman and Septimus Warren Smith appear to have experienced loss, and only Septimus has fought in the trenches. Through Septimus, Woolf contextualizes the pain of sexual suppression within the bodily and psychic fragmentations of war; in his fragmented thought patterns, she writes her own "madness" across the boundaries of gender and class.

Warner's "My Shirt Is in Mexico" and "A Love Match," in contrast, celebrate the ironies and even the joys of two very different closets. "My Shirt Is in Mexico" was published in the *New Yorker* on January 4, 1941; by the time Warner wrote it, Paris was occupied; Southampton and Bristol, the ports to the east and north of Dorset, where she shared a house with Valentine Ackland, had been heavily bombed, and an incendiary bomb had fallen through their roof onto the spare room bed. The story is about a temporary respite from the war. It is set on a train crowded with the soldiers, evacuees, baggage, and noise of wartime where Sylvia (the narrator) and Valentine edge their way to the buffet car, which, they find, "belonged to a different world." There they hear a tale about cruising, gay codes, and the closet that belongs to their irretrievable prewar lives of hopeful communist activism.

"A Love Match" was first published in the *New Yorker* in 1964 under the perhaps more apposite title, "Between Two Wars": its incestuous love story is engendered by shell shock and loss after the Battle of the Somme. What develops, however, is a lifelong romance between brother and sister that heals two psyches but ends in literal fragmentation by a bomb in the Second World War. This love affair enveloped by violence is nurtured through twenty years of peace in carefully guarded secrecy in a humdrum provincial town. Of the tales of the closet that I consider in this chapter, "A Love Match," celebrating incest, is the least concerned with shame.

Who Gets to Come out of the Closet

Allatini's *Despised and Rejected* focuses on two interlocking themes: homosexuality/lesbianism and conscientious objection to military conscription. Its representation of gay and lesbian desire is neither distanced by irony—as in Warner's *Mr. Fortune's Maggot*—nor disguised by the elisions and doublings of the stream-of-consciousness narrative of *Mrs. Dalloway*; in its idealism and melodrama—though definitely not in its socialist, internationalist message—it resembles Hall's *The Well of Loneliness*. The crosswritten explicitness of its homosexual romance between two conscientious objectors contrasts, however, with the increasing shadowiness of its representation of lesbian desire: the initially lesbian heroine falls hopelessly in love with the gay protagonist and is reduced to a merely choral figure at the end. In *Despised and Rejected*, gay empowerment and heroism are paralleled by lesbian invisibility. This imbalance, as well as the conflation of sexual radicalism with socialism, reflects the influence of Edward Carpenter's ideas on lesbian as well as gay writers who grew up between 1900 and 1920 as dissidents from the dominant ideology.

Toward the end of *Despised and Rejected*, there is a specific allusion to *Towards Democracy*, Carpenter's Whitmanesque poems celebrating socialism and comrade love. Alan Rutherford, the gay, socialist conscientious objector, lends his copy to Sinn Fein exile Conn O'Farrell. In this case the book does not function, as it so often did, as a kind of gay code—O'Farrell is happily heterosexual—but instead as a communication between two different kinds of revolutionaries. Carpenter is important in *Despised and Rejected* not just as a "gay writer" but because he connected an analysis of heterosexual culture—the (mis)education of ruling-class men, the subjection of workers and women, the waste of intermediates' talent—to a critique of capitalist industrialism. More central than *Towards Democracy* to understanding *Despised and Rejected* are Carpenter's socio-/sexological books, *Love's Coming-of-Age*, *The Intermediate Sex*, and, in the utopian use of evolutionary theory in the final pages of the novel, *Intermediate Types among Primitive Folk*. They are the source for Allatini's powerful representation of the link between compulsory heterosexuality and imperialist capitalism.

In her analysis of *Despised and Rejected*, Claire M. Tylee emphasizes the cultural interconnection between its themes of homosexuality and conscientious objection:[5] "Belligerence had been bound into the very definition of masculinity, and . . . homosexuality and the refusal to kill were intimately related in their defiance of the established notions of manhood."[6] Tylee traces these notions of manhood from ideas about progress and degeneracy in Charles Darwin's *The Descent of Man* and Herbert Spencer's *Principles of Sociology*:

> [A] man who was not courageous or pugnacious was effeminate. . . .
> if "effeminate" men predominated in a culture, the civilisation was

either not yet properly evolved, or was past its prime and on the way to extinction. . . . aggressive manliness was . . . essential for the maintenance of the British Empire. . . . Furthermore, women must unselfishly submit to breeding the 'masculine' type of man, who would ensure the stability and growth of British civilisation. On this depended the world's moral progress out of savagery.[7]

The political intensity of *Despised and Rejected* lies in the clarity with which it presents the bourgeois world constructed by this dominant ideology in peacetime and in war, and then opposes it to Carpenter's ideal of the socialist bond of comrade love as it unites and inspires a group of conscientious objectors after the passing of the Military Service Act in 1916. The political and social background of the narrative is depicted with relentlessly material specificity; this naturalism is deepened by the almost operatic intensity with which the two main characters think, write, and finally speak about both their sexuality and the horror of the war.[8]

Dennis Blackwood, a composer, is writing an opera when the novel opens. He rarely visits his family in suburban Eastwold, where most of the men remain public schoolboys all their lives. According to Mrs. Blackwood, her husband and twelve-year-old Reggie—a *"manly boy"*—"are more like friends than father and son." Dennis, on the other hand, angered his father as a boy because he would never "play with soldiers or steamers or any of the usual toys."[9] Mr. Blackwood could well come straight out of Carpenter's chapter on "Man the Ungrown" in *Love's Coming-of-Age*:

> This ungrown, half-baked sort of character is conspicuous in the class of men who organize the modern world—the men of the English-speaking well-to-do class. The boy of this class begins life at a public school. . . . A certain standard . . . of schoolboy honor and fairness is thumped into him. It is very narrow and conventional, but at its best rises as high as a conception of self-sacrifice and duty, though never to the conception of love. . . . The boy never learns anything after he leaves school. . . . He glides easily into the higher walks of the world—backed by his parents' money. . . . [He] can marry pretty well whom he chooses, or console himself with unmarried joys; and ultimately settles down into the routine and convention of his particular profession—a picture of beefy self-satisfaction.[10]

Carpenter calls the late-Victorian product of this ruling class "a society ungrown, which on its material side may approve itself a great success, but on its more human and affectional side seems at times an utter failure." Twenty years later, its product is the war, in which the young men of Eastwold dutifully sacrifice themselves: Clive Blackwood is congratulated by his father on losing an arm for his country; Doreen Blackwood's fiancé is killed.[11]

Dennis Blackwood and Antoinette de Courcy meet in June 1914 at the Amberhurst Private Hotel where the Blackwood family is vacationing—apparently the perfect setting for a prewar heterosexual romance. They have both desired same-sex love in the past, but their attitudes to their desires have been totally different. Antoinette, as long as she is ignorant of sexology, delights in her love for women.[12] Dennis, on the other hand, miserably suppresses his desire. As a schoolboy he had wanted to conform so entirely to public school conventions that he not only ran away from Eric Rubenstein, the younger boy to whom he felt attracted, but also concealed his own gift as pianist and composer. Being "musical" is code for being homosexual: both are "different"—unmanly, overexpressive, emotional.[13]

By 1914, Dennis has come out as a musician but not as a gay man: even after he meets Alan Rutherford, he continues to run from the "secret terror that . . . had been part and parcel of his being, since the first dawn of adolescence. . . . He must be for ever an outcast among men. . . . Abnormal—perverted—against nature—he could hear the epithets that would be hurled against him and that he would deserve. Yes, but what had nature been about, in giving him the soul of a woman in the body of a man?"[14] Besides expressing Dennis's shame and fear of discovery, this inflated language sounds as if he's been reading the wrong sexologists: Karl Heinrich Ulrichs, certainly, but also Richard von Krafft-Ebing, with his emphasis on morbidity and perversion. When they meet again in 1916, Alan's matter-of-fact, Carpenter-like tone deconstructs this jargon: "'You've been brooding too much in secret, Dennis, you've grown morbid. Why will you persist in regarding [our love] as something vicious and degenerate? For people made as we are it's natural and beautiful to love as we love, and it's perversion in the true sense to try and force ourselves to love differently.'"[15] They finally make love the night before Alan goes to prison as a conscientious objector—an ironic counterpart to the heterosexual couples who consummate their love before the man leaves for the front.

Allatini's depiction of the home front—both in patriotic Eastwold and among the dissidents in Miss Mowbray's tea shop—is remarkable for its documentary detail. Events among the women at Eastwold mirror many of those recounted at Buxton in Vera Brittain's *War Diary*. The domineering Mrs. Ryan and her daughters have started sewing classes by the beginning of 1915; Mrs. Brittain and Vera begin taking first aid classes in October 1914. Mrs. Ryan leads the unremitting assaults on Mrs. Blackwood's loyalty to Dennis when he refuses to enlist. "We women of England must give *all* our sons," she says;[16] Vera Brittain recounts a "quite rude" attack on her mother by a neighbor who expressed her astonishment that Edward Brittain had not shown as much eagerness to enlist as her own son and said that "we should give our sons to fight for their country."[17] Critical representations of such competitive middle-class jingoism became common in war novels written in the 1920s, but was rarely voiced as early as 1918.[18] In this, too, Allatini's counterculture reportage put her way ahead of her time.

The gradual hardening of Dennis's resistance to the war is precisely situated within current events. In 1914 he simply refuses to play the "great war game" just as he refused to play with soldiers as a child. It is no game to him because he envisions "being sent out . . . deliberately to maim and shatter the bodies of men as young as himself, the bodies of men as young as Alan."[19] At the end of 1915, when local tribunals are set up under the Derby Scheme to "encourage" enlistment by registering all men of military age, Dennis meditates on the fact that the machinery for forced military conscription is now in place.[20] By January 24, 1916, when the Conscription Bill is passed, he is back in London, making common cause with the other war resisters at Miss Mowbray's tea shop. By the spring, Vera Mansfield's husband has chosen to go to prison rather than further the war effort by taking noncombatant service, and Alan's appeal to the Central Tribunal has failed, so that he is expecting arrest and imprisonment as soon as the police catch up with him. As an "absolutist" conscientious objector, he refuses to work in prison and is tortured. By the end of the novel, in July 1916, Dennis has also refused the option of noncombatant service and is in prison, doing hard labor. Allatini's passionate accuracy grounds the oppositional propaganda of her novel in day-to-day current events.[21]

Besides the dating of events in the novel, there are several actual identifications to be made of its places and people. Miss Mowbray's meticulously described tea shop, for example, is almost certainly the one Ethel Mannin recalls visiting in 1916 or 1917: "an underground tea place called The Cave where tea-for-two was served in alcoves, and the lighting was dim, and *women smoked.*"[22] It seems very likely that the journalist and leader of the war resisters, Neil Barnaby, was modeled on Clifford Allen, chairman of the No-Conscription Fellowship. Sylvia Pankhurst writes that he was "a frail young man afflicted with curvature of the spine . . . regarded almost as a saint by thousands of his followers. One could hardly realise that he had been satisfied to work as business manager of the jingo *Daily Citizen* until it ceased publication."[23] Barnaby tells Antoinette that he and Miss Mowbray were "on the staff of the 'Daily Standard' [till] the paper went bust." Now he edits a pacifist paper called *The Dove.*[24] Saintly, sane, and intellectual, he is more severely disabled than Clifford Allen, who continued his political work in prison: refused exemption from military service despite his deformed spine, Allen spent more than two years in jail as an "absolutist" like Alan Rutherford in the novel. Another particularly specific allusion turns the torture and humiliation suffered by conscientious objectors (COs) into a courageous joke. When COs were first arrested they were taken not to prison but to the regiment they were supposed to join. At this point they were under military jurisdiction and required to wear uniform. If they refused to do so, their clothes were taken away; if they were lucky, they received a blanket instead.[25] Alan, denied his exemption and expecting arrest, anticipates this predicament, campily proclaiming that "one really ought to practise beforehand how to wear one's blanket in the most artistic and effective manner. . . . By next week I shall no doubt be quite an authority on the latest fashions in bedclothes."[26]

On the whole, Allatini presents her dissidents convincingly. They bolster up their courage with long political speeches; they eat Welsh rarebit and cake; they gossip and joke. Benny Joseph, a Jewish actor, maintains that he can't possibly fight because he has "an aunt in every port." At the end of the novel, he's the only free man besides Barnaby; he has suddenly been granted a medical exemption after being turned down twice by tribunals and even undergoing arrest. (There is nothing wrong with his health; this is another indication of the arbitrary absurdities of the system.) He's delighted, of course, but there's no one except Barnaby and Antoinette to rejoice with him:

DAILY SKETCH. FRIDAY, APRIL 14, 1916.

IRELAND'S MOST UNPOPULAR LANDLORD DEAD.

DAILY SKETCH.

GUARANTEED DAILY NETT SALE MORE THAN 1,000,000 COPIES.

No. 2,215.   LONDON, FRIDAY, APRIL 14, 1916.   [Registered as a Newspaper]   ONE HALFPENNY

A CONSCIENTIOUS OBJECTOR'S FIRST DAY IN THE ARMY.

This is the first photograph to be published of a Conscientious objector actually in the Army. It was taken at Kingston Barracks yesterday. That we are unable to present him in smarter or more soldierly guise than in this nondescript garment suggestive of the accretion of a medieval anchorite is due to the man's own refusal to don khaki. All that he would consent to wear, after being stripped for medical examination at Kingston, was this Army blanket, which has been his only attire for two days.
—[Photograph exclusive to the Daily Sketch.]

3. *Eric Chappelow's First Day in the Army. Daily Sketch*, London, April 14, 1916.

the others are in prison or dead, killed by British soldiers in Dublin or by German soldiers at the front, or even by their own hands at home in London. Not all these COs are heroes: Everard, another actor, gives in and joins his regiment, as does Harry Hope; Oswald Forsyth, an eighteen-year-old poet who has been working for

Barnaby's newspaper, kills himself after confessing to Antoinette that he's afraid of every alternative: going to the front as a soldier or noncombatant or going to prison as a CO.

Allatini's sympathetic portrayal of Oswald Forsyth is an answer to the stereotyping and persecution of COs, or "conchies," as cowards. She may, indeed, have been responding directly to May Sinclair's jingoistic 1917 bestseller, *The Tree of Heaven*. Like Allatini's Blackwoods, the Harrison family in *The Tree of Heaven* is humiliated by their son Michael's unwillingness to enlist. He too is a poet; when he finally decides to enlist, he feels a fear like Forsyth's, the fear that he had formerly refused to acknowledge:

> What shocked Michael was his discovering, not that he funked it now, which was natural, almost permissible, but that he had funked it all the time. . . . Funk, pure funk, had been at the bottom of all he had said and thought and done since August, nineteen-fourteen; his attitude to the War, his opinion of the Allies, and of the Government and of its conduct of the War, all his wretched criticisms and disparagements—what had they been but the very subterfuges of funk?[27]

As Sharon Ouditt points out, this passage "might have come from a propagandist pamphlet insisting that conscientious objection is nothing but cowardice."[28]

It is also useful to compare Sinclair's Michael and Allatini's Dennis as artists. One of Michael's "subterfuges of funk" is his belief that he should avoid the war as an act of individualism, cherishing his art and "the hardness of his mind"; this belief is subsumed in a D. H. Lawrence–like epiphany when he observes a troop train greeted by a band of bagpipers at a station in Scotland:

> Solemnly . . . the Highlanders played to their comrades. Michael did not know whether their tune was sad or gay. It poured itself into one mournful, savage, sacred cry of salutation and valediction. When it stopped the men shouted; there were voices that barked hoarsely and broke; voices that roared; young voices that screamed, strung up by the skirling of the bagpipes. The pipers played to them again.
>
> And suddenly Michael was overcome. Pity shook him and grief and an intolerable yearning and shame. For one instant his soul rose up above the music, and was made splendid and holy, the next he cowered under it, stripped and beaten.[29]

In his subsequent meditation, he realizes that what had threatened him had been "this collective war-spirit, clamoring for his private soul"; he now sees the war as "the greatest War of Independence. . . . the Great War of Redemption" in which he will immerse himself and sacrifice his individuality. But Dennis's music was collaborative even before the war, when he was composing an opera based on a play by Neil Barnaby. During the war, he starts writing an internationalist symphony; while he awaits arrest he tries obsessively to complete this work, which will resolve the chaos and horror of war into the unity of peace.[30] His art had never been merely individualist like Michael's, even though it had reflected the pain of his sexual suppression and the "tortured dissonances and scurrying arpeggios" of war.[31] His symphony resolves the distinction between the private and public in internationalist politics.

Certainly *Despised and Rejected* can seem portentous at times, especially in what Ouditt calls the "set piece political speeches,"[32] but I find its style preferable to the "exalted spiritualized vagueness" of Michael Harrison's epiphany.[33] Suzanne Raitt's observation that "[t]he war in Sinclair's fiction is a perversely bodiless affair" heightens my appreciation of Allatini's insistent embodiment of the wounded in the macabre procession of bodiless legs and feet that constantly passes by the blurred basement windows of Miss Mowbray's tea shop.[34] For Allatini, war and love are physical.

These bodiless legs and feet form the climax of a series of images of amputation and disfigurement in the novel. The opera that Dennis is composing in 1914 is based on a dramatization by Barnaby of Hans Christian Andersen's fairy tale "Karen and the Red Shoes." In the tale, Karen is punished for her vanity about her red shoes by having to dance whenever she wears them; finally they stick to her feet, so she has to dance all the time. She persuades the local executioner to cut off her feet with his axe, but when she tries to go to church on her crutches, the feet and shoes dance in ahead of her. With his characteristically sadistic sentimentality, Andersen finally permits Karen a deathbed repentance scene. Neil Barnaby's decision to dramatize this story reflects his attitude to his disability, with a "fine massive head sunk between rounded shoulders; one leg shorter than the other";[35] he walks with crutches, like many of the wounded men in the London streets. Barnaby's body disgusts and embitters him: encouraging Dennis in his decision to resist conscription, he says, "'And keep in mind that it's better to write music that will live, than to help to fill the world with things that look like me—and worse.'"[36] So Dennis goes back to work on his opera, but he finds his composition distorted by "music horrible and unreal, that in itself constituted a nightmare from which there was no escape. Like Karen . . . who was compelled to dance on and on in the red shoes she had so ardently desired . . . so was Dennis compelled to listen without respite to this nightmare music, that was like an evil spell upon him."[37] He escapes this obsession only when he starts writing his internationalist war symphony.[38]

The nightmares of war and love, sexual fear, and fear of imprisonment and mutilation are connected by structural themes and metaphors throughout *Despised and Rejected*. Dennis suffers so intensely from sexual repression that when he finally allows himself to sublimate his desire for Eric Rubenstein by sitting down at the piano he feels as if he has been released from prison.[39] In 1914, after meeting Alan, Dennis's homosexual panic reappears, at a costume party given by Mrs. Ryan. The masquerade of the closet is painfully enclosed in the absurd society masquerade: "For him the whole scene was imbued with that feeling of horror and despair which characterizes a nightmare . . . [P]art of himself was being tortured, beating against prison bars. . . . crying out for help, for understanding to a world that would neither help nor understand, but condemn him to eternal suppression, eternal loneliness."[40] The overwriting in the last sentence recurs with apparent inevitability whenever Dennis or Antoinette speak or think about their "inversion." Their shame and despair arise from their belief in the ideas of the more repressive sexologists. This is especially apparent in the case of Antoinette.

Dennis's love for Alan is intertwined in the novel with his attempted "romance" with its heroine—a romance doomed to failure precisely because it is *not* physical. Antoinette is lively, assertive, attractive to both men and women—altogether unlike the stereotypical female invert;[41] when she and Dennis meet before the war, she is happily pursuing an older woman. Now, as during the crushes she experienced at boarding school, she feels at her most alive: at school, however mistakenly, she had longed to be eighteen and meet a man. But the men she had met were disappointing, their kisses repulsive or unsatisfying, so she is delighted to feel so intensely attracted by the mysteriously unattached Hester. Like Dennis, Antoinette has never actually made love, but her celibacy is free from anxiety: "It seemed disappointing, but not in the least unnatural, that all her passionate longings should have been awakened by women, instead of by members of the opposite sex."[42] She is happy in her desire because she is not aware that it's "abnormal"; she lacks the self-consciousness and knowledge that make Dennis miserable. He shares them with her all too soon, however; immediately he notices her preoccupation with Hester and wonders "if he [has] at last found the answer to a riddle."[43] The riddle is how to live in the world as a closeted gay man; its answer: marry a nice lesbian.

The anxiety of the closet can still today drive both gay men and lesbians into unsatisfactory heterosexual relationships that often involve the kind of deception and self-deception evinced by Dennis Blackwood. Dennis's excuse is that he believes that Antoinette has recognized his "difference" just as he recognized hers. And Antoinette is also dishonest at first: her disappointment in Hester, who has turned out to be heterosexual, and her family's insistence that she marry, drive her to pretend that she returns the passion that Dennis pretends to feel. They both wish they could fall in love; Antoinette's tragedy is that she does so just as Dennis gives up this charade and unaccountably vanishes. When they meet again and he explains that they are both "tainted" by a "kink of abnormality," she believes him and feels that she lives in an "inverted world [that] she had not anticipated being left alone in"—as she is when Alan reappears in Dennis's life.[44] Since she and Dennis believe that inversion is innate and permanent, it is possible for Antoinette to suffer simultaneously from her unrequited heterosexual love for Dennis and from her "terror and loneliness of the Ishmaelite, outcast among men and women."[45] It is hard not to become impatient at this point in the novel; Allatini permits no glimmer of opposition, or even common sense, to penetrate this fog of ideology. I suspect that she was too attached to her story to do so.

I am inclined to identify aspects of Antoinette's situation with Rose Allatini's, as Jonathan Cutbill does. He points out that at the end of the novel "Antoinette is the only one left without a personal answer. . . . trapped in her family, refusing to marry, but unable to seek out the love she needs," and he thinks that perhaps "Antoinette was too close to her author."[46] Allatini was born in Vienna of Polish and Italian parents in about 1890, and was raised in London; Antoinette too has grown up in England; the idiosyncrasies of her unassimilably French parents and grandmother are caricatured throughout the novel. Perhaps the addressee in Allatini's mysterious dedication of *Despised and Rejected*, "TO YOU WHO MADE ME UNDERSTAND," was gay and male and may have introduced her to Carpenter's writing. Whatever she understood about herself and others, however, did not prevent her from marrying the composer Cyril Scott in 1921; they had two children and finally separated twenty years later. From 1941 until her death in about 1980 Allatini lived in Rye with Melanie Mills, who also published romances under several names. The two women supported themselves through their writing.[47]

If Allatini wrote fiction about lesbians later in her life, it has yet to be unearthed; it might differ considerably from the misogynist ending of *Despised and Rejected*, where Barnaby condoles with Antoinette, "I'm afraid you're the symbol of what has to be sacrificed to the love between man and man."[48] She is reduced to a merely choral figure in the last scene of the novel, where Barnaby reflects on Dennis's "maternal . . . virile and yet tender" passion for Alan, seeing it as "a wonderful motive-force that might accomplish much."[49] He makes clear that Allatini intended the allusion to Christ in the novel's title to refer to the sufferings of gay men in a homophobic society; women's suffering is immaterial.[50] Isaiah-like, Barnaby prophesies redemption, saying,

> "[The] time is not so far distant when we shall recognise in the best of our intermediate types the leaders and masters of the race. . . . From them a new humanity is being evolved. . . . For out of their suffering . . . will arise something great—something God-given: the human soul complete in itself, perfectly balanced . . . combining the power and the intellect of the one with the subtlety and intuition of the other; a dual nature, possessing the extended range, the attributes of both sides, and therefore loving and beloved of both alike."[51]

Allatini's exclusion of lesbians from this utopian vision reflects her source. Both in *The Intermediate Sex* and in *Intermediate Types among Primitive Folk*, Carpenter presents inverts as developing special powers of leadership as a result of their combination of masculine and feminine characteristics and their position as cultural outsiders.[52] His connection of this development with evolutionist theory is evident in the subtitles of both books: *A Study of Some Transitional Types of Men and Women* and *A Study in Social Evolution*. Although he takes care to include women in his theories about sociology and sexology, the focus of his utopian evolutionist writing is almost exclusively on men.

The representation of lesbianism in *Despised and Rejected* certainly seems to exemplify Lillian Faderman's early view of sexology's influence on lesbians: that once they learned that their love was a morbid inversion of heterosexuality, many of them repudiated it, fleeing into marriage instead. Yet in fact what Faderman blamed the sexologists for was the "morbidification" not of sexual desire but of romantic friendships, in which desire, she thought, was probably repressed and sublimated.[53] Antoinette, however, differs from the lesbians Faderman is concerned with, both in her knowledge and acceptance that her desire for women is sexual and in the fact that it has never been reciprocated, sexually or otherwise: there has been no romantic friendship, no relationship in which it might have been possible to make lesbian love. I find it completely convincing that Antoinette should feel unreciprocal love for a man, also—indeed, her pretended passion for Dennis becomes intensely authentic at the very moment that his moral and/or physical revulsion puts an end to his own performance—because her interactions with her mother, father, and grandmother make it abundantly clear that she is not used to being loved. Antoinette's love for a man cannot rescue her from the lesbian limbo most characteristic of her time—renunciation of desire.

Despised and Rejected *and* Censored to Death

Five months after its publication in May 1918, *Despised and Rejected* was banned and all unsold copies were destroyed ("burnt by the hangman," according to Virginia Woolf).[54] On October 10, 1918—one month before the armistice—its publisher, C. W. Daniel, was found guilty under the Defence of the Realm Act (DORA), of "making statements . . . likely to prejudice the recruiting, training, and discipline of persons in his Majesty's forces."[55] Daniel had been fined and imprisoned for pacifist publishing activities in 1917; now his fine was heavy: £460. The revolutionary Labour Party newspaper, the *Herald*, asked readers for contributions to help him pay the fine and avoid its alternative: ninety days' imprisonment.[56]

Both the presiding magistrate and the prosecutor, who charged that the book was "a pacifist pamphlet in disguise of a novel," seem to have been determined to condemn the book under DORA rather than the Obscene Publications Act.[57] Yet the magistrate, Alderman Sir Charles Wakefield, commented on its representation of sexuality; *Despised and Rejected* was an "immoral, unhealthy, and most pernicious book, written to attract a certain class of reader for the personal profit of the publishers."[58] One wonders whether that euphemistic "certain class of reader" signifies a mad rush of homosexuals desperately seeking pornography. They would have been disappointed. The emphasis is odd, too, in light of the military rather than moral language of the verdict.

Solomon Eagle (J. C. Squire) of the *New Statesman* appears also to have been disturbed by *Despised and Rejected*. He attributed "the authorities'" evasion of the obscenity issue to "the evil odour of a recent trial still cling[ing] to the air."[59] He was referring to the Noel Pemberton-Billing trial that had taken place from May 29 to June 5, 1918, which had been both notorious and absurd.[60] The memory of this event may underlie Wakefield's strange reference to "a certain class of reader"—the same hordes of effete German spies who had watched Maud Allan dance *Salome*? Perhaps he was a reader of *The Vigilante*. The coyness of Eagle's allusion may be partly attributable to his "liberal" embarrassment at sharing the bigotry and homophobia of the crassly jingoistic and prurient Pemberton-Billing.

Eagle's account of the banning of *Despised and Rejected* is the only response I have found that urges freedom of speech for pacifists but not for perverts:

> The book . . . was mainly devoted to two themes: moral perversion and conscientious objection. In the author's opinion the two things, to both of which she appeared sympathetic, go very largely together. . . . Had the book been prosecuted as offensive to public decency, I, for one, should not have said a word against the conviction. . . . But the authorities . . . fastened entirely on the Pacifist side of it. There they seem to me to have been acting in a manner which gravely endangers a necessary freedom of speech. . . . One wishes that publishers could unite to protect themselves, although peculiar circumstances (which almost stopped my self from mentioning this harsh suppression of political opinion) might well give them a distaste for defending this particular author and book.[61]

This passage follows immediately after Eagle's clearly respectful obituary comments on Robert Ross; he is full of praise for Ross and for his work as Oscar Wilde's editor and literary executor. Still, about *Despised and Rejected* Eagle is as euphemistic as the magistrate, and he is unable to let the matter go: he returns to the subject in his column two weeks later, ponderously exonerating C. W. Daniel of knowledge of the novel's perversity. We seem here to have an example of homosexual panic: Solomon Eagle appears thoroughly ambivalent about homosexuality. His misogyny shines out quite clearly, however.[62]

In its trial, as in its idealism and its explicit representation of homosexuality and lesbianism, *Despised and Rejected* looks forward to Hall's *The Well of Loneliness*; but it is important to remember that this little-known book was banned for opposing conscription, a political position that would have been anathema to Hall. Allatini's politics, as well as her crosswriting, situate her novel as a forerunner of postwar writings on war by such critics of imperialism as Virginia Woolf and Sylvia Townsend Warner. Unlike Hall's Mary Llewellyn and Stephen Gordon, Antoinette never gets to act on her lesbian desire; although her narrative point of view is crucial to the novel, her story is one of suppression. She is a mere onlooker on the dilemma of the conscientious objectors and, finally, on the romance plot: Dennis's struggle out of the closet into the arms of Alan Rutherford. In this respect, Allatini is one of the lesbian modernists who chose to crosswrite, focusing on gay men rather than lesbians in her representation of reciprocal desire. Her novel makes clear the connection between crosswriting by early-twentieth-century lesbian novelists and the absence of earlier nonstereotypical representations of lesbianism. It was comparatively unthreatening to Clemence Dane to depict the seductive Clare Hartill in *Regiment of Women* (1917) and then to condemn her as a vampirish predator: she was following a recognizable lesbophobic tradition established by such novelists as Charles Dickens, in his representation of the dangerously dissatisfied Miss Wade. But there was no tradition of positive lesbian representation available for Allatini.[63] Antoinette, potentially so complex and nuanced a lesbian creation, is thus left with her drama unresolved. It would take the passage of seven postwar years before Virginia Woolf's *Mrs. Dalloway* would find a way to represent both lesbian and gay sexuality within a sustained critique of militarism and an elegy for the lives lost in the First World War.

The Soldiers Return: Shell Shock and Forbidden Love

Fiction written during the First World War tends to fall into two categories: propaganda or escape—and sometimes both. *Despised and Rejected* is propaganda against the patriarchal imperialism that required military conscription as well as compulsory heterosexuality. *Regiment of Women* is simultaneously a work of eugenicist propaganda for heterosexuality and motherhood and an escape back to the time when the English pastoral romance was unblighted by war. Rebecca West's *The Return of the Soldier* (1918) is not at all concerned with propaganda, and it is certainly escapist in its representation of romance, shell shock, the (empty) luxuries of the very rich, and the pastoral idyll. My interest is in its representation of class and shell shock as a predecessor of *Mrs. Dalloway* (1925). We know that Woolf read *The Return of the Soldier* when it came out in 1918; in both narratives, the connection between shell shock and forbidden love is pivotal.[64]

West uses the war merely as a backdrop for romance. The only symptom of shell shock her Chris Baldry suffers is the familiar plot device of amnesia.[65] He forgets the last fifteen years of his life—his beautiful house, his business responsibilities, his pretty, spoiled wife, Kitty—and longs instead for Margaret Allington, whom he courted long ago when her father kept the pub at Monkey Island on the Thames. The story is told by Chris's cousin Jenny, an unreliable Jamesian narrator who describes Baldry Court, its environs, and every trick of the soft English light in painstakingly sensitive detail.[66] The reader discovers early that Jenny is in love with her cousin; it is she, not Chris, who has nightmares about his death amid the dismembered limbs and mud of no man's land. Margaret, who conveniently lives nearby in a respectable working-class poverty that disgusts fastidious Jenny, is fetched to comfort our hero; her transcendently selfless love is depicted with a cloying religiosity. Meanwhile, Kitty frets and sends for doctors to return her husband to his soldier self. Chris, the focus of all three women, is barely characterized: his most significant attribute is his swift double return—first from the front to his home as an amnesiac and then—in little more than a week—back to the front and most probably his death. He is cured of his pleasant delusion by a briskly skillful Freudian—another convenient device that provides the novella's conclusion.

The emotional barrenness at Baldry Court, where Kitty presides over heartless magnificence, contrasts with lost young love on romantic Monkey Island—a prewar pastoral idyll like Warner's Fanua in *Mr. Fortune's Maggot* or Woolf's Bourton in *Mrs. Dalloway*. There is a clear, if sentimental, connection between Margaret's class, the pastoral romance, and her curative maternity. Jenny feels snobbish horror at Margaret's shabby clothes and her home in a suburb where the women in front of the shops have faces "sour with thrift."[67] Her love for Chris makes her want his happiness, but she is intensely jealous of Margaret's power to provide it. At the end of Chris's week of amnesiac respite, she finds them both under a tree, where Margaret's "yellow raincoat ma[kes] a muddy patch . . . against the clear colors of the bright bare wood." Chris lies "in the confiding relaxation of a sleeping child" while Margaret watches over him. They remind Jenny of the working class:

> I have often seen people grouped like that on the common outside our gates. . . . It has sometimes seemed to me there was a significance about it. . . . But . . . it was not until now . . . that I knew that it was the loveliest attitude in the world. It means that the woman has gathered the soul of the man into her soul and is keeping it warm in love and peace so that his body can rest quiet. . . . That is a great thing for a woman to do.[68]

Jenny's primitivist idealization of Margaret's earth-mothering powers is the reverse side of her snobbery. One of this narrative's unresolved problems is the fact that West does not sufficiently distance her unreliable narrator, so that the reader is required to participate in Jenny's final stereotyping of motherhood as selfless and poverty as noble.[69] The demonization of Kitty is a welcome relief.

What Kitty most enjoys is control—like Woolf's sinister Sir William Bradshaw, who worships the goddess Conversion and prescribes compulsory rest for his patients. The trivialities that manifest Kitty's need for control are sometimes comical: there is a scene in which she passes the time by "holding a review of her underclothing."[70] And she believes, like Woolf's Dr. Holmes, in the curative value of effort. West's Freudian doctor doesn't, however:

> "I've always said," declared Kitty, with an air of good sense, "that if he would make an effort . . . "
>
> "Effort!" He jerked his head about. "The mental life that can be controlled by effort isn't the mental life that matters. You've been stuffed up when you were young with talk about a thing called

self-control—a sort of barmaid of the soul that says 'Time's up, gentlemen,' and 'Here, you've had enough.' There's no such thing. There's a deep self in one. . . . The superficial self . . . makes, as you say, efforts . . . [and erects] the house of conduct."[71]

Kitty does not fail to get her way in this story. It is Margaret, however, who gives Chris back to the war.

Disappointingly but all too believably, West's up-to-date psychiatrist collaborates with Margaret and Jenny in the restoration of Chris's memory. The decision is really Margaret's; it is presented as a moral triumph: "'The truth's the truth,' she said, 'and he must know it.'"[72] Her renunciation of her lover consigns him to almost certain death: once Chris remembers his duty, he of course returns to the front. The young man softened and feminized by amnesia stiffens into the war hero: "He walked not loose-limbed like a boy, as he had done that very afternoon, but with the soldier's hard tread upon the heel. . . . he would go back to that flooded trench in Flanders . . . to that No Man's Land where bullets fall like rain on the rotting faces of the dead."[73] He will return to the landscape of Jenny's bad dreams that alone in this novel reflect the reality of the war in the trenches.

The bitter irony in Jenny's recognition that Chris is marching to his death—she tells exultant Kitty that he looks "[e]very inch a soldier"—shows her rejection of the heroic veneer that enables Chris to return to the house of conduct and the war. But this moment of realism on the book's last page comes too late to block the impact of the romance plot with its lost young love and heroic self-sacrifice. *The Return of the Soldier* acquiesces to the sacrifice of young men to war even though, in 1917 when West was writing her book, the horrors of trench warfare were widely reported both in newspapers and on film.

West's use of the term *shell-shock* is itself quite up-to-date.[74] The first date for the word listed in the *Oxford English Dictionary* is a 1916 quotation from the medical journal *The Lancet*. Headlines of articles in the London *Times* in 1916 and 1917 refer to neurasthenia, neurasthenics, nerve disease, or "war-shaken men" until June 14, 1917, when the term *shell-shock* first appears.[75] It seems possible that West read the *Times* articles, which give prominent coverage to the work done by Sir John Collie, the doctor who was president of the special medical board on neurasthenia and functional nerve disease.[76] Collie took great pains to emphasize the very real physical suffering that shell shock entails; he was determined to show that soldiers were not cowardly malingerers. Yet none of the symptoms he described appears to affect Chris Baldry;[77] amnesia is Baldry's only symptom, making particularly transparent West's use of shell shock as a mere plot device.

West's priorities in writing *The Return of the Soldier* appear to have been the pastoral romance plot, the Jamesian narrative technique, the theme of class difference, and the elegiac representation of the deaths of Chris and Margaret's two-year-old sons, who are the same age that West's son Anthony was when she was writing the novel.[78] She was twenty-three when she wrote *The Return of the Soldier* and was living with Anthony at Alderton in temporary retirement. Alderton is near the real Monkey Island, which Anthony's father, H. G. Wells, used to visit with West; like her novel's Chris Baldry, Wells had known the island as a boy.[79] West wrote her first novel out of her immediate experience; the war, despite Jenny's nightmares and Chris's convenient shell shock, remains an abstraction.

Virginia Woolf was forty and embarking on her fourth novel in 1922 when she undertook her representation through Septimus Warren Smith of shell shock, homosexuality, and suicide. Its closeness to her own experience made the writing of Septimus's "madness" a constant struggle, but she sought help in fact, not romance. "I am now in the thick of the mad scene in Regents Park," she wrote in her diary. "I write it by clinging as tight to fact as I can, & write perhaps 50 words a morning."[80] Her primary source for Septimus's thought-processes and behavior was certainly her own periods of "madness," but her representation of shell shock seems to have been written also out of current events as a specific reaction against the *Report of the War Office Committee of Enquiry into "Shell-Shock"* that was presented to Parliament in August, 1922, two months before "Mrs. Dalloway ... branched into a book."[81] Above all, Woolf's representation of Septimus's last day is informed by her passionate opposition to the medical/military establishment. In *Mrs. Dalloway*, only Septimus and Doris Kilman oppose the postwar, ruling-class values embodied in the Dalloways and their essentially exploitative colonialist circle.

By 1922, the official attitude toward shell-shocked veterans had hardened into a determination to blame the victims rather than the conditions of war: this eagerness to rewrite military history appears

4. *Landscape*. IWM Q10711. Photograph used with the permission of the Trustees of the Imperial War Museum, London.

5. *Resting*. IWM Q872. Photograph used with the permission of the Trustees of the Imperial War Museum, London.

6. *Death Above*. E.C.P. Armées, France.

7. *Death Below*. IWM Q2041. Photograph used with the permission of the Trustees of the Imperial War Museum, London.

both in the *Report of the War Office Committee of Enquiry into "Shell-Shock"* and in the coverage of the report in the *Times*. A main concern—revealing both the ideological focus of the committee and the report's function as propaganda—is the inadequacy of the term *shell shock*: it "overlooks" the likelihood of a "predisposing cause" of neurosis in the individual and "concentrates attention on the *exaggeration* of stimulation *incidental to every battle*."[82] The writer of this editorial appears to have erased from his memory the distinguishing features of the "stimulation" encountered in such events as the Battle of the Somme.[83] Lord Southborough, the committee's chairman, who contributed two *Times* articles on the report, exults that shell shock was "exploded by the Committee."[84] A second editorial sums up briskly that the term *shell shock* is "but a new name for . . . a condition in which . . . the individual, *abandoning resistance*, yields to circumstances. Such *surrender* . . . is the real issue."[85] Here the victim becomes both a coward and a traitor—punishable by death. *Shell shock* is, of course, the term that Woolf uses in her novel.[86]

Several writers emphasize exaggeration, reducing shell shock to hypochondria. Lord Southborough also mentions "neurasthenia" and "hysterical symptoms": the soldiers are now reduced to women.[87] Sue Thomas points out that doctors advocated the same treatment for shell shock as that used for the female malady "hysteria."[88] This was the actual treatment Sir George Savage prescribed for Woolf, and the fictional treatment Sir William Bradshaw proposed for Septimus, prescribing "rest in bed; rest in solitude; silence and rest; rest without friends, without books, without messages; six months' rest; until a man who went in weighing seven stone six comes out weighing twelve."[89]

Woolf's satirical attack on Bradshaw is exceptionally bitter and direct. She grounds her indictment, however, in an understated detail, Bradshaw's conversation with Richard Dalloway at the party. Gradually, Clarissa realizes that they are talking about Septimus's suicide:

> That Bill probably, which they wanted to get through the Commons. . . . They were talking about this Bill. Some case Sir William was mentioning, lowering his voice . . . about the deferred effects of shell shock. There must be some provision in the Bill . . .
>   Sinking her voice . . . Lady Bradshaw . . . murmured how "just as we were starting, my husband was called up on the telephone, a very sad case. A young man (that is what Sir William is telling Mr. Dalloway) had killed himself. He had been in the army." Oh!

thought Clarissa, in the middle of my party, here's death she thought.[90]

In the middle of Clarissa's party there's also a polite conspiracy about legislation to make the incarceration of such "cases" as Septimus's mandatory. The reiteration of the word "Bill" is remorseless. Woolf herself had been incarcerated for weeks at a time in Burley Park, Jean Thomas's "private home . . . for ladies with mental problems."[91]

What is particularly threatening, however, about the conversation at the party is Richard's willingness to listen to Bradshaw, whom he doesn't like—"'didn't like his taste, didn't like his smell.'"[92] Richard, who cares about the female vagrants and Armenians (or Albanians), who recognizes that Hugh Whitbread is an intolerable ass, is inseparably allied by his class interests—social status, education, money, and work—to "Holmes and Bradshaw. . . . [t]he brute with the red nostrils" that hunts Septimus to his death.[93] Even Peter Walsh, who was once "a prey to revelations" and who still believes that he "dislikes India, and empire, and army," values "civilization" and admires the "very fine training" of the soldiers—"boys of sixteen"—who pass him in Whitehall.[94] The fact is that everyone at Clarissa's party is implicated in Septimus's death, in the bloodbath of the war, in the ruling-class conspiracy of patriarchal, capitalist imperialism.

This is the alliance that Septimus ignores when he at first fails to develop the manliness essential to the conduct both of business and of war. Mr. Brewer, the paternal managing clerk at Sibleys and Arrowsmiths where Septimus worked before the war, notes that he looks weakly and advises football, the working-class equivalent to cricket as inculcator of manly strength.[95] It was Septimus's unmanly romanticism, rather than a desire to "play the game," that made him "one of the first to volunteer. . . . He went to France to save an England which consisted almost entirely of Shakespeare's plays and Miss Isobel Pole in a green dress walking in a square. . . . There . . . he developed manliness; he was promoted; he drew the attention, indeed the affection of his officer, Evans by name."[96]

In the trenches, William Shakespeare and Miss Isobel Pole won't suffice; manliness—or masculinity, "the way men assert what they believe to be their manhood"—is obligatory.[97] That manliness was compatible with, or virtually inseparable from, homoerotic bonding is made amply clear in the writings of Wilfred Owen and Siegfried Sassoon. Masculinity, the homoerotic, and the cauterization of feelings were necessary to the soldier's performance of his duty—to his assent to the military discipline that trained men to face virtually certain death.

Septimus's inability to feel, then, was common during the war and presumably remained common for some time among those soldiers who returned.[98] Woolf describes in her diary the lack of affect she noticed in two survivors, her brother-in-law Philip and Nick Bagenal. The bomb that wounded Philip Woolf simultaneously killed his brother, Cecil. After visiting Philip in the hospital, Woolf wrote, with the authority of her own experience about the repression of grief, "To me, Philip looked well; though there was that absent-mindedness which one sees in Nick [Bagenal]. I suppose to Philip these days pass in a dream from which he finds himself detached. I can imagine that he is puzzled why he doesn't feel more."[99] What Woolf explores in Septimus is much more than puzzlement: by 1923, his inability to love and grieve and his fear of his sexuality have been repressed so long that they surface in uncontrollable swings of both perception and mood.

Septimus's repression of feeling after the war is distinguished by his "panic . . . sudden thunder-claps of fear . . . appalling fear"; the thunder-claps echo his shell shock, but he is afraid also because of guilt about his repression of his desire for Evans (96–98). This repression is the "sin" from which follows the "crime" of marrying without love and his being "so pocked and marked with vice that women shuddered when they saw him in the street" (101). He veers from seeing all love and beauty as obscene—Shakespeare is full of loathing for "the sordidity of the mouth and the belly"—to seeing his repression of love as the sin for which he is condemned to death (98). He is simultaneously the criminal and the redeemer, the fugitive and the poet (107). It is through this intensity of hallucinatory "madness" that we see him reach the point where he can acknowledge his love, greet his lover, and celebrate his death as marriage and the fruition of desire.

As a poet, Septimus dramatizes his life, his relation to Rezia, his suffering, and his death. He makes up the story of his life while he and Rezia walk up Bond Street, like Woolf making up her novels while she walked on the Sussex Downs or around Tavistock Square:

> "Now we will cross," [Rezia] said.
>   She had a right to his arm, though it was without feeling. He

out of the window defying Holmes—"'I'll give it you!' he cried"—yet
Holmes's feet on the stairs impel him to that action (165). He had
already felt pressured to kill himself some days earlier because
"[h]uman nature. . . . Holmes was on him. . . . The whole world was
clamouring: Kill yourself"; yet a moment later he envisioned himself as the drowned sailor, accepting that "the dead were with him"
and calling out to Evans (102–3). Is it Septimus's struggle through
"madness" that breaks through his despair, or is his acceptance of
love and death just resignation—a side effect of his status as victim
of the war, the class system, the doctors? Even when we consider
Septimus's death by itself, without Clarissa's response to it, we confront what Christine Darrohn calls "undecidability." At the end of
Mrs. Dalloway, according to Darrohn, "we do not know whether to
celebrate or pity Septimus, we do not know whether to admire or abhor Clarissa."[102]

What I particularly like about this comment is that strong word,
abhor. I abhor Clarissa's frivolity, snobbery, and cowardice, her suppression of her lesbian sexuality, and her appropriation of Septimus's
death. My response to *Mrs. Dalloway* reflects my own experience of
growing up as a Jewish lesbian in conformist, misogynist England before Stonewall: I have always felt an uneasy identification with Doris
Kilman. Acceptance of modernist "undecidability" in this particular
novel has been exceptionally difficult. Yet the narrative demands
some such acceptance from the reader.

Clarissa's initial recoil from Septimus's death causes a recoil from
her party: she needs to deal with her own fear of death by imagin-
ing his. She imagines his physical pain—"through him, blundering,
bruising, went the rusty spikes"—and then admires his defiance, flinging life away in order to preserve the "thing . . . that mattered." In
Clarissa's moment of projection—she envisions that Septimus died
"holding his treasure," preserving his passion rather than "defac[ing],
obscur[ing]" it as she has her love for Sally Seton—Woolf celebrates
and validates Septimus's suicide (203–4).

The narrative further unites Clarissa and Septimus in his echo
of her recurring memory of the lament that the rustic brothers sing
over Fidele's grave: "Fear no more the heat o' the sun / Nor the furi-
ous winter's rages." Nothing in this scene from *Cymbeline* is what it
seems: the brothers are not rustic but sons of the king; Fidele is not
a boy but their cross-dressed sister, and Fidele/Imogen is not dead

but sleeping. Septimus believes that the dead are alive; he engages in gender masquerade when he designs Mrs. Peters's hat, and he indeed "fear[s] no more" as he undertakes his journey to meet his beloved. The haunting lyricism of the dirge, too, seems pertinent to Septimus's death, but mostly inappropriate to Clarissa.[103] Yet she too needs to fear no more: she is very afraid. Again and again in *Mrs. Dalloway*, her lyrical delight in the surface of things—the weather, her orderly house, her relationship with her servants—is shown up as a defense against her horror of aging and death.

Clarissa encounters the lines from *Cymbeline* in an open book displayed in Hatchards's shop window; she reads them to distract herself from thoughts about death: "Did it matter then . . . that she must inevitably cease completely . . . ?" (11–12). On her return home from Bond Street, in a moment of thwarted social ambition, the words "fear no more" recur: expressing Clarissa's shock at the discovery that Lady Bruton has not invited her to lunch, they seem entirely incongruous. But the intensity of her disappointment reveals to Clarissa that "she feared time itself . . . the dwindling of life" (34). She is afraid that without social successes she will have no "exquisite suspense" to distract her from the emptiness of her days. It is after this that she climbs the stairs to her attic room, "feeling herself suddenly shrivelled, aged, breastless"—a strangely Tiresias-like image of old age—and, standing alone by her narrow bed, she recalls sexual desire (35). But the women to whom she was attracted seem oddly depersonalized, unlike the vibrant presence of Sally Seton in the idyllic natural world of Bourton. Throwing her love away has rent Clarissa's heart from her body.

Hearing the heart in the body telling him to fear no more, Septimus is not afraid of death; beyond it Evans is waiting in "the meadow of life" (154, 28). Yet to Clarissa, the heart in the body announces only death:

> [T]he heart in the body which lies in the sun on the beach says . . . that is all. Fear no more, says the heart. Fear no more, says the heart, committing its burden to some sea, which sighs collectively for all sorrows, and renews, begins, collects, lets fall. And the body alone listens to the passing bee; the wave breaking; the dog barking, far away, barking and barking. (45)

Only the heart counsels courage, consigning its sorrow and loss to an unspecified, sighing sea; only the body, split off from the heart, remains alive, listening to the sounds of the natural world. And the insistently barking dog has been deserted, abandoned; it signifies the breaking of faith.

At the end of the day, Clarissa's final use of the words from *Cymbeline* merely gives her courage to reassemble her social self and return to her party—even though she knows that to do so is to "wreathe about with chatter . . . let drop every day in corruption, lies, chatter . . . [the] thing there was that mattered" (204). Woolf has thus endowed Clarissa with clearsightedness: she is able to look below the surface that she has constructed and cherished and see her life for what it really is. No one else in the novel has this ability; Peter Walsh, Lady Bruton, and Sally Seton Rosseter believe in their fantasy selves. I admire Clarissa's courageous insight but find all the more abhorrent her willful blindness to the sufferings of others.

Clarissa's immediate response when she reads "Fear no more the heat o' the sun" on her walk down Piccadilly reflects her habit of callousness: she makes use of the war to distract herself from Shakespeare's reminder of death. The self-serving clichés with which the governing class justified four years of slaughter roll sonorously through her head: "This late age of world's experience had bred in them all, all men and women, a well of tears. Tears and sorrow; courage and endurance; a perfectly upright and stoical bearing" (12). The shorthand superficiality of Clarissa's thoughts about the war reflects not only guilt about her insulation from the sufferings of her own class, like the otherwise enviable Lady Bexborough, but a determination to distance the whole war experience. At no point does she connect Septimus's suicide to events at the front, even though she has heard Sir William Bradshaw mention "the deferred effects of shell shock" (202). "The War was over"; it barely affected her life (6). This is one reason for condemning her identification with Septimus as an appropriation of his suffering.

The other reason, of course, is Clarissa's rigid adherence to the ranks and exclusions of the class system in her relations with everyone else in the novel. But she doesn't personally know Septimus, and it suits her to speculate no further about his class than about his war experience. It would have been impossible for her to identify herself with his suicide had she noticed him that morning in Bond Street; she would not have been able to see beyond his "shabby overcoat"

(17). It is a clear signifier of class, like Doris Kilman's mackintosh, although the latter is particularly damning in Clarissa's eyes: it at once conceals and proclaims its wearer's monstrous lesbianism.

One of the central ironies of *Mrs. Dalloway* is the fact that the character who—to the present-day reader and at moments, to herself—is the most obviously lesbian is the least obvious to the other people in the narrative. They can't recognize lesbianism in Clarissa just because she's *not* a grotesque, gender-dysphoric invert—because she is impeccably dressed. She has her moments of anxiety at the beginning of her party when she feels that "it [is] all . . . falling flat" (186), but never for a moment is she anxious about her clothes. Indeed, mending her green evening dress had soothed her "sudden spasm" that morning—a spasm of anxiety about both lesbianism and aging (41–42). She knows that the mending will be therapeutic: her decision to mend the dress is part of the process of pulling herself together that started at the looking glass following her disturbing recollections of lesbian desire. And at her moment of triumph, escorting the prime minister down the room, Peter Walsh sees her "[catch] her scarf in some other woman's dress, unhitch it, laugh, all with the most perfect ease and air of a creature floating in its element" (192). Clarissa's ease in handling this potential social disaster may be a product of euphoria at having attained her social peak; but it is also the fruit of years of conformity to the rigid class and sex/gender norms that underpin patriarchal imperialism.

The couple at the party who are most at home in their clothes are most at home also in this hierarchy: those prize products of the ruling class, Lord Gayton and Nancy Blow: "They looked; that was all. That was enough. They looked so clean, so sound. . . . " Clarissa knows that they can neither talk nor think, but she loves them all the same, particularly admiring the way that Nancy, "dressed at enormous expense by the greatest artists in Paris, stood there looking as if her body had merely put forth, of its own accord, a green frill" (196). A young, rich, heterosexual woman's body can be so easy to clothe in the liberated 1920s that it seems simply to secrete a frill.

Doris Kilman's body secretes, too, if we are to believe Clarissa: she perspires anxiously, abjectly, beneath the rainproof armor of her green mackintosh (14). Humiliated by Clarissa's nervous, triumphant laughter, Doris locates the source of her abjection in her body—that "unlovable body which people could not bear to see"; she feels that no clothes suit her even though "she might buy anything" (143). Yet in fact, as Woolf shows in the example of Nancy Blow, she can't buy anything that counts. Beauty is easy to come by for the rich and upper class; it is probably available to the girls shopping near Bond Street, "buying white underlinen threaded with pure white ribbon for their weddings" (21). Such underclothes would have been hand-made.[104] Beauty is not for sale, though, in the Army and Navy Stores, where Doris, independent but degradingly poor, shops for a mass-produced petticoat, moving so blindly and speaking so portentously that "the girl serving her [thinks] her mad" (144).

The "yellowish raincoat" worn constantly by Margaret Allington, the lower-middle-class heroine of Rebecca West's *The Return of the Soldier*, is an interesting predecessor of Doris Kilman's mackintosh. Both narratives contrast the conspicuous consumption of the rich with the makeshifts of poverty. A raincoat will do in a pinch in all seasons to protect its wearer from the weather and to conceal any inadequacies in the clothes underneath. Doris needs hers, too, as armor or camouflage for her unlovable lesbian body.[105] Yet both West's Jenny and Woolf's Clarissa see the raincoats as aesthetic crimes against their superior sensibilities. What really threatens Jenny, however, is Margaret as a class "primitive," with her maternal power to make Chris Baldry happy; what threatens Clarissa is her sense of the primeval power of her adversary and her uneasy suspicion that Doris mirrors the strong emotions of hatred and desire that she tries to suppress in herself.

Clarissa displaces onto Doris the feelings that conflict with her wish to be supremely civilized; but at her party, in the midst of her success, she feels relief in thinking about Miss Kilman: "That was satisfying; that was real. . . . She hated her; she loved her" (193). The intensity of her convictions and her desire, and her uncompromising challenge to Clarissa—mackintoshed, petticoated, gooseberry-eyed and all—make *Kil-man* strangely impressive.

Woolf represents lesbian sexuality as monstrously primeval in her portrayal of Doris Kilman. Admittedly, it is through Clarissa Dalloway's horrified, snobbish, sexually suppressed eyes that we see Kilman stand on the landing "with the power and taciturnity of some prehistoric monster, armoured for primeval warfare" (139). Clarissa appears to have swallowed whole the primitivist idea that inverts are "degenerate," retrogressing to an earlier stage in evolution. We are shown, though, that Miss Kilman simultaneously exists in the London of 1923 as a historian, a pacifist, a feminist intellectual, and a bemused outcast from the consumer culture; Woolf is far too critical of the dominant ideology to reproduce a mere stereotype.[106] Nonetheless, there is a certain horror in the representation of Doris Kilman: she may not be monstrous, but her possessive, obsessive desire for Elizabeth, her hunger, her misery, her unremitting intensity are at once heroic and fearsome. Woolf offsets Clarissa's nostalgic memories of a youthful, privileged, lesbian romance with Kilman's uncomfortable, insistently physical presence. The depiction of lesbian sexuality in *Mrs. Dalloway* is noticeably ambivalent.

Pink Icing and a Narrow Bed: Mrs. Dalloway *and* Lesbian History

Among the multiple doublings and otherings that structure *Mrs. Dalloway*, the intense and mutual hatred that bonds Clarissa Dalloway and Doris Kilman provides perhaps the strongest connection between people in the novel. It demonstrates a main theme of the novel: women's deprivation of political, economic, and sexual agency and power. Lady Bruton is debarred by her sex from ruling "barbarian hordes"; she cannot get her letter about emigration printed without men's help. Clarissa makes the safest marriage she can; both she and Sally Seton settle down to bear children for the patriarchy; now Sally can't stop gushing platitudes, and Clarissa, like Septimus Warren Smith, finds herself unable to feel. Miss Kilman loses her teaching job during the war because Kilman was Kiehlman in the eighteenth century and she refuses to vilify all Germans indiscriminately. So here she is, in her dirty mackintosh; bristling with bitterness and oozing self-pity; poor, greedy, lonely, and lesbian. Indeed, it is hard to like Doris Kilman; I find myself reading her as my own spectral Other as well as Clarissa's and Lady Bruton's.[107]

According to Helena Michie in *The Flesh Made Word: Female Figures and Women's Bodies*, the heroines of British novels don't usually eat; when they do, food is a metaphor for sex.[108] We never see Clarissa Dalloway eating. Doris Kilman recognizes that her greed is sublimation; she feels that "except for Elizabeth, her food [is] all that she live[s] for; her comforts; her dinner; her tea; her hot-water bottle at night." Yet her baffled longing for the cake with pink icing that is eaten by the child at the next table, and her miserable, frustrated fingering of two inches of chocolate éclair—these do make her pathetic and absurd (143–45). No wonder critics find Doris hard to stomach: she's the lesbian predator who fails; one can't get much more abject than that.

One way for the lesbian critic to provide a reading of *Mrs. Dalloway* that doesn't either ignore Miss Kilman or collapse ignominiously into abjection is to recognize that Doris's life contains more than her desire. She cannot be ignored: even to a stranger, such as Mr. Fletcher—retired from the treasury, praying to his accessible God in Westminster Abbey—she has power; she's impressive (148). Socialist, pacifist, and a lesbian historian, Kilman plays an important role as an outsider, opposing with her solitary feminist consciousness the structures of the patriarchy in Woolf's reconfigured history of the aftermath of the First World War. Rather than identifying with Doris Kilman's abjection, the lesbian critic might try to emulate her skills as a historian.

Miss Kilman lost her teaching job at Miss Dolby's school partly because "the family was of German origin; spelt the name Kiehlman in the eighteenth century; but her brother had been killed" (137). The ironic juxtaposition is powerful. Presumably he was killed defending the empire against those Germans with whom Doris was accused of sympathizing. There is plenty of historical evidence for the cruel, often absurd, persecution of Germans in England during the war. Sylvia Pankhurst writes that the anti-German riots were a result of deliberately organized propaganda; Vera Brittain's *War Diary* demonstrates all too clearly that the propaganda convinced the educated middle class.[109] Karen Levenback points to Woolf's source in her 1918 diary entry about meeting Louise Matthaei, a classicist who lost her job at Newnham because her father was a German.[110] The London *Times* recounted another case like Kilman's on May 13, 1915, reporting, "A distinguished English woman archaeologist, whose family has been resident more than 80 years, can obtain work nowhere because she has a German name."[111]

Claire Tylee adopts Clarissa's viewpoint on Kilman's loss of her job. "Kilman," she writes, "has made the War into a personal grievance that stands for all her bitterness against life."[112] But anti-German prejudice lasted long after the war was over, and Doris Kilman's career is indeed ruined. It is also important to realize that a history teacher at Miss Dolby's school did not have the status of either a distinguished woman archaeologist or a fellow and director of studies of even a women's college at Cambridge. Doris Kilman is not only a victim of jingoism and bigotry, she's a lower-middle-class lesbian; as she tells Elizabeth, her "grandfather kept an oil and color shop in Kensington" (145).

Clarissa Dalloway reads history, too, for enjoyment: Baron Marbot's account of Napoleon's retreat from Moscow—a soothing bedtime story about hypothermia, starvation, and death that took place a long time ago. Knowledge of more recent events is not, for Clarissa, a priority. Trudi Tate has made abundantly clear that her confusion and dismissal of "the Albanians, or was it the Armenians" is not only frivolous but callous (133).[113] Clarissa "cared much more for her roses than for the Armenians." Her ignorance reflects her cold indifference to cruelty and suffering.

Clarissa can afford to live in ignorance because she is protected by her class position, guarded by the "civilization" that is admired by Peter Walsh when he hears the bell of the ambulance carrying Septimus's body away—the same "civilization" that is exposed during the course of the novel as greed for wealth and power (167). Doris Kilman, however, is lamentably vulnerable in the world of imperialist commerce. Victoria Street attacks her with "the assault of carriages, the brutality of vans" (142).[114] She has been humiliated by Clarissa and is further undermined by the traffic of prosperous consumers, "all those people passing—people with parcels who despised her." It is in this context that she reveals her abjection to Elizabeth: "'I never go to parties. . . . People don't ask me to parties. . . . Why should they ask me? . . . I'm plain, I'm unhappy.'" Hearing herself, she summons her education to her defense: "She was Doris Kilman. She had her degree. She was a woman who had made her way in the world. Her knowledge of modern history was more than respectable." But in the Army and Navy Stores—temple of imperialist consumption or "consumer sanctuary," as Reginald Abbott has called it—the feminist intellectual is powerless; she must lurch, hat askew, through "all the commodities of the world" (146–47).[115] And even when she turns to Westminster Abbey for sanctuary, Doris Kilman's approach to her God is rougher than the paths of those insiders, Mr. Fletcher and Mrs.

Gorham; she struggles and shifts her knees, "so tough [are] her de-sires" (148). Unable to sublimate her love through either food or religion, Kilman is abandoned to rage and frustration in a seemingly unchangeable, classist, heterosexist society.

Lady Bruton, the third lesbian historian in *Mrs. Dalloway*, has a social position that makes struggle for the self at once irrelevant and pointless, for Lady Bruton is a hollow woman. From the outside, her identity seems as unshakable as the empire, but really, as Kathy Phillips has pointed out, there's absolutely nobody at home.[116] Even the food at Lady Bruton's luncheon party is merely a "profound illu-sion" (115). Her identity, such as it is, comes ready-made with her class position, her ownership of Shakespeare (whose works she mis-quotes as effortlessly as she sublimates her sexuality), and her unques-tionable right to present herself as a "spectral grenadier" (199).

The British Grenadier is an imperialist icon, immortalized in an eighteenth-century broadside ballad whose martial tune is still broad-cast every year during that desperately nostalgic military parade, the Trooping of the Colour.[117] Grenadiers "were men of exceptional phy-sique and distinctive attire,"[118] and Woolf mentioned them twice in her diary during the writing of *Mrs. Dalloway*. On December 15, 1922, describing her first meeting with Vita Sackville-West, Woolf presents her as "a grenadier; hard; handsome, manly; inclined to double chin." The second entry, written on December 21, 1924 just as she was fin-ishing retyping the novel, refers more affectionately to "dear old ob-tuse, aristocratic passionate, Grenadier like Vita."[119] The British Grenadiers of the song stood for patriotism, masculine strength, and military victory—qualities that Woolf mocks by endowing Lady Bruton with them as she reconfigures imperial history with herself as glorious leader: "If ever a woman could have worn the helmet and shot the arrow, could have led troops to attack, ruled with indomi-table justice barbarian hordes and lain under a shield noseless in a church, or made a green grass mound on some primeval hillside, that woman was Millicent Bruton" (199). This fantasy's population seems a somewhat mixed bunch (Boadicea, a nineteenth-century Indian army officer, a stone effigy, a neolithic nabob?), but they have impe-rial qualities in common: violence, militarism, and righteousness. Lady Bruton is certainly hard, manly, and obtuse; like Vita Sackville-West in the two diary entries, she is presented satirically, in contrast to the lyrical representation of Clarissa Dalloway's sapphist romance;

8. *Vita Sackville-West and a British Grenadier*. Portrait of Vita Sackville West, *Lady with a Red Hat*, by William Strang. Courtesy of Glasgow Museums, Art Gallery and Museum, Kelvingrove. Painting of a British Grenadier courtesy of Bryan Fosten.

above all, the diary entries make clear that Woolf created Lady Bruton as a sexual invert, a lesbian who experiences herself as a man.

In the course of this novel fairly bursting with lesbians, Lady Bruton, Doris Kilman, and Clarissa Dalloway are all presented with flowers; only Clarissa can accept them gracefully. Doris rejects the patronage behind Clarissa's gift; she squashes the flowers all in a bunch, as Elizabeth remembers dispassionately (145). Hugh Whitbread's carnations are also received without thanks: Lady Bruton takes them silently "with her angular grim smile" (115). Later, however, Hugh feels confident enough to indulge in a familiarity intensely resented by Milly Brush, who recognizes the patriarchal heterosexist enemy as clearly as Sally Seton did when Hugh assaulted her in the smoking room. He says to Lady Bruton, "Wouldn't they [the carnations] look charming against your lace?" Lady Bruton has no choice; she has to obey the dictates of gender subordination and good manners, but her body language expresses her resistance: "Lady Bruton raised the carnations, holding them rather stiffly with much the same attitude with which the General held the scroll in the picture behind her; she remained fixed, tranced" (116). Her class privilege cannot enable her to transcend this discomfort.

I believe that Ethel Smyth, a lesbian much admired by Woolf long before the two women met in 1930, was a model for Woolf's exuberant, satirical portrait of Lady Bruton. Smyth's father was a general. Woolf read *Impressions That Remained*, the first volume of Smyth's autobiography, in 1919, and commented on it both in her diary and in a letter to Lytton Strachey. The letter describes seeing Smyth at a concert, "striding up the gangway in coat and skirt and spats and talking at the top of her voice"; the diary entry ends, "Friendships with women interest me."[120] In her letter to the *New Statesman* defending the intellectual status of women against the sexist arrogance of "Affable Hawk" (Desmond MacCarthy), Woolf cites Sappho and Ethel Smyth, connecting them characteristically by writing, "And now to skip from Sappho to Ethel Smyth."[121] In 1921, Woolf reviewed Smyth's *Streaks of Life*, remarking that during the previous two years Smyth had become "one of those whom we carry about in the mind to think of at odd seasons."[122] There are also the imperialist details: Smyth's father went out to India at the age of fifteen, was made "responsible for roads, transport, communications, law and order, life and death, in a district as big as Yorkshire" the following year, and later, during the mutiny, did an Indian sergeant the honor of hanging him with his own hands.[123] Smyth's father, her conservative politics, and her manly clothes and voice probably underlie Woolf's depiction of Lady Bruton as an imperialist invert.

Lady Bruton's lesbian sexuality, however, has been successfully sublimated in her pet cause, emigration—the population of the colonies with the "master race"; emigration, the object of desire, "round which the essence of her soul is daily secreted, becomes inevitably prismatic, lustrous, half looking-glass, half precious stone; now carefully hidden in case people should sneer at it; now proudly displayed" (121). The precious stone recalls Clarissa's wrapped-up diamond, which represents both her clitoris and her memory of romance; it recalls also the diamond she summons in her looking glass, the hard-surfaced, pointed self she presents to the world (40, 42). Yet Lady Bruton's looking glass is potentially also a source of humiliation, reminding us of Doris Kilman's anguish when she lurches in front of the mirror in the Army and Navy Stores. This mirror can gratify Millicent Bruton's vanity as her father's daughter, as a woman who confers with the prime minister. But she cannot get her letters about emigration published in the *Times*; Hugh Whitbread's sexism embarrasses her; as a woman without a man, her power is an illusion. Woolf's upper-class invert, however protected by both privilege and obtuseness, is an object of derision: as grenadier, she's spectral; as general, she's grotesque; as imperialist dreamer, she's absurd.

Mrs. Dalloway critiques imperialism in its multiplicity of forms: classism, militarism, war, racism and gender oppression, sexological theory, and internalized homophobia. I read the novel now as a survey of suppressed lesbianism (or homosexuality, in the case of Septimus) whose motive force was Woolf's growing interest in Vita Sackville-West. With her sharp eye for class difference, Woolf delineates the socially acceptable ways by which the rich lesbians distract themselves from their sexual frustration. The poor women, on the other hand—Doris Kilman, Milly Brush, possibly even Ellie Henderson—must endure the pain of repression, be it raging or resigned. And at the novel's heart, Clarissa Dalloway stands rigid and solitary beside her narrow bed, recreating her memories of lost lesbian desire.

Between Two Wars: Memory and Desire

The First World War appears in all of Woolf's novels from *Jacob's Room* to *Between the Acts*; it is present in *A Room of One's Own, Three Guineas,* and a number of her essays as well. Sylvia Townsend Warner, in contrast, wrote very little about the war after her elegiac ending to *Mr. Fortune's Maggot* (1927), in spite or perhaps because of the grief and rage the events of the war caused her.[124] Her attitude to the Second World War was complex: she was a dedicated antifascist but at the same time profoundly skeptical about the political and military leaders' methods and motives. Nevertheless, Warner was never a pacifist: while others were signing the Peace Pledge during the 1930s, she was busy with the class war.

An episode of the class war forms the climax of each of Warner's historical novels of the thirties and forties. The massacres of the working class in Paris at the end of the 1848 Revolution conclude *Summer Will Show*; a deadly skirmish between peasants and soldiers ends *After the Death of Don Juan* (1938), a political fable set in the eighteenth century but actually about the Spanish Civil War. *The Corner That Held Them* (1948), which Warner wrote at odd moments throughout World War II, tells the story of thirty-three years in the life of a nunnery. It starts with the Black Death and ends in 1382 after the suppression of that hopeful, angry journey of the people to the young king in London—the Peasants' "Revolt."

But in the real world during the five years after 1939, political activism was out of the question, and sustained writing became impossible: for middle-aged, unmarried women like Warner, the days were devoured by unremittingly tedious tasks. A letter to Nancy Cunard conveys her irritation:

> I sometimes feel exactly like a bombed building, with a cloud of dust rising up from my ruined chambers. . . . Now I have a notice on my table telling me to attend at the Labour Exchange with a view to taking up employment of national importance—which means they will try to put me into a laundry. If I had taken to myself a husband, lived on him and made his life a misery . . . I should not be troubled with any of this. Being kept by a husband is of national importance enough. But to be femme sole, and self supporting, that hands you over, no more claim to consideration than a biscuit.[125]

It is understandable that many of the stories about the Second World

War collected in *A Garland of Straw* (1943) and *The Museum of Cheats* (1947) are bleakly ironic rather than celebratory or sad. The light-hearted humor of "My Shirt Is in Mexico" is a shining exception.

The paradoxical fact that Warner's life in the thirties as a lesbian communist was more open and free than her life as a liberal hetero-sexual in an adulterous relationship during the twenties is reflected in her exuberant representation of homosexual codes in "My Shirt Is in Mexico"; the narrative bubbles with her pleasure in the sometimes surprising camaraderie that can lighten the isolation of the closet. Now she can put herself and her companion Valentine Ackland into a story about leftist politics and gay sexuality; they participate in the humor of a brief flirtation between two strangers on a train.

The story is set on the London-to-Plymouth train, which is crowded with the soldiers, evacuees, and bundles of baggage of wartime. Sylvia is the first-person narrator; she and Valentine are on their way back to Dorset. They edge their way to the buffet car, which "belonged to a different world, with its clean, light-painted walls and red leather upholstery." The conversation that the women have with the seem-ingly unromantic attendant—"a middle-aged man with a good face, innocent and humane like a rabbit's"—belongs to a different world, too.[126]

The label on Sylvia's bag brings them together, starting a friendly discussion of the beauties of the scenery and socialism in Mexico. (None of them has been there; Sylvia's bag is borrowed.) "Now we all looked at the label, which was printed with a gay scene of flowers and white-clothed tourists riding on festooned mules." But their shared escape fantasies cease when the man says, "I've got a shirt in Mexico." With minimal but characteristic prompts from Sylvia and Valentine, he tells the story behind this bizarre statement: "'It's an uncommon thing to say, isn't it? Oil shares, now, or a cousin—that's to be expected, But not a shirt. It all happened before the war, be-cause of a German gentleman, a refugee. I noticed him the moment he came in—he sat down at that table over there—and I thought to myself: Now, he's somebody.'"[127] The relaxed, confiding speech pat-terns convey both the working-class speaker's comfort with his middle-class audience and the immediacy of his memory of the meet-ing. Together, he and his listeners escape from the compulsory jin-goism of war into an internationalist past.

This observant, chatty man, seemingly expert at enlivening a dull job, manages to get into conversation with his "somebody"; soon they are talking about the traveler's destination—he's going to embark at Plymouth for New York—and the lightness of his suitcase. From there, they get on to clothes, of which the political exile owns predictably few, but he isn't worried:

> "What's more, he seemed so pleased with what he *had* got. Made me feel his suit to see what good wool it was and told me all about a wonderful pair of silk pyjamas he'd been given. And you could tell from the way he spoke he was the sort of gentleman who knows about clothes—quite a dandy, in fact. . . . Then all of a sudden it flashed on me he could have my shirt. It was a very nice shirt. Providential, really—I'd bought it that very morning. . . . I always like to buy my shirts in London. You get a better style. . . . Wasn't I lucky to have it with me, though?"
>
> "You were," said Valentine. "I can't wish anyone better luck than that."[128]

Extremely generous herself, Valentine approves this act of generosity. And as a cross-dressing butch—"quite a dandy, in fact"—she can appreciate the value of a well-tailored shirt. No wonder the attendant looked at the two women "as though [they] were already friends of his" when he first brought them their drinks; he was responding, whether consciously or not, to their lesbian intimacy.[129] No wonder, too, that he is acquainted with sailors: "'Living in Plymouth, naturally I know a lot about New York, so I could tell him things he'd find useful.'"[130] "Naturally": Warner is making a closet joke out of the stereotype of the gay man cruising the quays. The story is an anecdote about the pleasures of mutual recognition in the closet.

Reading "My Shirt Is in Mexico" requires a familiarity with codes—the moral code of life in the closet and the codes of talking or writing within it. The verbal and literary codes are necessitated by social and legal oppression; the crosswritten romance itself becomes code in the hands of E. M. Forster in *A Room with a View* or Oscar Wilde in *The Importance of Being Earnest*: both works code homosexuality as the heterosexual norm. One of the more pleasurable products of the necessity of such codes is the verbal and visual discourse of camp. The moral code of the closet requires a certain skill so that one doesn't "out" one's interlocutor while letting him know that one is gay—and perhaps interested in sex. Sometimes all that's needed is a look, but the enjoyment of the encounter is heightened by the codes of mutual revelation and flirtation—an art at which this buffet-car attendant is an innocent, exuberant master. All that detail about the clothes, of course, is homosexual bonding: the attendant and the exile, and then Valentine, are united in delight in that shirt: "But what I liked best was the way he opened the parcel and looked at the shirt most carefully—how the buttons were fastened on and all. Examined it all over, he did. If he had just taken the parcel, that wouldn't have been the same thing, would it?"[131] Indeed it wouldn't. Sylvia, narrator and writer, reads the codes and reencodes them for the pleasure of her readers.

The buffet-car attendant, on the other hand, proves unexpectedly complicated; his "innocence" is crucial both to the lighthearted mood of "My Shirt Is in Mexico" and to its tantalizing ambiguity. I read the story as a comedy in which one vital point is intentionally left unclear: whether or not the buffet-car attendant is conscious that he's gay. There's that "good face, innocent and humane as a rabbit's." The story is enriched by the possibility that he may not fully know why he is telling it or why he has treasured the letter that his "gentleman" wrote.

This comedy has a happy ending. The final twist of the plot explains how the shirt arrived in Mexico even though the traveler remained in New York. The buffet-car attendant has his letter with him:

Often read, always carefully refolded, the thin sheet of paper already had the air of something beginning to be historic:

"March 11th, 1939.
Dear Friend:

I have to tell you how I have made good journey and am settled here in New York City. And I have meet other friends here also, and I find some work shortly. And the beautiful shirt you gave me, it is not ungratefully that I bestow it to a comrade going to Mexico when he has greater need than I. I do not forget the kindness. I hope you are well and make always new friends. I thank you again.

    Cordially,
    RENATUS LEUTNER.
P.S. New York is very fine."[132]

Renatus himself is very fine: courageous, courteous, concerned about that little Marxist matter of who has greater need. He seems fully conscious of the sexual undercurrents of making friends on the train. And he is generous in his hopes for his friend's future friendships as well as in his redistribution of that shirt. *Renatus* Leutner's name reveals his origin in Warner's and Ackland's lives: he represents a dear friend of theirs from that now "historic" world before the war, the German writer and communist exile, Ludwig Renn.[133]

When Renn came to stay with Warner and Ackland in Dorset in 1939, they were going through a difficult time: Ackland's lover, Elizabeth Wade White, was also staying with them, and Warner had moved into the spare room. Many years later, Warner recalled Renn's exiled condition and the welcome relief he provided to their *ménage à trois*:

> He had no passport, for he was a stateless person. He had no money, he had no future, he had sat starving behind barbed wire at Argelès, he had an unhealed wound, he had seen the bitter defeat of his cause. He had kept his interest in humankind and his slightly frivolous goodwill. His presence was so restorative. . . . [S]eeing [Elizabeth] in one of her fits of gloom, he said: "Now we will dance," bowed a court bow, put his arm around her waist and waltzed with her on the lawn.[134]

A letter from Renn to Warner written in Mexico on March 30, 1942 makes quite clear his interest in homosexuality; he mentions that the book he is writing about prehistory will examine the origins of homosexuality, and he asks Warner for help on lesbian aspects of this apparently primitivist project. Ludwig Renn is a worthy original for that lighthearted, flirtatious comrade, Renatus Leutner, on the London-to-Plymouth train. And "My Shirt Is in Mexico" is a loving commemoration of Renn's visit and survival, and of the courage and battles of another war in the communist, internationalist 1930s.

In 1964, nineteen years after the end of the Second World War and fifty years after the beginning of World War I, Sylvia Townsend Warner, seventy years old, wrote her "nice calm story about incest."[135] Warner's use of shell shock in "A Love Match" is the trigger of her plot, as it is in West's *The Return of the Soldier* and Woolf's *Mrs. Dalloway*. Originally titled "Between Two Wars," Warner's story depicts two lives structured and encompassed by destruction. The First and Second World Wars shock into love and then into death the incestuous sister and brother, Celia and Justin Tizard.

The symptoms of Justin's shell shock are numb detachment, hallucinations, and nightmares through which he talks incessantly in his sleep. Awake, he is most comfortable gazing at the ground. His sister meets his train at Victoria when he comes home on leave after the Battle of the Somme:

> There were some pigeons strutting on the platform and he was watching them when a strange woman in black came up to him, touched his shoulder, and said, "Justin!" It was as though Celia were claiming a piece of luggage, he thought. She had a taxi waiting, and they drove to her flat. . . . The room smelled of polish and flowers. There was a light-colored rug on the floor and above this was the blackness of Celia's skirts. She was wearing black for her fiancé. . . . Looking round the room, he saw Tim's photograph on her desk. She saw his glance, and hers followed it. "Poor Tim!" they said, both speaking at once, the timbre of their voices relating them. . . . Compassion made it possible to look at her. . . . But he could not see her steadily for long. There was a blur on his sight, a broth of mud and flame. . . . When she showed him to his bedroom she stepped over mud that heaved with the bodies of men submerged in it.[136]

The compassion brings on the hallucinations: numbness, as in the case of Septimus Warren Smith, is much safer than feeling.

The Tizards pass their first two days together in desultory sightseeing. Justin does not speak of his hallucinations, nor does Celia tell him of her two sleepless nights on the living room couch trying to distract herself from the "ghastly confidences" of her sleeping brother in the adjoining room: that we don't hear what he actually says is an example of Warner's telling use of understatement.[137] The third night, Celia falls into the sleep of exhaustion, wakes up suddenly at some outcry or exclamation, and runs next door "to waken the man who, if she could awaken him, would be Justin, her brother Justin." She embraces him; he wakens and drags her toward him: "They rushed into the escape of love like winter-starved cattle rushing into a spring pasture."[138] Their urgency is naturalized; it marks the beginning of a romance that will lead to twenty-five years of loving incestuous companionship.

The Tizards' attitude to their breaking of the primal incest taboo is remarkably practical. At first they don't envision their relationship—or Justin—as having any future after he returns to the front, but they are lucky: he is wounded in the leg, gangrene sets in, and he has been sent to a hospital near London, where he "was ravaged with fret and behaving with perfect decorum when Celia was shown in—dressed all in leaf green, walking like an empress, smelling delicious. For a moment the leaf-green Celia was almost as much of a stranger as the Celia all in black had been. When she kissed him, he discovered that she was shaking from head to foot."[139] The siblings know that for them this love—depicted here with an economical explicitness that is characteristic of Warner's representations of desire—will be for life, and so, like innumerable British sexual outlaws, they take refuge after the war in France; five years later, when Justin is offered a job in the relentlessly respectable provincial town of Hallowby, they decide to risk cohabitation in England. The rest of "A Love Match" doesn't focus on romance; it is a narrative of day-to-day life in a humdrum, middle-class closet.

Warner's diary for 1930 recounts how an event similar to the start of the Tizards' romance marked the beginning of her long, loving, and humdrum relationship with Valentine Ackland: Sylvia, too, ran next door to kneel by the bed and comfort not a brother, but her friend.[140] And she and Valentine spent most of their next thirty-nine years together living in Maiden Newton, a Dorset village small enough to make gossip inevitable. Their closet shared with the Tizards' the quality of instant respectability. What couple could be more above reproach than a pair of literary ladies or "a disabled major and his devoted maiden sister"?[141]

Celia arranges the closet in "A Love Match": she chooses an out-of-the-way house surrounded by a high wall; she decides that if they don't have friends they will "become odd," and so they should go to church—but "not too often or too enthusiastically, as it would then become odd that they did not take the Sacrament."[142] Soon an invitation to join a rather elderly group of whist players enables them to indulge in that most genteel of pastimes. At home, they revel in their impenetrable disguise: "Returning from their sober junketings Justin and Celia, safe within their brick wall, cast off their weeds of middle age, laughed, chattered and kissed with an intensified delight in their scandalous immunity from blame. They were a model couple, the most respectable couple in Hallowby, treading hand in hand the thornless path to fogydom."[143] Their delight in the closet's ironies is entirely comparable to that of a lesbian couple enjoying "scandalous immunity from blame" because they are perceived as dried-up old maids.

"A Love Match" expresses a sexual radicalism that is perhaps more extreme than anything Warner wrote in her fantasy novels of the 1920s, not because it crosswrites lesbianism as incest but because its lovers live so calmly predictable a "married" life. Celia does just what is expected of a woman: she comforts the returning soldier; then she looks after him during his depression, planning and organizing the practical and social details of their lives in order to safeguard his peace of mind. By 1936 their normality is so established that her marching in communist demonstrations seems as minor an eccentricity as Justin's gammy leg. And so they live in settled contentment until Justin, predictably enough, acquiesces sufficiently to the blandishments of a young woman to make her want to unsettle them.

Age, not infidelity, is what changes the balance of power within the Tizards' relationship. Celia is the elder; she is disempowered when jealousy prompts Justin's young woman to write anonymous letters. These address Celia as "Hag," taunt her with being "ugly, ageing and sexually ridiculous," and list the names of neighbors who know about her "loathsome performances."[144] Anonymous letters have long been a feature of the closet; they are a staple of spy novels and of the real-life sex scandals routinely headlined in the British press, but the letters in "A Love Match" do not result in any kind of public exposure; the intense pain they cause is private. Instead of blackmailing Celia, they have "ripped through her self control and made her cry with mortification."[145] It is typical of Warner that she uses anonymous letters to represent the sexual humiliation of a middle-aged woman: the British, like North Americans but unlike the French, believe that sexually active women should be young. But as Justin points out, the letters are not dangerous: there may have been speculation about the Tizards among their genteel neighbors, but "even if they do know, they weren't informed at a public meeting. Respectable individuals are too wary about libel and slander to raise their voices individually."[146] Whatever gossip there is, nothing in a town like Hallowby or Maiden Newton will ever be said to the scandalous couple themselves.

One night in 1941, a bomb falls just across the road from the Tizards' house, and the explosion brings down their roof. Foe, the greengrocer's son, who has known the Tizards since he was a boy, is one of the rescue workers who

> followed the trail of bricks and rubble upstairs and into a bedroom
> whose door slanted from its hinges. . . . A dark bulk crouched on

the hearth, and was part of the chimney stack, and a torrent of slates had fallen on the bed, crushing the two bodies that lay there.

The wavering torchlights wandered over the spectacle. There was a silence. Then young Foe spoke out. "He must have come in to comfort her. That's my opinion." The others concurred. Silently, they disentangled Justin and Celia, and wrapped them in separate tarpaulin sheets. No word of what they had found got out.[147]

It is war, not incest, that is a monstrous invader of lives in "A Love Match," from the heaving mud on the threshold of Celia's room in 1916 to the chimney stack crouching on the hearth. The First World War brings grief to Celia and fearful horror to Justin; World War II brings them death. Warner's nice calm story persuades us that falling in love with one's sister could happen to any shell-shocked soldier on leave; we know that the Tizards' death could have happened to any British couple asleep in bed during the war; it would have happened to Warner and Ackland in 1940 if they had been sleeping in their spare room when the incendiary bomb came through the roof. Incest and perhaps all other forms of deviant sexuality are naturalized in "A Love Match"; what is unacceptable is war.

5

WRITING AND REWRITING STEPHEN GORDON

"Not an Exemplary Young Negro": Inversion, Primitivism, Nationalism, and Redemption

It is arguable that in forgoing crosswriting entirely and instead writing a bildungsroman focused on one particularly unmistakable invert, Radclyffe Hall was a far braver writer than either Sylvia Townsend Warner in her various forms of crosswriting or Virginia Woolf in her stream-of-consciousness explorations of homosexuality and lesbianism. Certainly *The Well of Loneliness* is more obviously centered on specifically lesbian politics than any other novel of the twenties. Both its accessibility and its notoriety stem from the fact that Hall adapted to her purpose the genre of popular romance. Like Clemence Dane's lesbian/heterosexual romance *Regiment of Women*, *The Well* explores forbidden love without crossing the boundaries of gender or class. Both novels explicitly endorse the values of imperial ideology.

An advantage of crosswriting is that it can provide the distance that enables a lesbian writer to free her narrative from the internalized lesbophobia that characterizes both *Regiment of Women* and *The Well of Loneliness*. In fact, many of the elements of *Regiment* are recognizable in *The Well*: its patriotic representation of a prewar pastoral England, its eugenicist insistence on motherhood, and its final melodramatic repudiation of lesbianism. The openness of Hall's representation of lesbianism was what made it unique. Hall saw her book as a work of propaganda to make inversion respectable. In response to a 1934 inquiry from Gorham Munson, she said that she wrote the book because "I wished to offer my name and my literary reputation in support of the cause of the inverted." She not only adopted for her protagonist the most recognizable lesbian stereotype available to her—the masculine-looking female congenital invert—but her letter to Munson claims the label *invert* for herself: "[B]eing myself a congenital invert, I understood the subject from the inside as well as from medical and psychological text-books." Speaking as a propagandist, she invokes congenitalism in the hope of gaining societal acceptance for herself and all the other inverted "target[s] for ridicule or condemnation."[1]

I am concerned with Hall's representation of inversion in *The Well* primarily as it connects with the other evolutionist, imperialist discourses in the novel—primitivism, degeneration theory, eugenics—and with the representation of nationality, class, and race in conjunction with sexuality and gender. However, it is difficult at present to mention Hall's reflection of the writings of sexologists—Karl Heinrich Ulrichs, Richard von Krafft-Ebing, Havelock Ellis, Edward Carpenter, and Sigmund Freud—without at least touching upon the critical debate about Stephen Gordon's sexual and gender identity. What is at issue is the meaning of Stephen Gordon's inversion not only within the novel but for current theories of lesbian sexuality, transsexuality, and female masculinity. *The Well of Loneliness* continues to be used as a tool for changing, or at least reformulating, discourses about the sex/gender system.

When lesbian critics write about Stephen Gordon's identity, they often tend to write about their own sexual and political identities as well. Several lesbian feminists writing from the 1970s on have seen Stephen as a self-hating, male-identified butch whose relations with other women were essentially oppressive of them as well as of herself. In "The Mythic Mannish Lesbian," Esther Newton countered their readings of *The Well* by redefining Stephen as a "mannish lesbian" whose representation continues to move lesbian readers because it confronts the "stigma of lesbianism" presented by those unassimilable masculine figures of abjection whom Hall wants to save from derision and condemnation. Newton's essay was a starting point for my own interpretation of *The Well*, as for significant new readings of it by Jay Prosser and Judith Halberstam.[2]

Prosser and Halberstam focus on Hall's use of inversion theory, in opposition to Teresa de Lauretis's controversial Freudian interpretation of the novel. All three writers center their readings on the crucial "mirror scene" in which Stephen repudiates her genitalia.[3] De Lauretis interprets the passage as a repudiation of masturbation that foreshadows Stephen's eventual renunciation of any autonomous, nonreproductive sexuality for women; she reads *The Well* as a fantasy of castration, fetishism, and desire. Her theory of sexuality prioritizes object choice—active desire between butch and femme women—to the point where she claims that "it takes two women, not one, to make a lesbian."[4] Both Prosser and Halberstam read de Lauretis as devaluing female masculinity, which their focus on inversion theory prioritizes. I also remain unconvinced by de Lauretis's complicated rewriting of Freud. Nevertheless, it seems to me, as it does to Jean Radford and Laura Doan, that Hall's representation of different strands of sexology in *The Well* is eclectic.

It is certainly clear that Stephen Gordon's sexuality is overdetermined. Despite Hall's eager espousal of the ideas of Havelock Ellis, she read other sexologists; she was familiar with Freudian theories as well. According to the Freudian model, Stephen is a lesbian because her father wants a boy and raises her as a boy, and, identifying with him, she desires women. There is a significant reference in *The Well*, also, to Edward Carpenter's hopeful replacement of the "invert" with the "intermediate." When Stephen, distraught after her mother has exiled her from Morton, discovers a book by Krafft-Ebing annotated with her name by her father, she can only mutter about "the Mark of Cain." But her benign ex-tutor, Puddle, has some comfort for her:

> "Why, just because you are what you are, you may actually find that you've got an advantage. You may write with a curious double insight—write both men and women from a personal knowledge . . . [W]e're all part of nature. Some day the world will recognize this. . . . For the sake of all the others who are like you, but less strong and less gifted perhaps, it's up to you to have the courage to make good."[5]

Nevertheless, despite these evidences of eclecticism, Stephen remains most obviously and intentionally a congenital invert—an embodiment of "a theory of homosexuality [that] folded gender variance and sexual preference into one economical package."[6]

The point at issue between Prosser and Halberstam is the meaning of inversion theory itself. In *Second Skins: The Body Narratives of Transsexuality*, Prosser sees Ulrichs' image of "the soul of a woman enclosed in a man's body" as "the popular trope for transsexuality";[7] he goes on to read Ellis's case histories as transsexual autobiographies. For Prosser, Stephen Gordon's grief in front of the mirror is the culmination of a number of "images of bodily lack" in *The Well of Loneliness*; many of them are "wrong body" tropes stemming from Ulrichs. "The implication," Prosser notes, "is that, as a female who ought to be a man, Stephen is incomplete."[8] Stephen is rejecting her body because it is insufficiently masculine, not insufficiently feminine, as de Lauretis argues. *The Well of Loneliness* is thus a narrative of transsexual longing.

I find Prosser's interpretation problematic because of its anachronism: nowadays, a female-to-male transsexual may not in fact undergo surgery or hormonal treatments, but he lives in a world where such possibilities exist, even if he is unaware of them. The word *transsexual*, therefore, has connotations that would not have existed for Radclyffe Hall, her readers, or her fictional characters. In *Female Masculinity*, Judith Halberstam writes,

> Toupie [Lowther] and Miss Ogilvy, the women in Havelock Ellis's surveys, and even Stephen Gordon seem much more closely related to what we now call a transsexual identity than they do to lesbianism. Indeed, the history of homosexuality and transsexuality was a shared history at the beginning of the century and only diverged in the 1940s, when surgery and hormonal treatments became available to, and demanded by, some cross-identifying subjects.[9]

I think Halberstam's acknowledgment of the divergence between transsexual and homosexual histories in the 1940s is crucial to understanding and expressing the *female masculinity*—Halberstam's useful term—of Stephen Gordon.[10] Her reading of the "mirror scene" identifies Stephen Gordon as a butch who desires other women but does not wish to be touched sexually herself—the kind of invert who will be called a "stone butch" in the 1950s; Stephen is confronting in the looking glass her "disidentification with the female body"; her clothed body, on the other hand, represents both her female masculinity and her desire.[11]

As both de Lauretis and Halberstam point out, the day before she stands naked and grieving in front of the mirror, Stephen is in London, buying luxurious clothes—gloves, pyjamas, a man's brocade dressing gown. They cannot comfort her, however, because Angela Crossby sees only her bodily lack and desires neither her masculinity nor her desire. Mary Llewellyn, in contrast, recognizes the sexual significance of Stephen's clothing: when they return to Paris as lovers, she examines the suits in the wardrobe, the shelves of shirts, crepe de chine pajamas, heavy silk masculine underwear. For Mary, these clothes become objects of desire; for Stephen, however, they constitute her gender identity.

I read *The Well of Loneliness* as primarily about female masculinity rather than sexual preference; although within inversion theory the two concepts are inseparable, the novel describes life on the gender cusp as a partially cross-dressing invert in far greater detail than desire. Stephen yearns painfully for Angela Crossby's love and for sex as the consummation of her love for Mary, but her sense of gender difference is what isolates her as an adolescent, exiles her as a young woman, and condemns her to a life of celibacy and Christlike intercession at the end of the novel. Contrary to the opinion of Sir Chartres Biron, the chief magistrate whose verdict consigned *The Well* to the flames, there is very little sex in this novel.

What particularly interests me, however, is Hall's identification of female masculinity with "primitive" sexuality. Her attempt to identify Stephen Gordon with racialized Others is problematic. Such cultural appropriations abound in modernist literature, but Hall's are particularly egregious: few writers offer such offensive evidence of precisely the racism and snobbery that they deplore. There are three central primitivist scenes. When Stephen declares her "grotesque . . . pitiful passion," Angela Crossby sees that there was "something rather terrible about her. All that was heavy in her face sprang into view, the strong line of the jaw, the square, massive brow, the eyebrows too thick and too wide for beauty; she was like some curious, primitive thing conceived in a turbulent age of transition."[12] The ideas behind this portrait form part of the racialized discourse of colonialism.[13] The "heavy" facial features, the excessively hairy eyebrows, the strange, ungendered "thing" belonging to a violent past—all these are out of place in "civilized" society. The importance to Hall of connecting inversion to "primitive" sexuality can be gauged from the fact that this passage is a virtually verbatim repetition of an earlier account of Stephen's appearance during a childish moment of frustrated chivalry; she wants to fight Roger Antrim because he has insulted her mother:

> She stood there an enraged and ridiculous figure in her Liberty smock, with her hard, boyish forearms. Her long hair had partly escaped from its ribbon, and the bow sagged down limply, crooked and foolish. All that was heavy in her face sprang into view, the strong line of the jaw, the square, massive brow, the eyebrows, too thick and too wide for beauty. And yet there was a kind of large splendour about her—absurd though she was, she was splendid at that moment—grotesque and splendid, like some primitive thing conceived in a turbulent age of transition.[14]

In the later passage, Stephen's "primitive" appearance is accentuated because of her unhappiness at Angela's brutal rejection of her, whereas for the prepubescent inverted child the emphasis is entirely on gender inversion rather than sexual desire. The child's unhappiness arises from the incongruity between the feminine clothes she must wear and her boyish physique and emotions: this is the first of her many experiences of acute gender dysphoria. At least the narrator, unlike Angela, sees her as splendid as well as grotesque.

The third primitivist scene contains a "real"—and degenerate—"primitive" with nothing splendid about him; it occurs in one of the vignettes of yearning and decadence that characterize the Bohemian life in Paris to which Stephen and Mary are banished. Jamie, the composer who will later kill herself, an invert whose music is made rigid and spiritless by her despair, throws a party at which two black musicians perform. Lincoln Jones plays the piano; his brother Henry, who sings spirituals, is described as "not an exemplary young Negro; indeed he could be the reverse very often. A crude animal Henry could be at times, with a taste for liquor and a lust for women—just a primitive force rendered dangerous by drink, rendered offensive by civilization. Yet as he sang his sins seemed to drop from him, leaving him pure, unashamed, triumphant."[15] Henry represents the dangerously displaced "primitive" of degeneration theory, the idea that certain racial types decay if displaced from their "proper" position and generate pathologies: slums, crime, prostitution, disease.[16] Henry would be a fine upstanding young man if only he lived in Africa, or perhaps Mississippi. In this passage, also, the idea of "primitive" peoples as separate, without their own history, outside of time, is significantly clearer than in the descriptions of Stephen. The invert can hope to develop beyond "transition" toward "civilization," whereas the true "primitive" is stuck.[17]

As a 1920s romance that reflects dominant cultural values, *The Well of Loneliness* celebrates whiteness as well as upper-class wealth at Morton, the Gordon family's ancestral home. First we have the idyllic childhood: heroic, protective father; heroic, dependent horse; peaceful countryside, hills like breasts. There are servants, stables, foxhunting, swans that nest on the lake. As a small child walking with her mother, Stephen notices the scents of the meadows and says, "'Stand still or you'll hurt it—it's all round us—it's a white smell, it reminds me of you!'"[18] This odd moment introduces the theme of Stephen's love for and disconnection from nature, which is identified with Anna in the novel; when Anna repudiates her daughter, the green world of the English pastoral, with its strangely white smell, will repudiate her too.[19]

Nothing can protect Stephen from the "unappeased love" of the invert; fatherless and twenty-one years old, she falls for Angela Crossby. In the mirror scene, she wants to maim her naked body even though it is "so white, so strong" a product of the ruling class in imperialist Edwardian England.[20] Its strength is weakened, its whiteness stained by her inversion. Peter, the male swan who guards his mate and cygnets on the lake, symbolizes the perfect whiteness no longer attainable by Stephen. Rejecting Stephen during her adolescence with a movement "like a disdainful negation," he sails off, "proud in his splendid, incredible whiteness."[21] His rejection is repeated by his son and heir during one of Stephen's alienated visits to her rejecting mother; Peter is so much more prolific than the barren invert can be. Again, her inversion darkens Stephen as well as displacing her. The novel's Garden of Eden, irrevocably lost Morton, is the patriarchal place of heterosexuality and whiteness.

The Well of Loneliness is a romance with an essentially Christian structure: on her journey through suffering to martyrdom Stephen finally becomes a Christlike figure who has "drained [the] cup to its dregs"—the cup in the garden at Gethsemane and the cup of martyred inversion: she will intercede through her writing for all the suffering inverts of the world.[22] But the novel is unorthodox in that it contains two Gardens of Eden: the second one is the lushly prolific tropical garden at Orotava in Tenerife, off the coast of Africa, where—ejected from Morton and her place in the ruling class—Stephen takes her class Other, Mary. They find "a veritable Eden . . . obsessed by a kind of primitive urge towards all manner of procreation" where Stephen, the invert who can't procreate, obsessively feels and heroically fights her desire for Mary.[23] But her response to "the dim blue glory of the African night" is inevitable: she eventually succumbs to her passion.[24] The erotic, exotic, slightly sinister setting permits a loss of rational control, a regression to the untamed self: here we have another trope of the primitivist discourse represented in Henry Jones's crude animal lust.

The novel's nationalist theme is as typical of romance as its primitivism: all the ethnicities of Britain are represented.[25] Sir Philip is firmly English—a "Gordon of Bramley," with Morton in the Malvern Hills as his "country seat," and Stephen takes her nationality as well as her gender identification from her father. The servants are all Shropshire people: Hall's sentimental representation of loyalty in old Williams the groom is emphasized by the insistently rustic dialect that identifies his origin in the peasantry of Merry England. Anna Gordon "is lovely as only an Irishwoman can be"; Stephen's beloved horse Raftery, named after the blind poet, also comes from Ireland.[26] And then there are the exiles in Paris. Mary Llewellyn is lower middle class and Welsh, much less privileged than Stephen and altogether deserving of her protection. Mary in her turn adopts a stray Welsh water spaniel whom she names David; they feel equally out of place walking in the Tuileries Gardens while Stephen is busy writing at home.[27] Jamie, the invert composer, and Barbara, her consumptive lover, are refugees from the Scottish Highlands. They had grown up together in the same village and been driven into exile by their neighbors' xenophobia. The focal point of these nationalisms is imperial Great Britain, in which Scotland, Wales, and Ireland are all subsidiary to England. We are given an idealized picture of the United Kingdom in which contemporary struggles around national identities, such as the vicious suppression by the English government of the 1916 Easter Rebellion in Ireland, have been completely erased. At the center of the picture stands upper-class Morton, from which Stephen has been thrust out into a foreign world where money may talk but British class privilege is irrelevant.

Patriotism is particularly celebrated in Hall's representation of the First World War. Stephen returns to England from Paris and lives temporarily in London along with the other awkward, courageous women who can find themselves in service to their country because "bombs do not bother the nerves of the invert."[28] Stephen is one of those who go off to become war heroes in Mrs. Breakspeare's Ambulance Unit. By 1928, there had been novels and autobiographies about the war that questioned its purposes, criticized its military and political leadership, and emphasized with more or less accurate detail the sufferings of those at the front.[29] Nothing like that sullies the patriotism of *The Well of Loneliness*. Unlike other war narratives written after the war, there is never a moment's doubt in this one that the British and French are heroes, while the Germans are villainous brutes. There are a few obligatory accounts of the sufferings of the wounded, but Stephen gets her scar and Croix de Guerre remarkably easily.[30]

The inverted Parisian world that Stephen and Mary inhabit after the war becomes progressively hellish, and their romance turns rapidly to melodrama. If Morton is Eden in this novel, the inverts' Paris is Hell, peopled by the "battered remnants of men whom their fellow men had at last stamped under" and who "must yet tap their feet to the rhythm of music" at Alec's, the most sordid of the gay bars.[31] Henry Jones as racial primitive acts as one of Hell's gatekeepers, mirroring Stephen's supposedly primitive sexuality. His musical genius, on the other hand, foreshadows Stephen's writing, the means by which she will rescue the damned and lead the inverts back into a mainstream society newly converted to tolerance. After sacrificing Mary to a marriage in the "Colonies" to breed children for imperialism, and after condemning herself to a life of celibacy and Christlike intercession, at last Stephen's "barren womb became fruitful."[32] She will give birth to novels that will make inversion respectable.

For me, the insuperable flaw in Hall's courageous attempt to change her culture's attitude to inversion is her assumption that she can erase homophobia in isolation from racism, classism, misogyny, and their basis in economics. In her 1934 letter to Gorham Munson, she wrote that she had intended *The Well of Loneliness* to present to the world her firm belief that "*the worthy* among the inverted . . . desire to form a part of the social scheme, to conform in all ways to the social code as it exists at present"[33] Hall's patriotic conservatism blinds her to the possibility that inverts, homosexuals, or lesbians just might stop conforming in order to make common cause with others who are oppressed. Other writers of her time, such as Virginia Woolf, Sylvia

Townsend Warner, and Rose Allatini, show their consciousness of the fact that homosexuals and lesbians do not fight for justice in a vacuum.

Jonathan Dollimore and Sonja Ruehl have both argued that *The Well of Loneliness* subverts dominant ideology by using the language of inversion theory as reverse discourse that empowers lesbian readers despite the novel's classism and conservatism.[34] Their argument is strengthened by Lucy Bland's claim that sexology enabled some women "to think about claiming a *sexual* identity"—to realize that they have other choices besides passive heterosexuality or celibacy.[35] It is ironic that a novel as racist, classist, and essentially misogynist as *The Well* should be perceived as empowering: the ideology it reflects, with the exception of its plea for tolerance of inverts, is not very far from that of Sir William Joynson-Hicks, the home secretary who ensured that it was brought to trial. Yet it certainly seems that, in the absence of a genuine alternative discourse, almost any representation can count as "reverse." For many decades, *The Well of Loneliness* provided the only widely available representation of lesbianism; even a book as problematic as this one is a lot better than nothing. It was the trial of *The Well of Loneliness* that ensured it a notoriety that has kept it in print ever since.

The Majesty of the Law: Patriarchal Bonding

Before *The Well of Loneliness* was published, Radclyffe Hall knew that she risked a censorship trial; three cautious publishers refused the book before Jonathan Cape accepted it, and Cape and Hall had some trouble negotiating liability for potential legal costs.[36] Of course Hall knew that she was challenging entrenched prejudices; indeed, she was preparing herself for martyrdom: during the evenings preceding publication, Una Troubridge read aloud to her Oscar Wilde's *De Profundis* and *The Ballad of Reading Gaol*, and Frank Harris's biography of Wilde. But neither her reading of Wilde nor her own experience as plaintiff in her 1920 slander suit against St. George Lane Fox-Pitt prepared her for the bigotry of the legal powers that massed against her; by suing the book—or its publishers—rather than its author and by refusing the testimony of witnesses for the defense, they completely deprived her of agency and voice.[37]

From the politicojudicial preparations for the trial through the hearing of Hall's appeal of the verdict, the proceedings against *The Well* were a travesty of justice—resembling in their unscrupulousness Noel Pemberton-Billing's 1918 machinations against Maud Allan. Indeed, the home secretary, Sir William Joynson-Hicks, had been a right-wing parliamentary crony of Pemberton-Billing ten years earlier. Joynson-Hicks was a Christian crusader against sex and communism. He was treasurer to the fundamentalist Zenana Bible Mission; as home secretary, he had the police scour the parks for violations of public decency, cracked down on prostitution, and harassed nightclubs and casinos. He had twelve leading communists arrested in 1925, secured a judicial ruling that made the Communist Party illegal, and had two hundred police raid a small Russian trade delegation. In *The Sink of Solitude* (1928), the anonymous verse lampoon that contains the famous Beresford Egan cartoon of Radclyffe Hall on the cross, Joynson-Hicks is called the "Policeman of the Lord."[38]

True to his generally high-handed approach to the law, Joynson-Hicks extralegally suppressed *The Well of Loneliness* before it was put on trial. James Douglas, editor of the *Sunday Express*, wrote a rabble-rousing front-page article, "A Book That Must Be Suppressed," on August 19, 1928, more than three weeks after *The Well* had been published to generally favorable reviews. Jonathan Cape immediately devised an ingenious two-step strategy to circumvent the banning and burning he rightly thought inevitable: he replied to Douglas's article in a letter to the *Daily Express* and sent copies of the book to the Home Office and the public prosecutor, undertaking to discontinue publication if they objected to it.[39] His second step was to have papier-mâché molds of the type prepared and flown to John Holroyd-Reece of the Pegasus Press in Paris.[40]

Following Douglas's article and Cape's offer to withdraw the book, there was a flurry of formal and informal conversations in Westminster and at the clubs. The director of public prosecutions, Sir Archibald Bodkin, was away, so Joynson-Hicks took the legal advice of his deputy, Sir George Stephenson, and had a "long private conference with the Lord Chancellor. We came to the conclusion that the book is both obscene and indecent."[41] Joynson-Hicks then replied to Cape asking him to withdraw the book, which he ostensibly did. Meanwhile, Stephenson had "informally consulted" Sir Chartres Biron, chief magistrate of the Bow Street Court, who would pronounce the book an "obscene libel" three months later.[42] Arnold Bennett, who had reviewed *The Well* favorably in the *Evening Standard* on August 9th, found Biron talking to James Douglas at the Garrick Club on August 22. "I set violently on Jimmy at once about his attack on Radclyffe Hall's Sapphic novel," Bennett wrote in his journal. "Jimmy was very quiet and restrained, but Biron defended Jimmy with *real* heat; so I went on attacking. I told Jimmy to come in and have lunch with me. He did. He said there was an imp in me.[43]

These scenes of patriarchal bonding at the Garrick Club, first between Biron of the judiciary and Douglas of the press and then more convivially between Douglas the conservative and Bennett the liberal, recall the meeting between Admiral Ernest Troubridge and St. George Lane Fox-Pitt at the Travellers' Club in 1920; their conversation led Fox-Pitt to slander Radclyffe Hall by calling her "a grossly immoral woman" and to say that Troubridge had told him that Hall had "come between [Lady Troubridge] and her husband and wrecked the Admiral's home."[44] The fact that Hall, practitioner of unnatural vice and wrecker of good men's homes, had won her 1920 slander case may have rankled the club gossips, the legislature, and the judiciary to such an extent that eight years later "[t]he Home Secretary, the newspaper editor, the Chief Magistrate, the government of the day, closed ranks to silence [Hall] and to show that she was, after all, 'a grossly immoral woman.'"[45] Hall's slander suit against Fox-Pitt may well have been on the minds of Sir Ernest Wild and Frederick Macquisten, too, when they described husbands wronged by predatory lesbians in their attempt to induce the House of Commons to vote in favor of criminalizing lesbianism and thereby scuttle the 1921 Criminal Law Amendment Bill. It is hard for patriarchs to forgive and forget sexual humiliation from a woman.[46]

Arnold Bennett's championship of *The Well* must have been ineffective, for on October 4, 1928, James Douglas ran a story in the *Daily Express* about the copies of the Pegasus Press printing of *The Well* that were pouring into England; he demanded action from the home secretary. Joynson-Hicks responded immediately by issuing a warrant to Sir Francis Floud, chairman of the Board of Customs, instructing that all copies of *The Well of Loneliness* be seized.[47] But he was foiled. When a consignment addressed to the bookseller Leopold Hill was held, Harold Rubinstein, representing the Pegasus Press, challenged the Board of Customs to justify its action. The Board members read the book but did not find it warranted censorship; Floud, their chairman, evaded Joynson-Hicks by writing to the chancellor of the Exchequer asking for permission to release the parcels being held.[48] So Joynson-Hicks had to lay fresh extralegal plans. He was helped by Bodkin, who instructed the police to shadow the released books through the mails, and by Biron, who issued warrants directing the police to search Leopold Hill's bookstore and Jonathan Cape's office and seize the 250 books when they arrived.[49] These actions enabled Biron to issue summonses against both Hill and Cape; the book could now be tried.

It is likely that the embarrassing tolerance toward *The Well of Loneliness* evinced by Sir Francis Floud and the Board of Customs motivated Biron's refusal to hear the numerous witnesses for the defense who assembled at Bow Street Magistrates Court on November 9, 1928. Chief Inspector John Prothero testified for the Crown, describing his seizure of the books and opining that *The Well* was objectionable and obscene. He was the only witness permitted to speak. In effect, Sir Chartres Biron constituted himself as sole judge of whether the book was obscene and would deprave and corrupt those who read it. It is unsurprising that at the end of his hour-long judgment on November 16, he concluded that the book should be banned because it neither condemned nor rejected "unnatural vice."[50] According to Diana Souhami, he used the phrase "horrible practices" eight times in his speech and offered a distinctly creative interpretation of the sexual scenes in *The Well*. Souhami quotes from the court transcript, "[T]he actual physical acts of these women indulging in unnatural vices are described in the most alluring terms; their result is described as giving these women extraordinary rest, contentment, and pleasure; and not merely that, but it is actually put forward that it improves their mental balance and capacity."[51]

One asks oneself what Biron was reading. The final travesty occurred when Bodkin informed Rubinstein that "it would not be appropriate nor practicable" to release copies of the book for the magistrates who were to hear Hall's appeal.[52] There were twelve of them; they heard the attorney general's evidence for the prosecution and then deliberated for all of five minutes.

The story of this banning ends as it began, with a scene of patriarchal bonding over luncheon, this time between Rudyard Kipling and Hugh Walpole. Joynson-Hicks had summoned Kipling and other literary witnesses for the prosecution to voluntarily attend the hearing, but they were not called upon to testify. Charles Carrington's *Rudyard Kipling* includes Walpole's account of Kipling's motivation: "'I asked him at luncheon whether he approved of censorship (apropos of this tiresome, stupid *Well of Loneliness*). No, he doesn't approve of the book. Too much of the abnormal in all of us to play about with it. Hates opening up reserves. All the same he'd had friends once and again he'd done more for than for any woman. Luckily Ma Kipling doesn't hear of this.'"[53] The problem with *The Well of Loneliness* was that it brought a blush to the cheek of the patriarchy, who had all been engaging in unnatural vice ever since public school. So much for their talk about protecting the young.

The banning and burning of *The Well of Loneliness* was multiply determined. Leigh Gilmore has argued that it was threatening because it was a romance—a book likely to be read by the working-class young; Adam Parkes compares it to Woolf's *Orlando*, which was published, unscathed, the same year.[54] Of course, it mattered that the book was infinitely more accessible to readers than *Orlando*, or Djuna Barnes's *Nightwood* or her privately published *Ladies Almanack*. There were plenty of highly literate working-class readers by 1928; "high modernist" texts, however, remained largely inaccessible to the judicial class.

For several decades most British women writers were frightened of representing lesbianism: self-censorship became the rule.[55] Yet *The Well*'s notoriety kept it available to lesbians despite its "exile," as Hall called the banning. There is ample evidence that, notwithstanding the pervasive gloom of its account of Stephen's suffering, the book has been helpful to many women seeking to establish their identity, both in Britain and elsewhere. For many of the working-class butch/femme narrators in *Boots of Leather, Slippers of Gold*, a study of the lesbian community in Buffalo, New York, during the thirties, forties, and fifties, it was the only available representation of lesbians. Although the authors decry "its depressing image of bars as seedy places," those telling their stories who mention *The Well* generally do so uncritically.[56] Ruth Ellis, the lesbian subject of Yvonne Welbon's 1999 documentary *Living with Pride: Ruth at 100,* says in the film that for her, living in Springfield, Illinois, during the 1920s, "everything was hush-hush. Everything was sort of secret-like. I didn't know anything about lesbians. We called them women-lovers. But I read that book, *The Well of Loneliness*, and that put me wise to something."[57]

Hall may have been distressed and depressed by its banning, but her book attained its goal.

Answering Radclyffe Hall: Not So Quiet . . . Stepdaughters of War

The representation of lesbianism after the trial of *The Well of Loneliness* posed narratological as well as legal hazards. The difficulty of representing the invisible lesbian that Rose Allatini had struggled with in 1918 was replaced by the problem of either opposing or refashioning Hall's stereotype of the tragic invert. Two 1930s novels confront that problem: Evadne Price's *Not So Quiet . . . Stepdaughters of War* and Sylvia Townsend Warner's *Summer Will Show* both challenge Radclyffe Hall's representation of lesbianism, along with her reproduction of imperialist patriotism.

Not So Quiet . . . Stepdaughters of War is a first-person narrative written in 1930 by the popular journalist Evadne Price under the pseudonym Helen Zenna Smith. Price had not been to the front; her narrative of Nell Smith's experience driving an ambulance behind the lines is based on actual war diaries by ambulance driver Winifred Young. *Not So Quiet* was ostensibly written as a reply to Erich Maria Remarque's 1929 antiwar best-seller, *All Quiet on the Western Front*; nevertheless, its bleakly frightening representation of service in a women's ambulance unit rewrites the sentimental patriotism of Hall's account of Mrs. Breakspeare's company of inverts in *The Well of Loneliness*. Stephen Gordon's impossibly unflinching heroism is countered by Nell's cynicism and "cowardice," while both Nell's lesbophobia and her lesbian desire—her lesbian panic, in fact—are Price's response to the notoriety of *The Well*.[58]

Not So Quiet exposes the horror of war as experienced by Nell on her nightly journeys between the railway station and the hospitals with her load of mutilated, sometimes crazed, usually dying soldiers; the potholed, icy road is driven without lights, at top speed when the ambulance is empty and as fast as it can go without jolting its cargo to death when it is loaded. Sometimes the women drive under enemy bombardment. The narrative reflects the stages of the transformation of Nell's terror into numbness and despair.

In *The Well of Loneliness*, there is one paragraph describing the wounded men who are carried in Stephen Gordon's ambulance; the

ambulance drivers are unharmed apart from a broken wrist, an in-
flamed eye, a minor flesh wound in the arm, and of course Stephen's
shrapnel wound in the cheek, which will leave a distinguished scar.[59]
Stephen does not drive alone; beside her is Mary Llewellyn, whom
she keeps as her codriver for as long as she can in order to protect
her from the other women's dangerous driving. As she drives, Stephen
is more conscious of the young woman beside her than of the men
in the back. In *Not So Quiet*, each young woman is solely responsible
for her ambulance and its load. Price emphasizes the difference between this exhausting and frightening reality and the lies that new
volunteers are told before they come out to the front: they are promised that they'll ride with another driver "for a month on probation"
when in fact they are on their own from the first night they arrive.[60]
Any wounded man who is still able to sit rides in the passenger seat.

Nell suffers terribly from fear and shame; she constantly accuses
herself of cowardice. One night her "sitter" sleeps beside her while
she hears screams, shouts, and blows from the wounded men behind
her. The strapped-down madman is screaming; soon the shell-shock
case joins in; a voice threatens to hit one of them with a stick. There's
a crash; it seems as if everyone is screaming. Nell is too frightened of
the dying man, the madman, the man with the face like raw liver to
stop and open up the back to intervene; she continues to drive, reit-
erating "I will not go and see. I will not go and see." Finally the
screaming is replaced by the dreadful moaning of the dying man; and
finally they arrive at Hospital Number Eight, which Nell had thought
they had missed in the dark.[61]

Not So Quiet consists of one long, surreal dramatic monologue.
At one point, Nell drives a dead man from a hospital mortuary to
the cemetery, a field where the dead lie in deep mud under the
clawlike branches of a bare tree that is called the Witch's Hand. The
flag is removed from the coffin for immediate recycling; the coffin is
lowered; the exhausted padre drones on; finally, two young buglers
in khaki sound "The Last Post." Nell's metaphor provides a specific
allusion to a surrealist model: "Once more the curtain rings down
on the drama that can already boast one of the longest runs on record.
When will the final performances be announced?"[62] Again we hear
an echo of the voice of Vernon Lee: Evadne Price is yet another war
writer familiar with the bitter irony of *Satan the Waster*.

Nell's mother's frantic pressure on the young to enlist is

symbolized by the sinister blessing of the Witch's Hand over their dead bodies. Evadne Price highlights the vicarious aggression of the women on the home front who shamed young men and women like Nell and Roy Evans-Mawnington into volunteering to die. The characterization of Mrs. Smith contributes to the postwar demonization of women of her generation, including many former suffragettes who propagandized for the war effort at home.[63]

Not So Quiet excoriates the callous, hypocritical jingoism with which Nell's mother and her neighbors in upper-middle-class Wimbledon compete as to who can sacrifice more children more heroically to the war. Her mother has "sacrificed" Nell and her sister already; she is about to send their brother to the front. Some of her activities are simply macabre: she has called their cat's three kittens Mons, Wipers, and Liège. Others are more practically harmful: like Radclyffe Hall and Mabel Batten in Malvern in 1914, Mrs. Smith is active in recruitment meetings. While Nell waits in misery at the station for the stretcher bearers to load up her ambulance, she fantasizes that she is showing her mother and Mrs. Evans-Mawnington, her mother's rival in "sacrifice," the spectacle of the wounded and dying men. She points out for their benefit a dying man spewing blood; a raving madman strapped down on his stretcher; a twitching, staring shell-shock case; a young boy like her brother Bertie who is coughing up his gas-shredded lungs; a man with a bellyful of shrapnel; a man whose face is pulp. Finally, she tries to prevent her guests from leaving: "Wait, wait, I have so much, so much to show you before you return to your committees and your recruiting meetings, before you add to your bag of recruits . . . those young recruits you enroll so proudly with your patriotic speeches, your red, white and blue rosettes, your white feathers, your insults, your lies. . . . "[64]

Nell's mother shows the usual patriotic enthusiasm for war babies. One of her letters recounts how "the new maid Jessie has just gone to a home to have a 'war baby' at the expense of the War Baby League"; Nell recalls "poor little Tanny, who was turned out to fend for herself three years ago."[65] The wartime obsession with birth to replace the dead conveys the disregard of individual life that is the reality of this war: behind the lines as at the front, the war is a nightmare of irrational violence from which the individual will almost certainly not awaken.[66]

The ambulance unit in *The Well of Loneliness* is led by Mrs.

Breakspeare, a war widow and mother who "look(s) like a very maternal general"; she has recruited the drivers in London and intervenes tactfully when the others complain that Mary always gets to ride with Stephen.[67] The equivalent role in *Not So Quiet* is played by the sadistic commandant who insists on the observance of an unnecessarily grueling routine and delights in handing out exhausting punishment duties to any driver who shows the slightest sign of individuality. Stephen Gordon's role as informal leader of the drivers is taken by Georgina Toshington ("Tosh"), who is the niece of an earl, almost as aristocratic as Radclyffe Hall's friend, the ambulance unit leader Toupie Lowther; Lowther, who was bulky and tall and lesbian and whose father was the sixth Earl of Lonsdale, was clearly a model of sorts for both Tosh and Stephen Gordon. Tosh is a carnavalesque figure who encompasses the power of both genders and is idolized by all the young women:

> There is something bravely comforting about the Amazonian height and breadth of Tosh. She has the hips of a matron—intensified by the four pairs of thick combinations she always wears for warmth, a mind like a sewer (her own definition), the courage of a giant, the vocabulary of a Smithfield butcher, and the round, wind-reddened face of a dairymaid. . . . I have adored her since the first night I arrived. . . . [68]

Tosh is a Bakhtinian life force in contrast with the commandant (or "Mrs. Bitch," as the drivers call her): she sends them to pick up the dying and to meet their deaths, and her gratuitous cruelty drives to madness and suicide Nell's friend and ally, The Bug. The heroic, bigendered figure of Tosh is suited to the surreal world behind the lines and taps into the unconscious of her companions; of course they all idolize her, and of course Nell ceases to care about anything and begins the process of becoming an automaton after Tosh dies in her arms at the side of the road, killed by a splinter of shrapnel.[69]

Tosh encompasses both the maternal energy embodied in Mrs. Breakspeare and the masculine courage and rationality of Stephen; prior to the explosion she appears indestructible, with life enough in her to best another figure of death besides the commandant. Returning to their bedroom later than the others one night, Nell hears whispers and stifled giggles from a cubicle across the hall and notices that Skinny, a driver in her group, is not in her bed. Eventually we learn that Skinny was in bed with her lover, Frost, and giggling, presumably, with pleasure, but Price prepares us for this revelation with some details about Skinny's appearance and bodily functions:

> [W]hen [Skinny] first awakens she reminds one uneasily of a corpse. Her face is yellow with the skin stretched tightly across the high cheekbones and there are queer bags under her eyes. Tosh says the bags mean kidney trouble. Certainly Skinny is out of her flea-bag every quarter of an hour. . . . When Skinny is asleep her rather large mouth pinches up tightly and greyly, and she is irresistibly like a photograph a gardener of ours showed me once of his mother, taken in the coffin after death.[70]

Skinny has the face of a skull, and a lower-class skull at that. Nell's violent recoil from Skinny is the product of lesbian panic, a symptom of her own desire for the motherly, protective, gigantic, bloody-minded, strangely pastoral Tosh.

Not So Quiet has been dismissed as sensational and clichéd, but such a judgment undervalues the power of the monologue's insistence on terror, shame, and waste. It misjudges too, the surreal representation of the detritus and filth of war: the dirt, rotting food, trench foot and gangrene, and the vomit, urine, excrement, and blood that the women clean out of their ambulances. Above all, it misses the complexity of this novel's reply to *The Well of Loneliness*.

Tosh leads her roommates in lesbophobic ostracism of Skinny, who complains that Tosh has called her a "something" and tried to get the commandant to move her out of their room. Tosh refuses to respond, Skinny attacks her physically, and word of this ruckus gets out to the commandant, who grills each driver in turn. When Nell suggests to Tosh that they shouldn't "cover" for Skinny—"there are some tales that ought to be carried"—Tosh maintains that she was wrong to let Skinny know that she knew: "'Personal dislike's a *queer* thing,'" she says. "'Her morals don't affect me one way or the other.'"[71] Then one of the drivers innocently tells the commandant that Tosh taunted Skinny for "not being able to attract men." Skinny and Frost are packed off for home, and the commandant has a private word with Tosh, whom she assumes to be the only young woman sophisticated enough to recognize lesbianism: "'You've got a faulty memory, Toshington. . . . I hope it continues faulty when this particular episode is discussed in the convoy.'" Nell and The Bug exchange a long look: "Silently we are asking how much or how little Commandant guesses."[72]

Officially, therefore, lesbianism in this novel is merely an unspeakable "something": Skinny and Frost are out of sight and should be out of mind. But there is a disquieting ambiguity among those who remain. Tosh has persecuted Skinny but does not condemn lesbianism. The commandant continues to visit her friend the matron in Hospital Number One. There has been an alliance between Mrs. Bitch and Tosh, the death force and life force of the unit. When Nell drives home on the night of the bombardment she thinks the ambulance in front of her is the commandant's and prays for a bomb to hit that ambulance instead of her own. But the ambulance is Tosh's, and the bomb takes her life. When sexual identity is ambiguous, other identities crumble. Nell is afraid of going mad.

Not So Quiet is uncompromising in its rejection of Radclyffe Hall's sentimental patriotism: Nell's interior monologue is a memorable rewriting of Stephen and Mary's war. But the representation of lesbianism is disquietingly lesbophobic, in spite of its interesting ambivalence: Skinny's death's-head conveys an unmistakable bigotry. But how is the reader to categorize the irresistibly comforting, aristocratically vulgar, lesbophobic and lesbian, maternal and monstrous, masculine and feminine life force and death force that is Tosh?

Evadne Price was too lesbophobic or too unconscious of her ambivalence to successfully redefine Hall's stereotype of the invert; that task was left for an unashamed lesbian Marxist, Sylvia Townsend Warner. In *Summer Will Show*, the arrogant, apparently heartless, upper-class Sophia Willoughby learns her revolutionary lesbian politics in Paris from February to June 21, 1848. Her teachers are her lover, the Jewish storyteller Minna Lemuel; Ingelbrecht (or Engels), for whom she delivers packages of *The Communist Manifesto*, and the communist Martin, who runs an underground factory making bullets out of scrap metal. All three die during the five days' class war in which, according to Raymond Postgate, "the problem of unemployment [was] solved by the massacre of the unemployed."[73]

Rewriting Lesbian Stereotypes in Summer Will Show

Evadne Price revises Hall's representation of women ambulance drivers in the First World War, but Warner, six years later, completes a more complex task: unwriting Hall's lesbian politics. *Summer Will Show* was Warner's first novel after she started living with Valentine Ackland; she began writing it following their visit to Paris in 1932 and finished it in December 1935; by that time they had been members of the Communist party for almost a year, and antifascists for two. Warner was quick to educate herself in lesbian literature, history, and sexology; these topics appear frequently in their letters from the early years of her relationship with Ackland. Ackland sends Warner a copy of Charlotte Charke's autobiography; Warner's difficult mother surprises her with the gift of a pomade pot with a picture of the Ladies of Llangollen on its lid; they read the sexologists Ellis, Bloch, and Krafft-Ebing; they have an ironic discussion of bisexuality.[74] It is unsurprising, then, that *Summer Will Show* reflects Warner's critique of literary representations of lesbianism as well as of revolutionary politics.

Intertextuality is basic to Warner's narrative strategy throughout her writing life; she uses allusion both to ground her apparently implausible narratives within literary history and to question and parody the politics, "history," and narratology of her predecessors. It is appropriate that in this novel, where the lesbian romance in Paris is precisely coterminous with the 1848 revolution, many of the allusions are to nineteenth-century French literary history. Warner's "unwriting" of Gustave Flaubert's *L'Éducation sentimentale* has received a great deal of attention since it was first noted by Terry Castle in her 1990 theorization of the lesbian triangular plot; later writers, in contrast, have emphasized the allusion's Marxist significance.[75] Quite another fictional genealogy seems more to the point, however, when we consider Warner's characterization of Minna Lemuel, the revolutionary Jewish storyteller: the representation, usually by women writers, of the powerful, sexually active, sometimes evil and sometimes doomed *femme artiste* in Madame de Staël's *Corinne*, Charlotte Brontë's *Villette*, George Sand's *Consuelo*, and Colette's *La Seconde*.[76] It is now abundantly clear that the intertextuality of *Summer Will Show* demonstrates that the novel is narratologically, politically, and sexually revolutionary.

Yet the roots of Sophia Willoughby's rebellion against both heterosexuality and the class system lie in the first part of *Summer Will Show*, set in England. Here, Warner's primary allusions are to British writers, for she is concerned with the whole question of English versus French nationalities; her own politics were internationalist. In her exhilarating, multiply allusive use of the fox as symbol of freedom, Warner both grounds her novel in the only obviously lesbian literary tradition available to her and rewrites some specifically British literary stereotypes of lesbianism.

Sophia Willoughby's social and sexual liberation starts in Dorset in the fall of 1847 with her sudden decision to go hunting. The fox in *Summer Will Show* sneaks away from the hounds, just as Sophia will free herself of the deadly constrictions of her life as an upper-class Victorian woman. Warner clearly wrote her hunting scene as a specific satirical response to a very different fox and hunt in *The Well of Loneliness*.

The hunting field is the chief setting for Stephen Gordon's male bonding with both Sir Philip, her father, and Raftery, her horse. After her father's death, however, Stephen can hunt no more; she finds herself identifying with the fox, "a crawling bedraggled streak of red fur . . . with the desperate eyes of the hopelessly pursued"; such is her sense of her own identity as an invert in county England.[77] She has not yet fallen in love with Angela Crossby or found in her father's study the volume of Krafft-Ebing with its marked passages about congenital inversion, but she already knows that she is an outcast. Later, she recalls this fox as the symbol of abjection in her encounter with a gay would-be brother in Alec's bar in Paris—one of the last stations on her journey toward celibate martyrdom. I am still shocked by the violence with which she disclaims sisterhood with this gay man:

> He bent forward, this youth, until his face was almost on a level with Stephen's—a grey, drug-marred face with a mouth that trembled incessantly.
>
> "Ma sœur," he whispered.
>
> For a moment she wanted to strike that face with her naked fist, to obliterate it.[78]

What saves Stephen from her gay-bashing impulse is a memory of the doomed fox "looking for God who made it"; violence is replaced by self-pity. She never stops longing for insider status.

It is instructive to compare this foxhunt with Sylvia Townsend Warner's. In 1847, Sophia Willoughby—conventional, rich, respectable, authoritarian—lives on her family estate, Blandamer, in Dorset, compulsively meticulous in looking after her inherited property and her two children. By the end of the year, however, her children have died of smallpox, which was contracted on a visit to the sinister lime-kiln man; the kiln's fumes, Sophia had hoped, would cure the children's coughs. After their death, she feels increasingly trapped in her role of lady of the manor and finds herself thinking obsessively about her husband's mistress in Paris, Minna Lemuel; Sophia has yet to meet Minna, but she has her conveniently pigeonholed as "a by-word, half actress, half strumpet; a Jewess; a nonsensical creature."[79] She decides to distract herself by going hunting.

The fox in *The Well of Loneliness* will inevitably be killed; hence the tragedy of identifying with "it"—Hall's distancing pronoun; the noble Raftery is always "he." But the fox in *Summer Will Show* is a survivor. Sophia also leaves the hunt, not because her neighbors disapprove of her—though of course they do—but because she has "discovered in herself a growing impression that she was out on false pretences, having in reality an assignation with the fox."[80] Unlike Stephen Gordon, Sophia is delighted to become a sexual and social outlaw; this fox is the precursor of liberty and joy. And Sophia will become a woman-identified lesbian; she may be a butch, like Valentine Ackland, to whom this novel is dedicated, but there's no room for Krafft-Ebing and congenital inversion in *Summer Will Show*.

These parallel yet contrasting foxhunting scenes indicate how consciously Sylvia Townsend Warner situated her novel in the most obvious lesbian literary tradition available to her and how, in claiming that tradition, she satirized Radclyffe Hall's attempt to make female inversion palatable to the patriarchy. She uses the fox as a symbol of freedom several times in the first part of her novel to emphasize the fact that Sophia is trapped in sexual repression because she is trapped in class privilege. Sophia first realizes this when she makes a solitary visit to Cornwall and discovers that she doesn't want to go home. She "snuffed" the fresh, earth-scented air, which, "so pure and earthy, absolved one back into animal, washed off all recollection of responsibilities; one waft of wind there would blow away the cares from one's mind, the petticoats from one's legs, demolish all the muffle of imposed personality loaded upon one by other people, leaving one free, swift, unburdened as a fox."[81]

Even before she leaves England and meets the anarchists and communists of the 1848 commune, Sophia signals her enlistment in the class struggle in her response to the richly deserved rebuff she receives from the lime-kiln man. She calls him "my man" when she visits him one night, with a sense of entitlement amounting to *droit de seigneur*, in the hope of conceiving a child to replace Augusta and

Damian. He gives her a lesson in economics as well as in class en-
mity in what may be the most powerful scene of the novel.[82]

> "Children do die hereabouts," he said. "There's the smallpox, and
> the typhus, and the cholera. There's the low fever, and the quick
> consumption. And there's starvation. Plenty of things for children
> to die of."
> "You speak with little pity, my man."
> "I'm like the gentry, then. Like the parsons, and the justices,
> and the lords and ladies. Like that proud besom down to Blanda-
> mer." He spoke with such savage intent that she leaped to her feet.
> But he had not moved.
> "Plenty more children, they say, where the dead ones came
> from. If they die like cattle, the poor, they breed like cattle too. Plenty
> more children. That's what I say to you. Rich and poor can breed
> alike, I suppose."
> "Eh?" he shouted, lumbering to his feet and thrusting his face
> into hers.[83]

Sophia flees in the dark; as she runs, she hears a woman's laugh. Yet
once the shock is over, she feels revived, stimulated, "as though a
well-administered slap in the face had roused her from a fainting-
fit."[84] She is even amused by the woman who has mocked her: "'His
vixen with him!' she exclaimed, and heard her chuckle sound out
over the silent field, coarse and free-hearted, a sound as kindred to
the country night as an owl's to-whoo or the barking of a fox."[85] For
a moment she has become the hardy, sneaking, thieving fox in the
night, liberated from the compulsory modesty that estranged upper-
and middle-class Victorian women from their bodies and their desire.

Warner must also have been aware of other literary predecessors
besides Radclyffe Hall as she wove these fox images into *Summer Will
Show*. She had certainly read David Garnett's whimsically misogynist
fantasy, *Lady into Fox* (1923), which focuses on the sad predicament
of a man whose wife suddenly changes into a fox and is finally destroyed in his arms by the hounds; she was probably familiar, too,
with tamed, vulnerable Foxy—Garnett's source for his lady/fox's death
scene—in Mary Webb's *Gone to Earth* (1917). Warner makes no explicit allusion to these well-known novels; they have little or no lesbian significance. She challenges, instead, the blatant lesbophobia of
D. H. Lawrence's short story "The Fox" (1922).

Lawrence is often mentioned in Warner's diaries and letters; both she and Ackland respected him as a writer, deplored attempts to censor and expurgate his work, and disliked his hostility to sexually active women. One reference to him in Warner's *Diaries*, from January 12, 1931, makes his relevance to their sexual lives abundantly clear:

> It was our most completed night, and after our love I slept unstirring in her arms, still covered with her love, till we woke and ate whatever meal it is lovers eat at five in the morning. She said, remembering *Lady C[hatterley's Lover]*, that Lawrence in heaven would be taken down a peg to see us, specimens of what he so violently disliked, loving according to all his precepts, and perhaps the only lovers that night really to observe them.[86]

Lawrence's themes of class and sexuality were definitely worthy of sly, parodic notice.

In "The Fox," working-class Henry Grenfel returns from the war to find two women living on the farm that used to belong to his grandfather. Although their physical relationship remains undefined, the women appear to be lesbians. Jill Banford cooks and keeps the house while Ellen March, with her "distant, manly way," does most of the work around the farm.[87] March also can have a dreamy, abstracted, distinctly unmasculine way with her, however: she can manage neither to protect the hens from the fox nor to fell the tree with which Henry eventually kills Banford; she's simply not manly enough. This is a gender disability wickedly satirized by Warner, for Sophia recalls with nostalgic pride the day in her childhood when she persuaded the estate woodman to let her fell a tree—before puberty ruled out such freedom: "The noise of the axe chiming through the silent plantation was in her ears, and the cry and harsh rustle of the falling tree."[88] And Sophia's relationship with Minna, of course, will make clear the irrelevance of Lawrence's hints that lesbians' sex lives are as limply amateurish as their farming.

For some time before Henry appears, March has been on the watch for the actual, animal fox that is stealing the women's hens. Then, standing there with her gun, March "lowered her eyes and suddenly saw the fox. He was looking up at her. His chin was pressed down, and his eyes were looking up. They met her eyes. And he knew her. She was spell-bound—she knew he knew her. So he looked into her eyes, and her soul failed her. He knew her, he was not daunted."[89] As soon as Henry turns up, March recognizes him:"But to March he was the fox. Whether it was the thrusting forward of his head, or the glisten of the fine whitish hairs on the ruddy cheek bones, or the bright, keen eyes, that can never be said: but the boy was to her the fox, and she could not see him otherwise."[90] And from there the story proceeds predictably and hypnotically, alternating matter-of-fact, increasingly charged dialogue with the repetitive, incantatory passages that signify, in Lawrence, intensifying desire. Inevitably and conveniently, Banford dies, crushed under the tree Henry fells; March marries Henry, and the couple prepare to emigrate to Canada. But he wants more, of course: she must give up her sense of responsibility and become dependent and sexually passive. "He would not have the love which exerted itself towards him. It made his brow go black. No, he wouldn't let her exert her love towards him. No, she had to be passive, to acquiesce, and to be submerged under the surface of love. She had to be like the seaweed she saw as she peered down from the boat."[91]

Seaweed moves only with the movement of the ocean—a fine symbol of sexual dependency. This Lawrencian misogyny as well as Radclyffe Hall's is what Warner attacks in her depiction of Sophia Willoughby's discovery of her active sexual and political desire in *Summer Will Show*. On the evening of their first meeting, Minna stands on the balcony, looking at the revolutionary barricade constructed in the street below, while Sophia watches her silently and waits: "Never in her life had she felt such curiosity or dreamed it possible. . . . Her curiosity went beyond speculation, a thing not of the brain but in the blood. It burned in her like a furnace."[92] This is the last glimmer of the lime-kiln fire, for now Sophia will attain the vixen's freedom; for the first time in her life she can experience sexual desire because "[h]ers [is] the liberty of a fallen woman now."[93]

For the most part, however, Sophia and Minna's lesbian love is depicted with an irony that is foreign to the solemnity and violence of the British blood-and-soil narratives of Mary Webb, Radclyffe Hall, and D. H. Lawrence. The violent ending of *Summer Will Show*—the deaths of Minna and Caspar and the painfully historical mass executions of the working class—is profoundly serious in meaning, but the second half of the novel is also full of wicked jokes. When Frederick Willoughby asserts his male prerogative by depriving his wife of her money, and Minna and her anarchist friends become increasingly impoverished, Sophia and Minna talk about becoming laundresses: "In England that is what we prescribe for fallen women."[94] And

Sophia takes to singing for a few francs in the streets of Paris. She sings English hymns in order to provide a living exemplum to accompany the anticlerical sermons of the anarchist sculptor, Raoul; they split the collection from the crowd, of course. Dury explains Raoul's scheme as follows: "It is his idea that you should accompany him as an escaped nun, thrust into a convent against her will, suffering untold atrocities—you know the sort of thing."[95] Indeed we do know the sort of thing he means. Sophia is to impersonate Sainte-Suzanne Simonin, the impossibly innocent narrator of Denis Diderot's prurient novel *La Religieuse*; her convent experiences culminate with the episode of the lesbian Mother Superior who has seduced a veritable harem of young nuns but finally becomes crazed with lust and guilt. The allusion is absurd, mocking the fears as well as the fantasies of the patriarchy, but it makes a fine, witty culmination to the lesbian revisions of this novel.

With these allusions to Hall, Lawrence, and Diderot, Warner reminds the reader of three very different misogynist representations of lesbianism: the doomed invert, the ineffectually mannish woman in need of a strong man's love, and the voracious corrupter of youth crazed by perverse desires. Each stereotype is neatly deconstructed by Warner's passionate irony. Yet Sophia and Minna's mutual attraction is rarely as straightforwardly expressed. Minna's habitual self-dramatization obscures deep feelings as much as Sophia's reserve, and Warner conveys the daily physical happiness of their love obliquely. Walking joyfully home, for example, Sophia observes "the houri-like curves of the feather bed" swelling from one of Minna's windows.[96] Later, sleepless and insistently planning their lives, Sophia wakes Minna up for a talk; it takes a little time to rouse her, but finally "[i]n the darkness there was a majestic and cat-like stir: Minna rousing, reassembling her pillows, propping herself to sit up and attend. The body that by day was heavy, ill-framed and faintly grotesque, at night assumed an extraordinary harmoniousness with its bed, became in suavity and sober resilience the sister of that exemplary mattress."[97] And once she's sat up Minna decides, of course, that she must have a biscuit.

Their discussion leads to a quarrel, and Sophia leaps from the bed. Later, she observes her beloved:

> Over the writing-table hung a mirror, and there she saw reflected . . . Minna candle-lit in bed. Her hand had just conveyed another biscuit

to her mouth. Her eyes were full of tears and she was munching slowly. Seeing that face, melancholy and gluttonous, Sophia forgot the anger of one who is in the wrong. Her whole being was ravaged with love and tenderness. Still holding the pen she sat and stared in the mirror, beholding as though for a first and a last time the creature who, but a few paces away, hung in the mirror as though in the innocence of a different world.[98]

I know of no more loving representation of a woman observed in bed than this crystallization of a moment of seeing when the beloved appears most separate, mysterious, and complete.

Warner's redefinition of lesbianism in *Summer Will Show* banishes the stereotypes of lesbian abjection because Sophia could, and most thoroughly did, choose to be an outlaw, a fox. As Warner wrote in her joyful diary entry for October 12, 1930, the day after her first night as a lesbian, "It is so natural to be hunted, and intuitive. Feeling safe and respectable is much more of a strain."[99] Throughout the narrative, however, we are constantly aware that love is circumscribed by the hardships and betrayals of the class war. Sophia learns a new politics from Minna, Ingelbrecht, and Martin; she survives to read *The Communist Manifesto*; but her two "primitive" Others, Minna and Caspar, are dead. She has been unable to learn anything from her relationship with Caspar, the young mulatto West Indian cousin whom she has neglected and killed.[100] She cannot escape responsibility for her class position within the structures of British imperialism simply because she falls in love and learns her communism in Paris.

Summer Will Show provides an overt representation of lesbianism, yet some readers have managed to overlook the sexual nature of the romance between Sophia and Minna. Claire Harman maintained as recently as 1987 that "lesbianism was not Sylvia Townsend Warner's theme in this book, although at points it seems implicit."[101] Anticommunism and lesbophobia can be quite distracting. There is no evidence that Warner was ever afraid of either. Nor is there evidence that she adopted any of the plot devices, such as vampirism, murder, suicide, or otherwise untimely death, that can indicate lesbian panic. The deaths in her novels always seem justifiable.[102] And unlike other lesbian novelists who published between 1928 and 1959, Warner was not induced by the banning of *The Well of Loneliness* to undertake conscious self-censorship.[103]

Censorship and Self-Censorship

The list of modernist novels banned under the 1857 Obscene Publications Act because of their representation of female sexuality is quite impressive, including D. H. Lawrence's *The Rainbow* and Norah James's *Sleeveless Errand* as well as *The Well of Loneliness*. Lawrence was unable to find a publisher for *Lady Chatterley's Lover* in England: he had it printed in Italy and then in Paris; pirated editions immediately sprang up in Europe and the United States; after his death, an "authorized" expurgated English version was published in 1932. Not until 1960, a year after a newer Obscene Publications Act introduced literary merit as an adequate defense against censorship, did Penguin Books defend its publication of *Lady Chatterley's Lover* and win its celebrated victory.[104]

We cannot know how many women were prevented from publishing or writing by legal and cultural lesbophobia, but the example of Rosemary Manning is well worth considering. Manning was born in 1911 and came out openly as a lesbian in London in the 1980s. She started her autobiographical novel, *The Chinese Garden*, in 1951 but abandoned it almost immediately. She rethought it a year later, erasing the autobiographical element; rewrote it again by 1955; and continued to revise it until 1961. Jonathan Cape published it in 1962—three years after the new Obscene Publications Act. The book is a remarkable representation of internalized lesbophobia and a specific response to *The Well of Loneliness*.

The Chinese Garden depicts Rosemary Manning's suppression of lesbian desire in 1928 at Bampfield, an English boarding school for girls. Its main theme is lesbian silence: the silence of suppression on the part of the teenage protagonist and of betrayal on the part of cross-dressing teachers who hypocritically expel students who have been found naked together in bed (and in possession of that "filthy" book, *The Well of Loneliness*). The teachers who founded the school served in an ambulance unit in the war; at Bampfield, discipline is spartan, living conditions are crude, and the landscape resembles that of the Somme. The novel's form is a double narrative; parts of the adolescent's story are told in the third person, though always from her limited point of view, while others are remembered and reflected upon by the now adult narrator. The tone of *The Chinese Garden* is both lyrical and melancholy; it is a memorable novel.

Manning's most notable other book is also a fictionalized autobiography with a lesbian theme; it reads like a meditation. *A Time and a Time* describes her 1962 suicide attempt after the end of a lesbian relationship, and her gradual recovery from despair. Its publication history is also of interest: although Manning wrote the book in the early sixties, she was prevented by her position as headmistress of a girls' school from publishing it under her own name until 1986; it came out under a pseudonym, Sarah Davys, in 1971.[105]

Publishers, of course, were wary of censorship, too. Warner wrote with irritation in her diary about a 1954 telephone call from her editor, Ian Parsons; he wanted her to cut both of the overt representations of homosexuality in *The Flint Anchor*. She countered with a wily combination of outright refusal and subterfuge; both passages appear in the published book.[106] Omitting Crusoe's declaration of love would have cut the heart out of her novel.

The Flint Anchor is a study of the Victorian hypocrisy that dominates the Barnard family, extinguishing both love and rage and producing instead drunkenness, fear, depression, heartlessness, and despair. The satire is sometimes hilarious but unremittingly dark. The love, joy, and generosity that are driven from the Barnard household are embodied and expressed by Crusoe, the bisexual fisherman, who declares his love for the emotionally anemic Thomas Kettle:

> Crusoe's hand fell on his shoulder. Even through the cloth of his coat he could feel that it was hot and hard as a blacksmith's tongs.
>   "You've got to hear me out, Mr. Thomas. For there's something I've been meaning to say." He paused and stood for a minute, looking out to sea, as if his words must be dredged from the waves.
>   "Do you see that there moon? There won't be a night of my life when I see that there old moon but I'll think of you. . . . Soon as I clapped eyes on you I took a liking to you, no more than a boy then. Now that I'm man grown, I love you. And I could go with plenty, and I go with some. But never as I'd go with you. . . . You don't love me. But I love you so strong, I was fair busting to tell it. . . . And now I have."[107]

Once again Warner uses crosswriting to castigate timidity and repression; she may be providing a corrective to the anxious pederasty of her Mr. Fortune, her "poor Timothy," too.

This book starts and ends with Sylvia Townsend Warner, who cannot, of course, have entirely avoided self-censorship, but who apparently contrived to elude both internal and external censors with remarkable self-knowledge and skill. The sexual politics in her writing reflect both her rejection of British mainstream culture and her deep involvement with British individuals, the countryside, and history. In her intellectual grasp and intensity, her rejection of national politics, and her manner of living an apparently irreproachable middle-class, ladylike life, I see her as the successor of the lesbian pacifist Vernon Lee and the companion-in-arms of her friend Nancy Cunard, the heterosexual activist and exile. All three castigated without fear the dominant culture to which they appeared to belong; all were sexual outlaws, disconcerting in their ability to live full lives and think for themselves without the tutelage of men. Perhaps it is not surprising, then, that the achievements of all three women writers are still underappreciated today.

Notes

For names cited repeatedly in the notes, the following abbreviations have been used:

RA   Rose Allatini
RH   Radclyffe Hall
STW   Sylvia Townsend Warner
VW   Virginia Woolf

INTRODUCTION

1. See Julie Abraham, *Are Girls Necessary?*, 61–78, on historical crosswriting in the novels of Mary Renault.
2. Radclyffe Hall figures fairly prominently in *Women of the Left Bank*, but she never regarded herself as a sapphist and in fact spent only about six weeks in Paris during her life. The idea that Una Troubridge and Hall were constant visitors there perhaps derives from Djuna Barnes's wicked satire of them as Lady Buck-and-Balk and Tilly-Tweed-In-Blood in *Ladies Almanack*, 18–20. Virginia Woolf writes about Sappho and sapphists, of course, but her modernism and her life were firmly based in England.
3. My anachronistic use of the word *queer* is intended to reflect the sexual ambiguity and/or inclusiveness of many of these writers and of their representations of sexuality. During these writers' lives, *queer* was used to indicate homosexuality only by homophobes or by queers themselves, for whom it became reverse discourse as part of the language of camp.
4. I am indebted to Jane Marcus for my "canon" of sexual radicalism.
5. Warner is also a remarkable writer of letters and diaries, but only selections of these have as yet been published.
6. There are two biographies of Warner. Wendy Mulford's *This Narrow Place: Sylvia Townsend Warner and Valentine Ackland* combines astute readings of Warner's published works with insight into her life with Ackland and their Marxist activism. Claire Harman wrote the official biography; *Sylvia Townsend Warner: A Biography* is more comprehensive than Mulford's book, reflecting Harman's access to Warner's diaries and other papers in the Dorset County Museum.

   Among British critics on Warner, see Maroula Joannou, "Sylvia Townsend Warner in the 1930s"; John Lucas, *The Radical Twenties*; Janet Montefiore, *Men and Women Writers of the 1930s*; Arnold Rattenbury, "Literature, Lying and Sober Truth" and "Plain Heart, Light

Tether"; and Gillian Spraggs, "Exiled to Home: The Poetry of Sylvia Townsend Warner and Valentine Ackland." Spraggs focuses on Warner and Ackland's jointly published 1934 book of poems *Whether a Dove or a Seagull*; Warner's poems in *Whether a Dove*, as well as some of her political poems published in periodicals, are omitted from Harman's edition of the *Collected Poems*.

Jane Marcus has done the most to publicize Warner's work in the United States, often focusing on her less-known stories and poems: she has written about Warner in *Art and Anger: Reading Like a Woman*; "A Wilderness of One's Own: Feminist Fantasy Novels of the 1920s"; "Alibis and Legends: The Ethics of Elsewhereness, Gender, and Estrangement"; "Sylvia Townsend Warner," and "Bluebeard's Daughters: Pretexts for Pre-Texts." Otherwise, see Barbara Brothers, "Flying the Nets at Forty: *Lolly Willowes* as Female Bildungsroman" and "Writing Against the Grain: Sylvia Townsend Warner and the Spanish Civil War"; Robert L. Caserio, *The Novel in England, 1900–1950* and "Celibate Sisters-in-Revolution"; Jane Garrity, "Encoding Bi-Location," and Robin Hackett, "Sapphic Primitivism in Modern Fiction."

For writing that focuses exclusively on *Summer Will Show*, see chapter 5, notes 75 and 76.

7. See Michel Foucault, *The History of Sexuality*, 53–54.
8. For a useful discussion of the development among legal theorists, philosophers, anthropologists, and ethnographers of the idea of "primitive" society, see Adam Kuper, *The Invention of Primitive Society*. For primitivism in the work and thought of modernist writers, artists, and psychoanalysts, see Marianna Torgovnick, *Gone Primitive*. David Theo Goldberg gives an impassioned critique of Torgovnick and the idea of "primitive" peoples existing outside of time in his *Racist Culture*. In *Banishing the Beast*, Lucy Bland provides an extremely helpful exposition of the effects on white middle-class and working-class Englishwomen of degeneration theory, primitivism, and eugenics. See also Elazar Barkan and Ronald Bush, eds., *Prehistories of the Future* for a particularly useful collection of essays on explorations, exploitations, and appropriations of "primitive" cultures by missionaries, ethnographers, artists, and writers.
9. See RH, *The Well of Loneliness*, 150, 52, 363.
10. See Eve Kofosky Sedgwick, *Between Men* and *Epistemology of the Closet*; an adaptation of Sedgwick's theory of homosexual panic to lesbians is offered by Patricia Juliana Smith in *Lesbian Panic*. For readings of *The Well of Loneliness* through Ellis or Freud, see Esther Newton, "The Mythic Mannish Lesbian," Elizabeth Abel, *Virginia Woolf and the Fictions of Psychoanalysis*, Teresa de Lauretis, *The Practice of Love*, Jay Prosser, *Second Skins*, and Judith Halberstam, *Female Masculinity*; I have also found useful Lucy Bland and Laura Doan, eds., *Sexology in Culture*, 1998. See also, on both Hall and Warner, Terry Castle, *The Apparitional Lesbian*, and Thomas Foster, "'Dream Made Flesh.'"
11. For a discussion of the source of Evadne Price's ambiguous representation of lesbianism, see chapter 5, note 58.

1. LESBIAN HISTORIES

1. George Orwell, "Shooting an Elephant," 19–20.
2. Ibid., 16.
3. See Annie E. Coombes, *Reinventing Africa*; Penny Summerfield, "Patriotism and Empire"; Ben Shephard, "Showbiz Imperialism"; and John M. MacKenzie, *Propaganda and Empire*. MacKenzie's description of the 1924–25 Empire Exhibition at Wembley (108–12) provides a particularly illuminating background for understanding Virginia Woolf's satirical critique in her essay "Thunder at Wembley."
4. Rosemary Manning, *A Corridor of Mirrors*, 51.
5. Antonia White, *Frost in May*, 188, 191.
6. VW, *The Pargiters*, 50, 38, 50.
7. VW, "A Sketch of the Past," 124–25.
8. Ibid., 130.
9. Woolf's silence about her fear, shame, and despair under George Duckworth's inspection was painfully overdetermined; around the time of this incident, he was invading her bedroom almost nightly and incestuously abusing her. See Louise DeSalvo, *Virginia Woolf*, 120–33, for a detailed account of Woolf's courageous and repeated breakings of silence about these events later in her life.
10. VW, "A Sketch of the Past," 125, 131.
11. On the interconnections between these men of science, see Marianna Torgovnick, *Gone Primitive*, 7–8.

12. Edith Lees was a lesbian who married Havelock Ellis; the six lesbian "cases" he included in the 1897 edition of *Sexual Inversion* were her friends' stories and her own.

13. Havelock Ellis and John Addington Symonds, *Sexual Inversion*, 87.

14. Michel Foucault, *The History of Sexuality*, 63, 53–54.

15. Lillian Faderman filled in Foucault's habitual blank about women when she critiqued *The History of Sexuality* in 1981 and blamed the sexologists for the "morbidification" of romantic friendship: now that close friendship had been labeled *inversion* "it was inevitable that many women fled into heterosexual marriage, or developed great self-loathing or self-pity if they accepted the label of 'invert'"; Faderman, *Surpassing the Love of Men*, 252. Faderman somewhat modifies this view in *Odd Girls and Twilight Lovers* (1991), but she still sees congenitalist theories as a negative influence on lesbian lives (41–61). See below for Lucy Bland's contrasting assertion of sexology's usefulness to women.

16. Lucy Bland and Laura Doan, *Sexology Uncensored*, 52.

17. For an explication of Hamer's research and its bearing on sexual identity, see Jan Clausen, *Beyond Gay or Straight*.

18. Lucy Bland, *Banishing the Beast*, 256.

19. The distancing irony of Woolf's diary entry about the conversation with Lytton Strachey fails to conceal her interest in inversion theory. "[H]e gave us an amazing account of the British Sex Society," she writes. "The sound would suggest a third variety of human being, & it seems that the audience had that appearance. Notwithstanding, they were surprisingly frank. . . . I think of becoming a member" (VW, *Diary*, vol. 1, 110).

    See chapter 4 for Allatini's use in *Despised and Rejected* of unhappy "trapped soul" and inspirational "intermediate sex" theories. For an analysis of the 1912 discussion of sexology in the *Freewoman*, see Judy Greenaway, "It's What You Do with It That Counts," 36–39.

20. Laura Doan, "Acts of Female Indecency," 205–6.

21. The Labouchère Amendment criminalizing "gross indecency" between men had been tacked on to the 1885 Criminal Law Amendment Act; that act also aimed to protect children from sexual abuse. The Labouchère Amendment made "Acts of Gross Indecency" between men of any age punishable by up to two years hard labor. This, of course, was the law to which Oscar Wilde owed his two years' prison sentence in 1896.

22. See chapter 5 for more on Joynson-Hicks' extralegal subterfuges that helped ensure the banning of *The Well of Loneliness*. For his association with Pemberton-Billing, see Philip Hoare, *Oscar Wilde's Last Stand*, 49 and 194.

23. See Jennifer Travis, "Clits in Court," for the argument that Allan's "professed knowledge of a discourse that women were supposed to be ignorant of was . . . a sure sign of her sadism, and, subsequently, lesbianism" (151) and that "what constituted Salome's (and, in turn, Allan's) "lesbianism," according to this trial, was the "violence" of her sexual arousal (153). Lucy Bland, in "Sexology on Trial," focuses on Pemberton-Billing's use of Krafft-Ebing's theory of congenital perversion to surprise and incriminate Maud Allan through her brother; Bland emphasizes orientalism and primitivism as well as sexology. For the political implications of the trial, see Hoare, *Oscar Wilde's Last Stand*, and Michael Kettle, *Salome's Last Veil*. See also Felix Cherniavsky, *The Salome Dancer: The Life and Times of Maud Allan*.

24. "The First 47,000."

25. "The Cult of the Clitoris."

26. Kettle, *Salome's Last Veil*, 144.

27. See Foucault, *The History of Sexuality*, 43; Bland, "Sexology," 184, and Travis, "Clits in Court," 157. The law's association of enlarged clitorises with "primitive" peoples who were unfit to govern themselves is particularly clear in the transcript of an 1811 lesbian libel case in Edinburgh.

    Marianne Woods and Jane Pirie, both teachers, sued Dame Helen Cumming Gordon for libel after she removed her "niece," Jane Cumming, from their school and induced all the other parents and guardians to remove their daughters, also, "for very serious reasons" ("State of the Process," 135; my references herein to the Woods/Pirie action are to the 1975 reprint of the original transcript *Miss Marianne Woods and Miss Jane Pirie against Dame Helen Cumming Gordon*. I include both section title and page number because each section is numbered separately.)

    Jane Cumming was actually the illegitimate Anglo-Indian child of Cumming Gordon's dead son. She had shared a bed with Miss Pirie in one of the two rooms where the students and teachers slept and had told her grandmother that her teachers' close friendship was sexual.

    Most of the seven Edinburgh judges' statements express their difficulty both in believing that women could experience desire for one another and in imagining how, if they did, they could satisfy it. They had less difficulty, however, in imagining that the Anglo-Indian adolescent, Jane Cumming, had fantasized the whole story, saying, "That this young woman's mind was contaminated, that she was no stranger to those impure ideas which she had imbibed partly from her Eastern education, and partly perhaps from that precocity of temperament which she owed to an Eastern constitution,—that her mind, I say, was familiar with such ideas, we have proof. . . . " ("Speeches of the Judges," 73)

Lord Woodhouselee is here elaborating on the earlier surmises of Lord Meadowbank, who had referred to "Hindoo laws" about "a peculiar conformation—an elongation of the clitoris." He was certain that "the imputed vice has been hitherto unknown in Britain" ("Speeches of the Judges," 7, 8). The Anglo-Indian adolescent was assumed to have invented her story; Cumming Gordon was found guilty.

Lord Meadowbank's certainty that no British women were lesbian was still sufficiently current in 1918 to enable Pemberton-Billing to capitalize on the orientalism in *Salome* and Maud Allan's foreign origin. For more on the Woods/Pirie case see Lisa L. Moore's account in her *Dangerous Intimacies*, 78–82.

28. Diana Souhami, *The Trials of Radclyffe Hall*, 105–6; emphasis added.
29. "Psychical Research"; emphasis added.
30. Quoted in Jeffrey Weeks, *Sex, Politics, and Society*, 105; emphasis added.
31. It seems likely that Lord Alfred Douglas, sometime lover of Oscar Wilde but now heterosexual, a friend of Pemberton-Billing, and a bitter enemy of Wilde's literary executor Robert Ross, may have brought Theodore Durrant's crime to Pemberton-Billing's notice. See Philip Hoare, *Oscar Wilde's Last Stand*, 78. Pemberton-Billing reprinted passages from Douglas's scurrilous satirical poem "The Rossiad" in *The Vigilante* during the weeks before the trial; he also called him to the witness box, where Douglas spoke about Wilde's "diabolical influence" and claimed that *Salome* "was founded on Krafft-Ebing" (quoted in Hoare, *Oscar Wilde's Last Stand*, 152). Pemberton-Billing took every opportunity to emphasize Allan's connection to Wilde.
32. See Bland, "Sexology," 187–92, on the uses of sexology in this trial. It is particularly ironic that Maud Allan was discredited by use of the congenitalist theory that implied so strongly that sexual perversions were not in themselves crimes.
33. *Satan the Waster* (1920) is a complex multigenre work consisting of the introduction, "Prologue in Hell," "The Ballet of the Nations" (published separately in 1915 and reprinted in *Satan the Waster*), "Epilogue," "Notes to the Prologue," and "Notes to the Ballet of the Nations." See Gillian Beer, "The Dissidence of Vernon Lee: *Satan the Waster* and the Will to Believe" for an account of Vernon Lee's "refusal to 'fit'" as a pacifist, lesbian intellectual:

    Vernon Lee's reputation as the cleverest woman in Europe was not unearned. Indeed, the specification "woman" was an important defence against her. Part of what made her threatening to the literary élite was that, if let loose, she might turn out to be the cleverest *man* in Europe too. Her frank lesbianism, or, in the language of the time, 'inversion,' opened the door between male and female intellectuals dangerously wide. (110; emphasis in the original)

    As early as the 1890s Vernon Lee's open sexual independence of men could enable her to challenge their intellectual hegemony.
34. Vernon Lee, *Satan the Waster*, 63.
35. Ibid., 102–3; emphasis and ellipses in the original.
36. According to Philip Hoare (*Oscar Wilde's Last Stand*), 107–8, and Michael Kettle (*Salome's Last Veil*, 52), Eileen Villiers-Stuart was actually an agent provocateur of the Lloyd George government sent to lure Pemberton-Billing into sexual indiscretions. Pemberton-Billing, however, charmed her into his bed and the witness box, where her lies rivalled in absurdity those of the insane Captain Spencer. The only other lesbian response to the Maud Allan trial that I have been able to discover comes from across the English Channel. The young French writer and photographer Claude Cahun (Lucy Schwob) wrote an account of the trial for the *Mercure de France* entitled "La 'Salomé' d'Oscar Wilde: Le Procès Billing et les 47,000 Pervertis du 'Livre Noir,'" (July 1, 1918, 69–80). Her article's emphasis on the need for freedom of artistic expression whatever the circumstances, in war or in peace, is audacious in a nation still suffering enormous losses in the First World War. Vernon Lee's priorities in her exposé of Pemberton-Billing's equation of peacemaking with perversion and homophobia with patriotism is more urgent: she wants to end the war. I have no doubt, however, that both writers' bravery in attacking Pemberton-Billing reflects their courageous sense of them-

selves as gender and sexual outlaws. See François Leperlier, *Claude Cahun: L'Écart et La Métamorphose*, 34–36.

37. See RH, *The Well of Loneliness*, 270–72, and "Miss Ogilvy Finds Herself"; in both narratives, however, inverts have a hard time after the Armistice. For a contrasting representation of invisible lesbianism on the home front, see Rose Allatini, *Despised and Rejected*.

38. Quoted in Jeffrey Weeks, *Sex, Politics, and Society*, 105.

39. See Emma Donoghue, *Passions between Women*, 59–61, for legal evidence of the use of dildos, and 206–12 for the representation of dildos in erotic narratives written by men. For Charke, see her 1755 autobiography, *A Narrative of the Life of Mrs. Charlotte Charke*; Donoghue provides an interesting reading of Charke's relationship with her unnamed friend as "one of the most moving accounts we have of a . . . loving interdependent . . . partnership between working women" (186). Two volumes of selections from Lister's diaries, *I Know My Own Heart* and *No Priest but Love*, have been published; see also Terry Castle, *The Apparitional Lesbian*, 92–106, and Moore, *Dangerous Intimacies*, 83–90.

40. See Martha Vicinus, "They Wonder to Which Sex I Belong," 439, 432.

41. Lillian Faderman, in *Surpassing the Love of Men*, contends that romantic friendships and boarding school crushes were probably platonic (142); her position is strongly critiqued by Lisa L. Moore in *Dangerous Intimacies*, 8–10. Martha Vicinus argues that we are too concerned with "knowing for sure" because "lesbianism can be anywhere without being mentioned" ("Lesbian History," 57–59).

42. Lister, *I Know*, 210.

43. Castle, *The Apparitional Lesbian*, 100.

44. Quoted in Martha Vicinus, *Independent Women*, 332.

45. Bland, *Banishing the Beast*, 230.

46. Hermione Lee, *Virginia Woolf*, 245. Lee is corroborated by Lucy Bland, in *Banishing the Beast*: "Unlike Berlin or Paris, London, as far as historians can discover, had no visible lesbian subculture before the first world war" (169). After the war, Bloomsbury's 1917 Club became largely bisexual (Lee, *Virginia Woolf*, 384); see Jane Marcus, *Virginia Woolf and the Languages of Patriarchy*, 167–69, for a discussion of the connection between the 1917 Club and the Cave of Harmony, where a more overtly lesbian and gay community of outsiders would meet in the 1920s.

47. VW, *Diary*, vol. 2, 216. See Nigel Nicolson, *Portrait of a Marriage*, 156–57, for Nicolson's opinion that his father could, and should, have acted with greater patriarchal authority to silence the gossip about Vita Sackville-West and Violet Trefusis during their three months together in Monte Carlo in the winter of 1918–19. He describes how "all Paris, all London hummed with it . . . the unmentionable had become mentionable." Since he states that their affair was kept out of the newspapers, I assume that "all" Paris and London was simply the upper-class society in which Vita, Violet, and their families moved.

48. "Love and marriage," of course, was the most profitable segment of what Gayle Rubin has memorably called "the traffic in women." See Rubin, "The Traffic in Women," 173–77.

49. VW, "Old Bloomsbury," 170.

50. Ibid., 172.

51. VW, *Letters*, vol. 4, 203. In 1979 Blanche Wiesen Cook entitled her groundbreaking article on the suppression of lesbian literary history "'Women Alone Stir My Imagination': Lesbianism and the Cultural Tradition."

52. VW, *Letters*, vol. 1, 208.

53. Ibid., vol. 3, 347.

54. Ibid., vol. 3, 375–76.

55. VW, "Old Bloomsbury," 173–74.

56. Vanessa Bell, *Selected Letters*, 84.

57. Smyth was in love with Singer for a number of years; in 1935, Woolf calls Singer "Ethel's old flame" (*Letters*, vol. 5, 451). Winnaretta Singer was the daughter of the American millionaire Isaac Singer; when she and Smyth met in 1903 she was living with her second husband, Edmond de Polignac, in Paris, where she knew Marcel Proust and was a notable patron of the arts. Smyth wrote about Singer in *What Happened Next*, her 1940 volume of autobiography, "As she is still a faithful and cherished friend of mine, I will only say here that of the new friends the new century brought me, none counted more in my life than she" (*Memoirs*, 262). A different note is struck by Woolf in a 1937 letter to Dorothy Bussy: "I saw . . . La Princesse de Polignac, née Winnie Singer, but whatever she was born she's grown into the image of a stately mellow old Tory, and to look at you'd never think she'd ravished

half the virgins in Paris, and used, so Ethel Smyth tells me, to spring upon them with such impetuosity that once a sofa broke" (VW, *Letters* vol. 6, 100).

58. Michael Baker, *Our Three Selves*, 125.
59. Ibid., 48.
60. Quoted in Souhami, *The Trials of Radclyffe Hall*, 52.
61. Ethel Smyth, *Memoirs*, 298–99.
62. See Djuna Barnes, *Ladies Almanack*, 18–19, for a wickedly satirical presentation of Troubridge's and Hall's lesbian politics in 1928:

> Lady Buck-and-Balk sported a Monocle and believed in Spirits. Tilly-Tweed-in-Blood sported a Stetson, and believed in Marriage. They came to the Temple of the Good Dame Musset, and they sat to Tea, and this is what they said:
> "Just because woman falls, in this Age, to Woman, does that mean that we are not to recognize Morals? What has England done to legalize these Passions? Nothing. . . . Therefore we think to bring the Point to the Notice of our Judges, and have it set before the House of Lords. For when a Girl falls in Love, with no matter what, should she not be protected in some way, from Hazard, ever attending that which is illegal?"

Barnes perceptively emphasizes the importance of legality to Hall. Her "belie[f] in Marriage" probably also reflects her desire for the "social respectability that would have been denied her growing up under the stigma of divorced parents"; Laura Doan, "Passing Fashions," 700.
63. Baker, *Our Three Selves*, 27.
64. Ibid., 81.
65. Helene Deutsch, "On Female Sexuality," quoted in Teresa de Lauretis, *The Practice of Love*, 63.
66. See Teresa de Lauretis, *The Practice of Love*, 58–65. She reads Deutsch's account of two lesbian analyses in "On Female Sexuality" as narratives of the authorization of lesbian activity by the analyst and/or the lover. My use of the 1950s terms *butch* and *femme* here reflects de Lauretis's use of them throughout her book, irrespective of the dates of the works she discusses.

    See chapter 5 for more details about theories of inverted/butch/transgender desire—or, in Judith Halberstam's useful phrase, *female masculinity*.
67. See Doan, "Passing Fashions," for an illuminating analysis of "boyish" fashions in London from 1918 to 1928. To wear man-tailored coats, collars, and ties, felt hats (but not trousers), and to have one's hair shingled or Eton-cropped was not necessarily a lesbian marker; it was fashionable. According to Doan, Hall followed the fashions of the day in her haircuts and capes and Spanish hat. Young women could pass—or perform—as boys; middle-aged women like Hall and Troubridge could construct an ambivalent style, passing as women of fashion and/or declaring their lesbianism. Women's fashions became unambiguously feminine again in 1928, partly because *The Well of Loneliness* trial firmly associated Hall's look with sexual inversion.
68. This photograph is reproduced in Baker, *Our Three Selves*. In the twenties, Hall and Troubridge would often be photographed and painted with dogs partially concealing their skirts and legs. An example occurs in Romaine Brooks's famous portrait of Troubridge with two dachshunds; see Doan, "Passing Fashions," 686–88, for an analysis of that portrait's representation of gender masquerade.
69. "Psychical Research," 4.
70. Baker, *Our Three Selves*, 123.
71. The *Daily Mail's* account of the first day of the slander trial features only a photograph of Admiral Troubridge; Hall, Una Troubridge, and Fox-Pitt all appear on the newspaper's back page, which is devoted entirely to pictures illustrating the news. The editors clearly believed that the most newsworthy aspect of the case was the wronging of so distinguished a member of the establishment as the admiral ("Spirits in a Slander Suit").

    It seems likely that Sir Ernest Wild and Frederick A. Macquisten had Hall's libel suit in mind when they scared the House of Commons into action in 1921 by describing husbands wronged by predatory lesbians. See Doan, "Acts," 209.
72. Baker, *Our Three Selves*, 124.
73. See Souhami, *The Trials of Radclyffe Hall*, for a differing interpretation of Hall's achievement in this slander trial. Souhami does not produce any new facts about the case, but she vigorously emphasizes the embarrassment not of Hall but of the patriarchy: "She was not going to be embarrassed into silence. She was a homophobe's nightmare: dykish, rich, unyielding, outspoken, successful with women and caring not at all for the small vanities of men"

(106–7). I still see Hall's 1920 performance as more abject than heroic, however; by insisting on Hall's agency, Souhami has made me admire not so much Hall's lesbian politics as Souhami's.

74. "£500 Damages."
75. Bland, *Banishing the Beast*, 290–91.
76. Souhami, *The Trials of Radclyffe Hall*, 119.
77. STW, *Opus 7*, 7–8.
78. STW, "The Way," 478.
79. See Valentine Ackland, *For Sylvia: An Honest Account* for details of her life before she met Warner. She had her first sexual relationship at finishing school in Paris when she was sixteen. By the time she was twenty, she was involved in her second meaningful lesbian relationship, had been engaged to one man, and had married and then separated from another. In October 1930, she was twenty-four years old and predominantly involved with women. Even today, lesbians and gay men often start their sexually active lives as heterosexuals or bisexuals; there is still considerable pressure to be "normal."
80. STW, *Diaries*, 70.
81. For a detailed account of the Vicarage case, see Judith Stinton, *Chaldon Herring* 109–19.
82. "Damages against Four People."
83. "Dying Author Carried into Assize Court."
84. Quoted in Stinton, *Chaldon Herring*, 109.
85. STW, *Diaries*, 69; editor's ellipses. *The Diaries of Sylvia Townsend Warner* (1994) is a woefully incomplete book. Its editor, Claire Harman, selected the single volume from thirty-eight notebooks that "run in total to almost as many words" as the five-volume *Diary of Virginia Woolf* (Harman introduction, viii).
86. See chapter 2, 53, for H. G. Wells's advocacy of "the sterilization of failures" in an address to the Sociological Society.
87. These facts formed part of Warner's evidence at the libel trial as reported in *News of the World* ("Dying Author Carried into Assize Court"). The headline refers to Llewellyn Powys, who was in the last stages of tuberculosis and gave his evidence in a whisper from a bath chair. It is indicative of the culture's sexism that neither Ackland nor Warner were described as authors, despite the fact that Warner had already published nine books, one of which had been a best-seller. Instead, they were called "literary ladies" by lawyers in court as well as in most of the newspaper accounts; *The People* emphasized these words in a subheading, "Two Literary Ladies," which is certainly derisive ("Dying Author in Court Drama"). Only the *Dorset County Chronicle* ("Damages against Four People") mentioned that Warner was an "authoress." Of course, the word *bluestocking* is the most obvious code for *lesbian* in British misogynist culture, but "literary *ladies*" seems particularly patronizing. Warner and Ackland lived much more modestly than Radclyffe Hall and were therefore more easily dismissed as eccentric old maids.
88. "Damages against Four People."
89. "Dying Author Carried into Assize Court."
90. Ibid.
91. Stinton, *Chaldon Herring*, 114.
92. Harman, *Sylvia Townsend Warner*, 139.
93. Quoted in Stinton, *Chaldon Herring*, 114.
94. Rattenbury, "Plain Heart, Light Tether," 46.

2. IMPERIAL IDEOLOGY AND LESBIAN WRITING

1. Carpenter's account in *My Days and Dreams* of the publication history of his pamphlet *Homogenic Love and Its Place in a Free Society* throws considerable light on the instant homophobia created by the Oscar Wilde trials. *Homogenic Love* was first published in a privately circulated edition of two thousand by the Labour Press in Manchester in January 1895. Carpenter writes:

Wilde was arrested in April, 1895 and from that moment a sheer panic prevailed over *all* questions of sex, and especially, of course, questions of the Intermediate Sex.

I did not include *Homogenic Love* in my proposed new book [*Love's Coming-of-Age*], nor had I any intention of including it; but when the mere existence of the thing came to the knowledge of Fisher Unwin he was so perturbed that he actually cancelled his Agreement with me, with regard to *Love's Coming-of-Age*, and broke loose from it. . . . Indeed, he was quite willing to sacrifice the expense he had already incurred (for the book was now partly set up) rather than go on with it. . . .

Being routed by Fisher Unwin, I went to Sonnenschein, Bertram Dobell, and others—altogether five or six publishers—but they all shook their heads. The Wilde trial had done its work; and silence must henceforth reign on sex-subjects. There was nothing left for me but to return to my little Labour Press in Manchester. (196–97; emphasis in the original)

The confusing publication history of Carpenter's writings about sexuality reflects not only the homophobic culture that he was attempting to change but also his pragmatism. That his caution was justified is demonstrated by the suppression of Havelock Ellis's *Sexual Inversion* in 1897. Carpenter had additional reason to be cautious since he and George Merrill were in constant danger of arrest and up to two years hard labor on the charge of "gross indecency" because they lived openly together as homosexuals.

2. Oscar Wilde, *The Importance of Being Earnest*, 406.

3. Significantly, in both this novel and the darker, more openly homosexual *Where Angels Fear to Tread* (1905), romance takes place not in England but in a primitivized Italy.

4. See George Moore, *A Drama in Muslin*, 322.

5. On Moore's sexual ambiguity, see Adrian Frazier, *George Moore*, 32–33, 156–57, and 347. Frazier reads Moore's Representation in *A Drama in Muslin* of the unhappy lesbian, Lady Cecilia Cullen, as "excoriat[ing] a woman-centered attitude to life" (127). Cecilia eventually decides to become a nun.

A more obvious instance of a gay man crosswriting sexuality as well as gender occurs a generation later in Compton Mackenzie's primitivist satire of wealthy lesbians, *Extraordinary Women* (1928). Like Wilde and Forster and unlike the young Moore, Mackenzie uses comedy to distance himself from his subject matter.

6. The best work of Bryher, Renault, and Yourcenar was historical; they each turned to history after writing two or more novels set in the present time, as did Sylvia Townsend Warner. Unlike Warner, however, all three appear to have been male-identified: Bryher spent her childhood longing to be a cabin boy and felt intolerably oppressed by gender norms until she escaped from her family and met H.D.; her crosswritten historical novels emphasize adventure more than romance. Renault's homosexual romances set in ancient Greece and Macedonia were bestsellers, while Yourcenar was the first woman writer admitted to the Académie Française. Both women were rewarded for celebrating masterful men who were heroes of patriarchal history—Socrates, Plato, Theseus, Alexander, Hadrian, and, in Zeno of *The Abyss*, the Renaissance *Homo universalis*. Warner's historical novels, in contrast, consistently satirized the powerful and pretentious.

7. Marguerite Yourcenar wrote in "Reflections on the Composition of *Memoirs of Hadrian*" that it was "virtually impossible to take a feminine character as a central figure. . . . Women's lives are much too limited, or else too secret" (327). "Cultural tyranny" is Gloria Anzaldúa's term; it "keeps women in rigidly defined roles" and molds them into obedient transmitters of the laws and rules made by men (*Borderlands* 16–17). The rigid rules for women in the Catholic Chicana culture that Anzaldúa describes parallel the compulsory conformity of women's lives in most middle-class late-Victorian homes.

8. See Mary Shelley, *The Last Man*, 131.

9. VW, *A Room of One's Own*, 143. Female soldiers are a common theme of eighteenth-century broadside ballads; these generally "resolved matters in the final verse with a happy marriage or other appropriate female destiny" (Vicinus, "They Wonder to Which Sex I Belong," 436). The appropriate destiny for Evadne, a heterosexually active woman, is death.

10. VW, *Women and Fiction*, 114. See Hermione Lee, *Virginia Woolf*, 525–26; Lee draws on Jane Marcus's groundbreaking lesbian reading of *A Room of One's Own* in Marcus's *Virginia Woolf and the Languages of Patriarchy*, 186–87.

11. VW, *A Room of One's Own*, 142–46.

12. Ibid., 141.

13. Ibid., 146–47.

14. VW, *Jacob's Room*, 132.

15. Woolf's sexually radical fantasy *Orlando* forms the bridge between the ambivalence of these partially crosswritten narratives and the biting satire of legal prurience in *A Room of One's Own*. *Orlando* confuses the issue of crosswriting by problematizing gender boundaries entirely. Its fictional biographer is at once insistently male (14–15) and "enjoy[s] the immunity of all biographers and historians from any sex whatever" (220). Woolf appears to be

crosswriting as long as her narrative concerns Orlando as a man; but in places he is a very girlish boy; her biographer crosswrites when he portrays Orlando as a woman, but then Orlando delights in deconstructing her gender by cross-dressing. When she dresses most clearly as a woman, during the densely murky nineteenth century, she and Shelmerdine seem most uncertain about one another's gender (252, 258). The jokes are not only about gender ambiguity but about the embarrassments of gender-specific language in a sex-/gender-ambiguous world. See, for example, the changes in pronoun number as well as gender when the narrator attempts to clarify the crucially inexplicit transgender moment: within three short sentences, "he" passes through "their" in order to become "her" and "she" (138). *Orlando* is not crosswritten: it is *about* crosswriting.

16. Terry Castle illustrates the interdependence of gay and lesbian high camp in the twenties and thirties in the photographs she reproduces in *Noël Coward and Radclyffe Hall: Kindred Spirits*. They include dramatically posed, overlapping binary portraits of Coward with Gladys Calthrop, Gluck with Nesta Obermer, and Troubridge with Hall (26–29). Castle comments that the binary portraits with lesbians for which Coward posed "might be considered coded symbolic tributes: expressions of fellow feeling, emotional identification, and love" and surmises that the lesbians' binary portraits may be evidence that they recognized Coward's tribute to them (30).

    In *Gluck: Her Autobiography* Diana Souhami reproduces sixteen remarkable photographs and paintings of Gluck, including the binary portrait with Nesta Obermer. Gluck was a painter who cross-dressed almost constantly and never, as an adult, used her birth name, Hannah Gluckstein. See Souhami, *Gluck*, 9–10 on Gluck's many nicknames and her reasons for choosing to be known by "this austere monosyllable."

17. Kathlyn Oliver's experience is just one example of the importance to lesbians of gay men's sexual permissiveness and experience throughout the twentieth century. See Lucy Bland, *Banishing the Beast*, 265–87, on the discussion of sexuality in the *Freewoman* and 290–93 on Oliver's letters to Carpenter. Emily Hamer gives an account of the same material in *Britannia's Glory*, 22–25, but reads Oliver's letters to the *Freewoman* as consciously "heterosexualizing" her history.

18. I use the term *in the closet* here to denote a lack of lesbian sexual activity in someone who actually *is* a lesbian. Being in the closet can also mean, of course, being a sexually active lesbian but keeping one's activity secret, at least from some of the people one knows. The range and ambiguity of the term *in the closet* reflects a continuing difficulty in defining lesbianism: "being" a lesbian without active lesbian sexual desire remains a debatable concept. See chapter 1, 20–21, for the critical controversy about the definition of "romantic friendships," and 23–24 on Woolf's intense feelings about the women whom she was "in love" with, such as Violet Dickinson and her sister Vanessa.

19. VW, *Letters*, vol. 2, 336.

20. Crossing class boundaries was notoriously difficult in England; see Wendy Mulford, *This Narrow Place*, 61–69, for a detailed, balanced account of Warner and Ackland's attempts to ignore or surmount class barriers in their political activities and everyday lives in Chaldon in the thirties. See chapter 3 for a comparison of Warner's class and race primitivism with that of her friends and fellow novelists T. F. Powys and David Garnett.

21. See chapter 3 for a consideration of Stevenson's influence on Warner's representation of Fanua and the Fanuans.

22. Warner demonstrates an extraordinary command and understanding of history throughout her writing life. All but her first two novels are set in the past, in the fourteenth, eighteenth, and nineteenth centuries. They reflect the respect for historical detail shown by her father in his articles on military history published in *Blackwoods Magazine* during the First World War. Yet Sylvia Townsend Warner's questioning of the political and cultural assumptions of the past, as of the present, was very different from her father's treatment of imperialist war as a necessity. While there is no doubt that Sylvia deeply loved her father and was shattered by his early death in 1916, I believe that Claire Harman overestimates George Townsend Warner's influence on his daughter's ideas; see Harman, *Sylvia Townsend Warner*, 20. Warner was a woman who thought things out for herself. Her 1962 story, "A Spirit Rises," on the other hand, demonstrates her father's centrality to the development of her poetic imagination; see STW, *Selected Stories*, 78–79.

23. Julie Abraham, *Are Girls Necessary?* 30–32.

24. Bonnie Kime Scott, *The Gender of Modernism*, 4–5. Scott's oxymoron, "traditional experimental," neatly undermines the canonization process: while its reference to writers such as

T. S. Eliot and James Joyce is absolutely clear, it is equally clear that canonization stultifies, depriving experimental work of its shock impact. The writings of the traditional modernists become increasingly hard to defamiliarize.

25. Abraham, *Are Girls Necessary?* 4–6.

26. Jane Marcus, "Bluebeard's Daughters," 27–28. See also Susan S. Lanser, "Queering Narratology."

27. Stephen Jay Gould, in *The Mismeasure of Man* (1981), notes that for eugenicist classifiers of intelligence the terms *idiot* and *imbecile* came to have technical rather than merely pejorative meaning: "[I]diots could not develop full speech and had mental ages below three; imbeciles could not master written language and ranged from three to seven in mental age" (158).

28. STW, *The True Heart*, 1–4. "Sukey" meant a general servant or slavey from about 1820, according to Eric Partridge's *Dictionary of Slang*, s.v. "Sukey." And indeed, in the Apuleius story Venus forces the former princess, Psyche, to become a slavey. A sukey can also be a tea-kettle; this definition explains the "finished tea-set" for which Warner thanked Ray Garnett (*Sylvia and David* 41); she had contributed the engraving of a teapot, cups, milk jug, and sugar bowl surrounded by leaves and flowers that appeared on the title page of the first British edition of *The True Heart*. Partridge's fourth and final definition of "sukey" is "Perhaps . . . a simpleton: mid-C.19–20." I was delighted to find this characteristic example of slippage within the terminology of degeneration theory.

29. In 1930, Warner and Ackland became aware that their neighbors, the Stevenson women, were mistreating their teenage maids, one of whom was named Lily Roberts. See chapter 1 for further details.

30. For Warner's feeling that she was living with Sukey, see her *Diaries'* entries for December 29, 1927; January 14; 1928 ("A hideous day with Sukey at Southend . . . "); August 8–21, 1928; and August 24, 1928.

31. STW, *The True Heart*, 73.

32. Ibid., 250–51.

33. Bland, *Banishing the Beast*, 60.

34. See Sander L. Gilman, "Black Bodies, White Bodies," for an account of the equation of the appearance of prostitutes with that of "primitives" in nineteenth-century medical writing. He includes illustrations taken from papers by Pauline Tarnowsky of prostitutes' "degenerate" faces with "abnormalities [including] asymmetry of features, misshapen noses, overdevelopment of the parietal region of the skull, and the appearance of the so-called Darwin's ear. . . . [which is] a sign of the atavistic female" (243). See also Lucy Bland, *Banishing the Beast*, in which she notes, "The new sciences of craniology and anthropometry 'discovered' that women shared with negroes a narrow, child-like skull and head in comparison to the rounded-head, small-jawed males of the "higher races" (73). There are reproductions of anthropometrists' photographs of "primitives" in Annie E. Coombes, *Reinventing Africa*, 138–39; according to Bland, these "provided a surrogate pornography for European middle-class males" (76).

35. This phrase was widely current: it was used by Darwin and can be found later in the writings of the socialist Edward Carpenter, who found the notion of "higher" and "lower" classes unacceptable. The idea of a hierarchy of "races" was prevalent from mid-Victorian times onward as part of the rationale for imperialist exploitation. The term "lower races" was used interchangeably with "primitives" and "savages."

36. Bland, *Banishing the Beast*, 74.

37. Adam Kuper, *The Invention of Primitive Society*, 4.

38. Ibid., 2.

39. Bland, *Banishing the Beast*, 57.

40. Ibid., 74.

41. STW, *The True Heart*, 110.

42. Ibid., 203–4.

43. Bland, *Banishing the Beast*, 76.

44. See chapter 3 for further discussion of primitivism in *Mr. Fortune's Maggot*.

45. Arnold Rattenbury, "Literature, Lying and Sober Truth," 231; emphasis in original.

46. Quoted in Bland, *Banishing the Beast*, 222.

47. See Lucy Bland's account of eugenics in *Banishing the Beast*, 222–49, and also Jeffrey Weeks, *Sex, Politics, and Society*, 126–38.

48. Bland, *Banishing the Beast*, 240.

49. STW, *The True Heart*, 185.

50. John M. MacKenzie, *Propaganda and Empire*, 122.

51. Paul Scott's four novels were made into a television series and were enormously popular in Britain in the 1970s. Profoundly nostalgic for empire despite their irony, they are postcolonial in date only.

52. Paul Scott, *The Towers of Silence*, 72.

53. STW, *The True Heart*, 199, 200.

54. Quoted in Bland, *Banishing the Beast*, 235–36.

55. Ibid., 225.

56. Ibid., 230.

57. Edith Lees Ellis, "Eugenics and Spiritual Parenthood," 69.

58. "Clemence Dane" is the pseudonym of Winifred Ashton (1888–1965). She was a teacher, actor, painter, sculptor, and a writer of numerous successful novels, plays, and screenplays. *Regiment of Women* was her first novel, followed by *Legend* (1919), which also has a lesbian theme. See Emily Hamer, *Britannia's Glory*, 84–88, for a discussion of the possibility that the "E. A." to whom Dane dedicated *Regiment* was the Elsie Arnold to whom she willed her house in 1956. Terry Castle, on the other hand, names Olwen Bowen as Dane's "secretary-companion" of many years; she also delightfully suggests that Clemence Dane and Radclyffe Hall were both Coward's "Lesbian muses," specifically in his characterization of Madame Arcati, the absurd medium in *Blithe Spirit*; see Castle, *Noël Coward*, 99–101.

59. Alison Hennegan, introduction to Dane's *Regiment of Women*, xiii.

60. The conscious courage behind the writing of the *The Well of Loneliness* makes me unwilling to suggest that it represents lesbian panic, which is generally a product of repression; the novel certainly manifests Hall's internalized lesbophobia, however.

61. See Angela Ingram's witty analysis of this novel's representation of lesbianism and spinsterhood in her "Un/Reproductions," 339–41.

62. Naomi G. Royde-Smith, *The Tortoiseshell Cat*, 287.

63. Ibid., 284. The representation of lesbianism Woolf's *Mrs. Dalloway* is too various for that novel to belong on Hennegan's list, but see chapter 4, **TK**, on the lesbian panic and class primitivism that underlie the characterization of Doris Kilman.

64. See Hall's letter to Newman Flower of Cassell, who had first option on *The Well*: "[N]othing of the kind has ever been attempted in fiction. Hitherto the subject has either been treated as pornography, or introduced as an episode as in *Dusty Answer*, or veiled as in *A Regiment of Women [sic]*" (quoted in Sally Cline, *Radclyffe Hall*, 235). Hall thought so highly of *Regiment* that in 1929 she asked Clemence Dane to dramatize *The Well of Loneliness*; see Castle, *Noël Coward*, 22.

65. Claire M. Tylee, *The Great War and Women's Consciousness*, 171.

66. For more on war babies, see chapter 5. In *The Great War and Women's Consciousness*, Tylee writes that nostalgia for an idealized, prewar, paradisal England is an aspect of the postwar romanticization of Empire (245).

67. Dane, *Regiment of Women*, 256, 254.

68. Ibid., 248.

69. See Hennegan, introduction to *Regiment of Women*, vi–vii; Hennegan sees *Regiment of Women* as part of the intensifying campaign against the spinster schoolteacher that was to continue throughout the 1920s and 1930s. Dane made another contribution to the debate in her essay, "A Problem in Education" in *The Women's Side*, 1926.

70. Dane, *Regiment of Women*, 220.

71. Ibid., 248.

72. Dane, *Regiment of Women*, 289. Roger's euphemisms and portentous silences make his diagnosis of Clare as an invert, or a lesbian, or (less probably) a sapphist abundantly clear, even though chivalry prevents him from speaking the name to Elsbeth or Alwynne. Only the spinster Elsbeth, who has clearly given anxious thought to the matter, uses the "medical" words "perverse" and "abnormal."

73. Dane, *Regiment of Women*, 213–14.

74. For a contrast to Dane's patriotic pastoral, see Jane Marcus, "Britannia Rules *The Waves*," 145, on Woolf's attack on imperialism in her parodic allusions to the Romantic poets.

75. For Constance Maynard's innocence, see chapter 1.

76. Sara Burstall, *English High Schools for Girls*, 160–61.

77. See Martha Vicinus, "Distance and Desire," 225–26, for a somewhat different reading of Burstall's attitude.

78. Bryher, *The Heart to Artemis*, 134. For another account of Bryher's schooldays, see her first novel, *Development* (1920).
79. Bryher, *The Heart to Artemis*, 131.
80. Dane, *Regiment of Women*, 31.
81. Ibid., 34–41.
82. Dane, *Regiment of Women*, 209.
83. See ibid., 110, for Miss Marsham's pleasant fantasy about Cynthia Griffiths "curled kitten-fashion on [her] austere white pallet."
84. Dane, *Regiment of Women*, 58.
85. Ibid., 74.
86. Ibid., 29.
87. Ibid., 210.
88. Ibid., 288.
89. Ibid., 335.
90. Ibid., 337. Elsbeth is accusing Clare of psychic rather than literal vampirism; see Nina Auerbach, *Our Vampires, Ourselves*, 101–12, on vampires who don't feed on their victims' blood but on "their energy, emotional generosity, self-control, creativity, talent, memories" (102). But see the discussion later in this chapter of the more literally vampirish aspects of Clare's lesbian kiss.
91. Eve Kosofsky Sedgwick, *The Epistemology of the Closet*, 186.
92. Ibid., 187.
93. Such novels include George Moore, *A Drama in Muslin* (1886), Helen Zenna Smith [Evadne Price], *Not So Quiet . . . Stepdaughters of War* (1930), Dorothy Bussy, *Olivia* (1949), Rosemary Manning, *The Chinese Garden* (1962), and Violette Leduc, *La Bâtarde* (1965). See note 26 above for examples of lesbian panic in novels of the 1920s and thirties that may reflect the influence of *Regiment of Women*. See also Patricia Juliana Smith, *Lesbian Panic*; after her first chapter on Woolf, Smith focuses on Muriel Spark, Elizabeth Bowen, and "postmodern" writers Brigid Brophy, Maureen Duffy, Beryl Bainbridge, Emma Tennant, Fay Weldon, and Jeanette Winterson.
94. Dane, *Regiment of Women*, 121.
95. Thanks to Bonnie Gray for insight into lesbian vampires.
96. Dane, *Regiment of Women*, 30.
97. Ibid., 300.
98. See Nina Auerbach, *Our Vampires, Ourselves*, 38–53. Particularly interesting from the point of view of lesbian primitivism is her reading of the group of women—in Sheridan LeFanu's "Carmilla"—with whom Carmilla first appears as "an elusive female community" (40). While Carmilla's "mother" deceives Laura's obtuse father into receiving Carmilla as his guest, "a hideous black woman, with a sort of coloured turban on her head . . . was gazing all the time from the carriage window, nodding and grinning derisively toward the ladies, with gleaming eyes and large white eyeballs, and her teeth set as if in fury" (LeFanu, "Carmilla," 286). Auerbach's reading sites intelligence and power in these women rather than in the laborious male authority figures Lefanu sets up.

    See also Joss Lutz Marsh, "In a Glass Darkly," 159–61. Marsh reads the black woman as "the originating point of the matrilineage that spawns Le Fanu's womanly monsters"; he also sees her as "the text's horror-principle incarnate . . . the primitive Victorian fantasy" that is embodied again in the tribal woman who laments Kurtz's departure on the river bank in Joseph Conrad's *Heart of Darkness*.

    What most interests me is the racialized tension in this scene between the intelligence of the white vampires and the power of the black one: she is clearly a product of the fascinated horror that underlies patriarchal degeneration theory: beneath every elegant white woman lurks a grinning black "devil."
99. LeFanu, "Carmilla," 291–92.
100. LeFanu, "Carmilla," 337.
101. Hennegan, introduction to *Regiment of Women*, xiii.
102. Dane, *Regiment of Women*, 345.
103. Even Elsbeth's likening of the lesbian teacher to a vampire is a stereotype; ten years later, Dane quoted a "sober headmistress" as saying, "I have known of at least four of these vampire women in my own experience, and have heard of many others. . . . I am responsible for over eighty boarders, so you may imagine I feel pretty strongly about this sort of love-making" (*The Women's Side*, 64).
104. Dane, *Regiment of Women*, 176.

105. In *Sexual Inversion* (1897), Havelock Ellis distinguished between the "actively inverted" woman and women "to whom the actively inverted are most attracted." The latter do not manifest the "more or less distinct trait of masculinity" that the "actively inverted woman" possesses (87).

106. In "From Sexual Inversion to Homosexuality," 116–23, George Chauncey sees sexology as part of the biological validation of the Victorian sex/gender system just as social Darwinism, with its biologically-based hierarchy of social development, was used to validate racism and colonialism. It is important to remember that the main British writers about lesbian and gay sexuality—John Addington Symonds (1840–1893), Edward Carpenter (1844–1928), and Havelock Ellis (1859–1939)—were all Victorians.

107. I emphasize the exclusively heterosexual content of the early editions of *Love's Coming-of-Age* because Sandra Gilbert and Susan Gubar have asserted in *Sexchanges*, xiii and 215–16, that Carpenter's 1895 pamphlet *Homogenic Love* was included in the first edition (1896), despite the ongoing scandal about Oscar Wilde. This is incorrect; the chapter "The Intermediate Sex" to which they refer appeared only in the fifth (1906) and subsequent editions of *Love's Coming-of-Age*; it was reprinted also as the second chapter of *The Intermediate Sex* (1908). Furthermore, this chapter was a reprint not of *Homogenic Love* but of a less explicit later article that had first appeared as "An Unknown People" in *The Reformer* (July–August 1897) and had been reissued as a pamphlet by Bonner in 1905. A version of *Homogenic Love* made its first book appearance in 1908 as the third chapter of *The Intermediate Sex*.

   Gilbert and Gubar's references to *Love's Coming-of-Age* are to the 1911 American edition published by Mitchell Kennerley. My references are to the third edition, published in 1902 by Swan Sonnenschein. See note 1 above for Carpenter's own account of the book's publication.

108. Carpenter, *Love's Coming-of-Age*, 66.

109. Ibid., 80.

110. Ibid., 70–71.

111. For more details about the 1897 suppression of *Sexual Inversion* see Weeks, *Sex, Politics, and Society*, 180–81.

112. Bland, *Banishing the Beast*, 257.

113. Elazar Barkan, "Victorian Promiscuity," 61. See this essay for Barkan's further arguments against Foucault's view that sexology formed part of the apparatus of repression and control.

114. See Wayne Koestenbaum, *Double Talk*, 43–61, on the sexual politics of Symonds's and Ellis's relationship.

   I use quotation marks to indicate my skepticism about the evidential value of Ellis's "cases" and to distance myself from his "confessional science." I was delighted to find that Carpenter also encloses "cases" in quotes when he cites *Sexual Inversion* in *The Intermediate Sex*.

115. Havelock Ellis and John Addington Symonds, *Sexual Inversion*, 34–35.

116. John Addington Symonds, *Male Love*, 149.

117. Ellis and Symonds, *Sexual Inversion*, 4–8.

118. Barkan, "Victorian Promiscuity," 59.

119. Marianna Torgovnick, *Gone Primitive*, 8.

120. See Judy Greenaway, "It's What You Do with It That Counts," 34–36, for a remarkably clear, economical exposition of Carpenter's evolutionism.

121. Carpenter, *Intermediate Types Among Primitive Folk*, 58.

122. Ibid., 59–60.

123. Ibid., 59; emphasis in the original.

124. Ibid., 170.

125. Ellis and Symonds, *Sexual Inversion*, 47

126. Sheila Rowbotham and Jeffrey Weeks, *Socialism and the New Life*, 82–83.

127. Eve Kosofsky Sedgwick, *Between Men*, 204. Here is a famous example of their influence: in his 1960 "Terminal Note" to *Maurice*, E. M. Forster writes that his novel was conceived on a 1913 visit to Millthorpe when "[Carpenter] and his comrade George Merrill combined to make a profound impression on me and to touch a creative spring. George Merrill also touched my backside—gently and just above the buttocks, I believe he touched most people's" (217). Edith Lees Ellis affectionately recalls sitting in the kitchen talking with Carpenter and Merrill while both men busied themselves with the household mending ("Personal Impressions," 57).

128. Dane, *Regiment of Women*, 215.

129. Ellis and Symonds, *Sexual Inversion*, 46.
130. Carpenter, *My Day and Dreams*, 28–32.
131. Dilip Kumar Barua, *Edward Carpenter*, 195–96.
132. There are some telling allusions to Sassoon's relationship with Carpenter in *The Regeneration Trilogy*, Pat Barker's spectacularly accurate fictional narrative of homosexuality, pacifism, psychoanalysis, and primitivism during the First World War.
133. Edward Carpenter, *Intermediate Types among Primitive Folk*, 111.
134. Barua, *Edward Carpenter*, 161.

3. CROSSWRITING THE "PRIMITIVE"

1. STW, *Letters*, 28.
2. The irony in this 1962 letter is very typical of Warner. She writes to William Maxwell, her editor at *The New Yorker* who had sent her some reviews, "I have never read any provincial reviews before. I am pleased to see that they lay stress on my moral tone. I sometimes think that I am alone in recognising what a moral writer I am. I don't myself, while I am writing; but when I read myself afterward I see my moral purpose shining out like a bad fish in a dark larder" (STW, *Letters*, 203).
3. Many of these fables, originally published in various left-wing periodicals, were collected in *The Cat's Cradle Book*, which was not published in Britain until 1960. The U.S. edition was published in 1940.
4. Warner did not actually join the Communist Party until 1935; her radical mastery of the facts and meanings of history was multiply determined. All her novels after *Lolly Willowes* and *Mr. Fortune's Maggot* are set in the past. Warner herself would probably have attributed her satirical realism to such predecessors as Defoe, Austen, and Stendhal. She was as learned and constant a reader as Virginia Woolf.

   See John Lucas, *The Radical Twenties*, on connections between the socialist and communist writing of the thirties and the sexual radicalism that preceded it during and after the First World War.
5. See STW, "Nelly Trim," in *Collected Poems*, 99–102, and "Elphenor and Weasel," in *Kingdoms of Elfin*, 23–37.
6. STW, *Flint Anchor*, 299.
7. Angela Woollacott, *On Her Their Lives Depend*, 41.
8. STW, "The Way by Which I Have Come," 475.
9. The name "Miaow" is almost certainly a derisive imitation of the "lady workers'" accent—an accent that must also have been Warner's. Her upper-class speech patterns are made particularly clear by her interviewers' use of italics in "Sylvia Townsend Warner in Conversation." STW, "Behind the Firing Line," 199.
10. Warner's comparative freedom from classism seems to have been exceptional. See Angela Woollacott, *On Her Their Lives Depend*, 41–42 and 162–87, on class relations between women in the munitions factories. Woollacott quotes several accounts of munitions work by middle-class women. Brenda Erwin, who was trained at Erith under the same scheme as Warner, describes in a series of patronizing clichés "so many precious memories" that enabled her "to understand the heart of the factory girl" (41). Naomi Loughnan's assumptions about her companions' intelligence reflect the stereotypes of degeneracy theory and eugenics: "They lack interest in their work because of the undeveloped state of their imaginations. . . . [T]hough their eyes may be swollen with weeping for sweethearts and brothers whose names are among the killed and wounded, yet they do not definitely connect the work they are doing with the trenches" (42).
11. STW, "Behind the Firing Line," 192–93.
12. Ibid., 202.
13. Early in her first novel, *Lolly Willowes*, Warner emphasizes the difference between prewar and postwar possibilities for young ladies. The spinster Laura's nineteen years of genteel servitude to her brother's family are compared to her niece's freedom:

    When Fancy Willowes had grown up, and married, and lost her husband in the war, and driven a lorry for the Government, and married again from patriotic motives, she said to Owen Wolf-Saunders, her second husband:

    "How unenterprising women were in the old days! Look at Aunt Lolly! Grandfather left her five hundred a year, and yet she could find nothing better to do than to settle down with Mum and Dad, and stay there ever since." (6)

    Until the success of *Lolly Willowes* in 1926, Sylvia lived on what would have been half of Laura's income.

14. From 1917 for more than ten years, Warner was a member of the Tudor Church Music Committee, funded by the Carnegie Trust. The committee gathered early music from churches and archives all over Britain, then collected and edited it in the ten volumes of *Tudor Church Music*. It was at this time, too, that Warner contributed a chapter, "Notation: The Growth of a System," to *The Oxford History of Music*.

15. STW, "East Chaldon and T. F. Powys," 68.

16. STW, "Theodore Powys and Some Friends at East Chaldon, 1922–1927," 16.

17. Ibid., 14.

18. Marianna Torgovnick, *Gone Primitive*, 8. Crusoe's communion with the moon does not prevent him from drowning in a prosaic, entirely unprimitivist subordinate clause near the end of *The Flint Anchor* (299). Warner's idealized fishermen are more reminiscent of the working-class George Merrill who became Edward Carpenter's lover than of the laborers and lovers in Powys's villages and pubs. For Carpenter's primitivist socialism, see chapter 2.

19. STW, "The Way by Which I Have Come," 478.

20. Rereading *Mr. Tasker's Gods* in 1967, Warner likens Powys's depiction of a clerical convention to Balzac and writes, "[M]uch better than I remembered, substantial and observant and unmannerismed . . . And of course it is Montacute: we were all too polite to say so" (*Diaries*, 310). Powys grew up unhappily in his father's rectory in Montacute, Somerset; the autobiographical element in the novel appears in the savage satire of the Reverend Hector Turnbull and the bewildered innocence of his neglected youngest son, Henry.

     In 1968, reading *Mr. Fortune's Maggot* in the new Viking edition ("*deformed* by idiot misprints"), Warner recognized Powys's influence: "Only the opening is weakened by too much T. F. P." (*Diaries*, 316; emphasis in the original). The novel starts with a funny, whimsical account of a conversation between Mr. Fortune and his archdeacon that is indeed reminiscent of Powys's clerics' absurdity.

21. STW, "Sylvia Townsend Warner in Conversation," 36.

22. STW, *Lolly Willowes*, 51. *Lolly Willowes* was a success on both sides of the Atlantic; it has recently received more critical attention than any Warner novel besides *Summer Will Show*. See especially Jane Marcus, "A Wilderness of One's Own," Barbara Brothers, "Flying the Nets at Forty," and Jane Garrity, "Encoding Bi-Location."

23. STW, *Lolly Willowes*, 103.

24. Ibid., 105. Later in her life, Warner voiced some reservations about *Lolly Willowes*: "So poor a welcome for the General Strike" (Arnold Rattenbury, "Literature, Lying and Sober Truth," 238). Repaying the war loan may be a safe investment, but it certainly doesn't hurry on the revolution.

25. STW, *Lolly Willowes*, 150.

26. Ibid., 247. Buck taught music and composition at Harrow School where George Townsend Warner taught history; later he may have helped Warner get her position on the Tudor Church Music Committee. Warner had several other lovers during her years in London; there are diary entries and a 1973 short story indicating some of the difficulties in her relationship with Buck, but her diaries also indicate her enjoyment of his intelligence. See *Diaries*, 12, 34, 36, 47–48, 52, and "The Foregone Conclusion."

27. STW, *Lolly Willowes*, 176.

28. Ibid., 121.

29. Ibid., 192–93.

30. Ibid., 195.

31. Jane Garrity, "Encoding Bi-Location," 243–44.

32. STW, *Lolly Willowes*, 247.

33. Garrity, "Encoding Bi-Location," 247–48.

34. The use of the word *Chinaman* was acceptable among most white Britons until very recently. Warner generally managed to avoid blatant racism in her writing, but see below for Laura's appropriation of slavery; see below also for the thin ice Warner treads in her characterization of Lueli in *Mr. Fortune's Maggot*. In "Sapphic Primitivism in Modern Fiction," Robin Hackett's analysis of the characterization of Caspar the West Indian in *Summer Will Show* throws further light on Warner's participation in the racism of her culture.

35. STW, *Lolly Willowes*, 200.

36. Ibid., 242.

37. John 20.15.

38. STW, *Lolly Willowes*, 228.

39. Is it possible that Kipling could have read the popular new novel by an upstart young woman and decided to administer a corrective in "The Gardener"?

40. Rudyard Kipling, "The Gardener," 213.
41. See Jane Marcus, "Registering Objections," on white feminist writers' implication in the various racial oppressions of the dominant culture.
42. STW, *Lolly Willowes*, 149.
43. See Christopher B. Steiner, "Travel Engravings and the Construction of the Primitive." Steiner demonstrates the importance of representations of "savage" dances to the maintenance of imperialist hegemony.
44. VW, *A Room of One's Own*, 75. Alice Walker's 1974 essay "In Search of Our Mothers' Gardens" usefully revises the racism in *A Room of One's Own*. Her novel *Meridian* (1976) provides a further corrective: the distinction between the work of a mother and the life of a mother in slavery is at the center of this narrative.
45. Christina Stead, *The Man Who Loved Children*, 458.
46. STW, *Lolly Willowes*, 153-65.
47. Garnett met Warner through Stephen Tomlin, with whom Garnett seems to have been in love. See Garnett, *The Familiar Faces*, 1-2, and 7-8 for his homoerotic account of his first meeting with Tommy and his enthusiastic but comparatively prosaic description of Sylvia.
48. See Peter Fryer, *Staying Power*, and Paul B. Rich, *Race and Empire in British Politics* on the increase in racism in Britain following the First World War. White working-class mobs repeatedly attacked demobilized Arab, African, and West Indian sailors in the seaports, while otherwise "liberal" journalists wrote impassioned articles about the "horrible sexual excesses" of black troops in Europe.
49. David Garnett, *The Sailor's Return*, 56.
50. Ibid., 188.
51. David Garnett, *Great Friends*, 167.
52. Garnett, *The Sailor's Return*, 131.
53. Ibid., 133. For Tulip's parenting skills, see 68-69.
54. Ibid., 72.
55. Ibid., 91.
56. Ibid., 188.
57. I have borrowed the phrase "jarringly racist antiracism" from Jane Marcus's forthcoming book about Nancy Cunard.
58. Warner's response to *A Man in the Zoo* was distinctly guarded: "It must have been difficult to write so unaffectedly about such a violent subject" (Sylvia Townsend Warner and David Garnett, *Sylvia and David*, 7).

    Garnett's *A Man in the Zoo* (1924) is an apparently lighthearted fantasy in which white, middle-class John Cromartie volunteers to become the zoo's example of *Homo sapiens*. For much of the novella he occupies a cage between the chimpanzee and the orangutan. Eventually, the zoo working committee decides to "establish a Man-house which should contain specimens of all the different races of mankind, with a Bushman, South Sea Islanders, etc., in native costume, but such a collection could of course only be formed gradually and as occasion offered" (100). Occasion offers Joe Tennison, a black man in a black bowler hat, who takes his place in the cage adjoining Cromartie's. This development is clearly intended to satirize the forthcoming Empire Exhibition at Wembley, but the blatantly bigoted depiction of Joe Tennison is a crudely unthinking reflection of the violent racism in Britain after the First World War. A year later, writing *The Sailor's Return*, Garnett had given some more thought to the matter.
59. Warner and Garnett, *Sylvia and David*, 23-24.
60. Ibid., 26-27.
61. Ibid., 30.
62. STW, *Letters*, 10.
63. Ibid., 10.
64. STW, *Mr. Fortune's Maggot*, 205.
65. In "The Presence of the Past" Ronald Bush traces the influence on T. S. Eliot and his generation of modernists of the anthropologists Lucien Lévy-Bruhl and Emile Durkheim. They critiqued the racist extremes of the British anthropologists from Edward B. Tylor to James George Frazer—the inventors of "primitive society"—but "continued to make unwarranted distinctions between the mentalities of scientific and prescientific men, otherwise primitives" (33). ("Prescientific" seems to me an interesting variant on the idea of peoples outside time.)
66. Chinua Achebe, "An Image of Africa," 255-56.

67. Joseph Conrad, *Victory*, 190.

68. The comparative rarity of pidgin English in Stevenson's South Pacific tales perhaps reflects his love of Samoan, a complex, subtle language he studied quite seriously; he translated "The Bottle Imp" into Samoan with the help of a missionary named Claxton. For his enthusiastic descriptions of the language, see his *Vailima Letters*, 48 and 170. But his letters also represent the European habit of speaking pidgin to "natives" when he describes his wife, Fanny, frightening one of the servants after the disappearance of three of their pigs: she pretends that she will punish the culprit by means of her personal "devil" (40–41).

69. STW, *Mr. Fortune's Maggot*, 50.

70. Ibid., 218.

71. In 1935, when Warner was alone at a friend's cottage finishing *Summer Will Show*, her lesbian Marxist novel set during the 1848 Paris Revolution, she wrote to Valentine Ackland, "One extraordinary stroke of luck. I wanted a dullish book in case I couldn't sleep, so I took R. L. Stevenson's memoir of Fleeming Jenkin." The luck lay in the sixteen-year-old Jenkin's unbiased description of "the volley in the B. des Capucines which set things off" (Warner and Ackland, *I'll Stand By You*, 139). Warner was glad of an account "with no political views"; her researches had led her to "Legitimists, Orleanists, Republicans [who] all told incompatible versions of the same events" (*Letters* 40).

Warner liked and admired Stevenson himself rather more than his fiction. In 1957, during a depressed phase of her forty-year relationship with Valentine, she wrote in her diary, "Both of us singularly exhausted. I . . . read Stevenson-Baxter letters. I wish, how I wish, I had a Baxter" (237). And in her eighty-fourth year she wrote to Maxwell about Stevenson's recognition of the moment of his death, "[S]uch an assumption of responsibility" (*Letters* 300).

72. STW, *Mr. Fortune's Maggot*, 10–11.

73. STW, "Behind the Firing Line," 195.

74. In March 1891, clearing and weeding farmland and missing his friends, Stevenson wrote, "Though I write so little, I pass all my hours of field-work in continual converse and imaginary correspondence. I scarce pull up a weed, but I invent a sentence on the matter to yourself; it does not get written . . . but the intent is there, and for me (in some sort) the companionship. To-day, for instance, we had a great talk. . . . " (*Vailima Letters*, 56).

75. Stevenson, *Vailima Letters*, 85; emphasis in the original. Traces of this passage remain in Warner's prefatory note to her novel: "In the island names the vowels should be pronounced separately with the Italianate vowel-sounds. Words of three syllables are accented on the second: Fanùa, Lueli."

Warner probably also knew the name of the Fijian island, Vanua Levu. Both Samoa and Fiji are between sixty and seventy degrees latitude south of England—the distance specified for Fanua in *Mr. Fortune's Maggot*. But Fiji is in Melanesia, while Samoa and Fanua are Polynesian (62). An interesting later example of the place-name in a primitivist work occurs in John Ford's 1937 film *The Hurricane*: the Polynesian protagonist escapes colonialist persecution by fleeing with his wife and daughter to "the forbidden place," an island named Fanua Inu. Perhaps Ford had read Warner's novel.

Fanua was also a woman's name in Samoa: Stevenson describes an interracial "marriage of G. the Banker to Fanua, the virgin of Apia" (*Vailima Letters*, 46–47). All the women present at this wedding were Samoan, while almost all of the men were European. Note that Stevenson writes very much as one colonialist man to another: he protects the identity of "G." while specifying Fanua's sexual purity. It is unclear whether his irony is at the expense of Fanua's character or that of the inhabitants of Apia in general.

76. STW, *Mr. Fortune's Maggot*, 10.

77. Ibid., 118.

78. Stevenson, *Vailima Letters*, 120; emphasis in the original.

79. I find Compton Mackenzie's good-humored allusion to a missionary stereotype in *Extraordinary Women* (1928) infinitely funnier than any I've read by Waugh. Mackenzie's exuberant satire—a sexually radical response to Norman Douglas's *South Wind*—places a variously outrageous group of lesbians on the Mediterranean island of Sirene (Capri). The Sirenesi differ from the Fanuans in that they are accustomed to visitors and they wish above all to profit from them:

    [T]he natives. . . . expected foreigners to show signs of moral sunburn within a few days of arriving; and when, as occasionally happened, foreigners visited the island and complained of the way other foreigners behaved the Sirenesi only suspected the critics of worse vices than those they criticized. Several worthy Englishmen and Americans had had to leave the island because the Sirenesi had accused them of appalling secret depravities to explain their censoriousness of others. It is not recorded that any missionary has ever visited Sirene, but if one should be inspired by this chronicle to do so the legend of his private life will mark a new epoch in sexual psychopathy. (133–34)

80. Stevenson, "The Isle of Voices," 390.
81. Stevenson, *Vailima Letters*, 365.
82. Torgovnick, *Gone Primitive*, 27.
83. STW, *Mr. Fortune's Maggot*, 223–24.
84. Ibid., 64, 5, 64.
85. Ibid., 65–66.
86. Stevenson, *Vailima Letters*, 167–68. "My rebel" was the Samoan chief, Mataafa. Stevenson was visiting him shortly before his brief, unsuccessful attempt to seize the throne from the Germans' puppet king, Malietoa. See Jenni Calder, *Robert Louis Stevenson: A Life Study*, 308–10, for an account of Stevenson's involvement in Samoan politics during the rivalry among Britain, the United States, and Germany for political and economic power in the Pacific Ocean. Calder maintains that Stevenson "had no intention of sticking to the imperialist rules" (309), and he certainly seems to have liked and admired Mataafa (*Vailima Letters* 169), but the use of "my rebel" is quite colonially paternalistic.
87. STW, *Mr. Fortune's Maggot*, 21.
88. Ibid., 62–63.
89. Thanks to Marianne Guénot for sharing with me her brilliant unpublished paper, "The Ambiguity of *Mr. Fortune's Maggot*." Guénot writes that "Warner may have felt the threat colonialism poses any exoticist project: to convey the ideology it denounces," and she cites Lueli's tendency to remain silent as one example of Warner's falling into that trap. Guénot sees Mr. Fortune's repression of his love as exemplifying the colonialist "denial of bisexuality in men"; he is able to grow and change because "Warner transplants her hero to an alternative/exotic world and uses an eroticized, exotic young man as a mirror, in which one reads the aberration of Western modern culture."
90. STW, *Mr. Fortune's Maggot*, 21.
91. Ibid., 203, 5.
92. Daniel Defoe, *Robinson Crusoe*, 38–44.
93. STW, *Mr. Fortune's Maggot*, 82–83. I can find no trace in Defoe of this wonderful "quotation" from Crusoe's diary; it must be a product of Warner's talent for parody.
    For Warner's lifelong devotion to Defoe, see Warner and Garnett, 66, and Warner, "Sylvia Townsend Warner in Conversation," 36. An allusion to *Robinson Crusoe* is also central to the representation of homosexual romance in Warner's last novel *The Flint Anchor* (1954); it is clear that for her Robinson and Friday were icons of comic homoeroticism. In both her novels, Robinson Crusoe's Christian colonialism forms an ironic contrast to Warner's representations of intense love between a "civilized" man and one from a "lower" class or "race"; the effect is to problematize assumptions of superiority, first in the world of each novel and then in Warner's own society—and ours.
94. STW, *Mr. Fortune's Maggot*, 26–27.
95. Ibid., 89–92.
96. Ibid., 134–35.
97. STW, *Letters*, 9.
98. See chapter 5 on the 1928 trial of *The Well of Loneliness* and various speculations as to why *The Well* was banned while other "lesbian" narratives were tolerated.
99. STW, *Mr. Fortune's Maggot*, 27.
100. Ibid., 185. An even clearer allusion to Wilde's "Ballad of Reading Gaol" occurs later: as Mr. Fortune works on the carving of a man, a bird, and a dog that he will give to Lueli as a substitute for his idol, "strange thoughts concerning [the idol] stole into his mind. Sometimes he thought the man was himself, listening to the parrot which told him how the doom of love is always to be destroying the thing it looks upon" (219).
101. STW, *Letters*, 11.
102. Torgovnick, *Gone Primitive*, 46.
103. In *Racist Culture*, Goldberg castigates Torgovnick for her use of "we" and "they," for the "unstated assumption throughout that the reader is one with the postmodernist 'we,' that the Primitive is in no position to read such a text" (158).
    He also attacks with impressive rhetorical power the notion that "primitives" live outside time:

It is a remarkable conceit this, to think of 'a people' having no history, no past, no movement from one time to another, frozen stiff like a wax figure in Madam Tussaud's or the Museum of Man. Remarkable in its arrogance . . . remarkable in its lack of self-conscious scepticism. . . . Remarkable, too, in its denial of the invented relationships between Self and Other in modernity and now postmodernity that have been necessary in making possible the standard of living achieved by the "civilized," "developed," "progressive," "historical" beings. If the Primitive has no history at all, it is only because the theoretical standard-bearers of Civilization have managed first to construct a Primitive Subject and then to obliterate *his* history. (157)

The emphasis is Goldberg's; I might have italicized "his" for a different reason: to critique the continuing obliviousness to gender issues of many activists in leftist politics.

I admire, however, the ideological clarity of Goldberg's focus on economic realities and his insistence throughout *Racist Culture* that "primitive society" is an invention and that the words "primitive" and "race" (but not "primitivist" or "racist" or "racial") are empty terms. He avoids collusion with the racism he deplores by his consistent, Foucauldian emphasis on the ways in which "racial knowledge" continues to be used as a means of political and economic oppression. His own language, in contrast with Torgovnick's, has both the precision and the difficulty of philosophical political theory.

104. STW, *Mr. Fortune's Maggot*, 227.
105. Ibid., 240.
106. Claire M. Tylee, *The Great War and Women's Consciousness*, 245.
107. STW, *Mr. Fortune's Maggot*, 221.
108. Ibid., 232.
109. *New English Dictionary*, s.v. "Maggot."
110. STW, *Letters*, 11.
111. E. M. Forster, "Terminal Note," in *Maurice*, 254.
112. STW, *Mr. Fortune's Maggot*, 241.
113. Although Warner wrote series of short stories about the same character, such as the Billy Williams stories in *A Garland of Straw*, these are not really sequels. "The Salutation" is an actual continuation of Mr. Fortune's life story after his setting out for the second time from the mission at St. Fabien.
114. STW, "The Salutation," 65.
115. STW, *Diaries*, 211.
116. STW, *Letters*, 251.
117. Ibid., 274.
118. See Warner's autobiographical story, "Battles Long Ago," for a witty account of this work: she managed to borrow and furnish two empty houses and set up several families in them. For a sheltered, privileged twenty-year-old, she certainly had a remarkable command of essentials.
119. Warner/Ackland Papers. I have been able to find little material from Warner's youth in the Dorset County Museum; several diary entries from later in her life recount her burning of letters and other documents. Only one note from Percy Buck survives: it is about musicology. Warner may have preserved Milner-White's letter because of its historical value as an account of an officer's "'camp horror' (rather than war horror)" (Milner-White, Warner/ Ackland Papers). There is also a series of postcards written to Sylvia by her father when she was working in munitions at Erith; entitled "Gurgling Gore," they tell a satirical, sometimes very funny story about war and red tape and treachery. They certainly reflect the close companionship this father and daughter shared.
120. STW, *Lolly Willowes*, 69–70.
121. Ibid., 72.
122. Ibid., 76.
123. Ibid., 177–78; emphasis added.
124. Vernon Lee, *Satan the Waster*, 115.

4. WAR STORIES: CROSSWRITING THE CLOSET

1. See chapter 3 on the war in *Lolly Willowes* and *Mr. Fortune's Maggot*. I place Warner alongside Woolf, West, and Barnes as one of the modernist "women of 1928" whom Bonnie Kime Scott contrasts with the "men of 1914" in her *Refiguring Modernism*. Scott compares their 1928 representations of sexuality with that of *The Well of Loneliness*. Warner's 1928 volume of poems, *Time Importuned*, cannot be figured as a response to Radclyffe Hall, but see chapter

5 for her Marxist lesbian novel *Summer Will Show* (1936), which revises with precision and wit the patriarchal lesbophobia of her predecessors, with a special focus on Hall and D. H. Lawrence.

2. There is no evidence that Woolf or Warner read *Despised and Rejected*, although Woolf met Allatini and knew about the banning of her novel. See VW, *Diary*, vol. 1, 246 and *Letters*, vol. 2, 336–37. Censorship appears to have silenced this novel effectively: it was not reprinted until the Arno edition of 1975 in New York and the Gay Men's Press edition of 1988 in London. It is now again available from Ayer Company Publishers.

3. On *The Last Man* as an early example of the use of crosswriting to depict politics, war, and forbidden love, see chapter 2.

4. For conflicting accounts of women's sexual "freedom" during the First World War, see Sandra Gilbert and Susan Gubar, *Sexchanges*, and Jane Marcus, "The Asylums of Antaeus." Pat Barker's *Regeneration Trilogy* offers a nuanced fictional representation of heterosexual women's and homosexual men's wartime encounters and romances. For war babies, see my accounts of Clemence Dane's *Regiment of Women* in chapter 2 and Evadne Price's *Not So Quiet . . . Stepdaughters of War* in chapter 5.

5. I purposely avoid the word *pacifism* in my discussion of *Despised and Rejected*. Of the conscientious objectors in the novel, only Strickland, the Christian, seems likely to oppose all war. Others who express their views are socialists who object above all to the demand of the ruling class that they kill other young men sacrificed to capitalist imperialism. I can easily imagine Alan, for example, fighting in a revolutionary war with as much if not more passion as he shows in refusing to fight in this one. Conn O'Farrell, who inveighs against the current hypocrisy about poor little Belgium in view of Britain's oppression of Ireland, is killed fighting in Dublin in the Easter Rebellion.

6. Claire M. Tylee, *The Great War and Women's Consciousness*, 123.

7. Ibid., 124–25. See also Raymond Williams, "Social Darwinism": he traces the development of Lamarckian evolutionary theory through Herbert Spencer—who coined the phrase "the survival of the fittest" in 1864—and the eugenics movement to the idea of a particular human "race"—the Anglo-Saxon, the Aryan, the Celts—as "the vigorous stock, the survivor in the competitive battle, inheriting a certain natural right to mastery." The justification of militarism was that "[i]f the competitive struggle produces the strongest human types, then clearly the strongest race must in no way be limited" (93).

8. Thanks to Corinne E. Blackmer for the notion that aspects of *Despised and Rejected* resemble opera.

9. RA, *Despised and Rejected*, 16.

10. Carpenter, *Love's Coming-of-Age*, 28–29.

11. See Angela Ingram, "Un/Reproductions." Ingram presents Eastwold as a breeding-ground for the "fascist 'germ' in patriarchy which . . . is nurtured in boys'-school team spirit and girls' marriage-competitions; it logically matures to compelling boys to kill other boys for the fathers' defense and to compulsory motherhood" (331).

12. Antoinette's name itself hints at her lesbianism. In the amateur theatricals taking place at the hotel, Antoinette is cast as Marie Antoinette, a part written especially for her by Rosabel Fayne, her admiring friend. See Terry Castle, *The Apparitional Lesbian*, 107–49, on Marie Antoinette as "a code figure for female homo-eroticism" (140) and Allatini as "the first English writer to invoke Marie Antoinette specifically as a lesbian icon" (141). Stephen Gordon and Mary Llewellyn are taken to Versailles by their knowing gay friend, Brockett, in *The Well of Loneliness*.

13. RA, *Despised and Rejected*, 78. Eric is a Jewish violinist: he is called "Ikey" and constantly bullied by Dennis's peers. Dennis is afraid to intervene. Allatini here pairs her Anglo-Saxon homosexual with a younger racial Other—like André Gide's North African boys in *The Immoralist* and *If It Die*, or Forster's Aziz in *A Passage to India*, or Warner's Lueli in *Mr. Fortune's Maggot*. All these exemplify the repeated connection between gay and "primitive" sexuality in modernist writing.

14. RA, *Despised and Rejected*, 107.

15. Ibid., 250. Carpenter attacks the notion that "Urnings" are effeminate, morbid, and degenerate in *The Intermediate Sex* (22–25 and 60–63). He asserts that the apparent nervousness of some inverts is an appropriate response to society's opprobrium and that doctors naturally encounter the morbid more often than the healthy. Dr. Albert Moll, for example, did his research "under the guidance of the Berlin police" (63).

16. RA, *Despised and Rejected*, 149.

17. Vera Brittain, *Chronicle of Youth: War Diary 1913–1917*, 91.
18. See chapter 5 for my discussion of a comparable representation of suburban jingoism in Evadne Price's 1930 war novel, *Not So Quiet . . . Stepdaughters of War*. Nell Smith, the narrator, presents her contempt for the Mrs. Ryans of her world in a satire of surreal intensity.
19. RA, *Despised and Rejected*, 150.
20. Ibid., 199. See Caroline Moorehead, *Troublesome People*, and John Rae, *Conscience and Politics*, for detailed accounts of conscription and conscientious objection in Britain during World War I.
21. It is likely that Allatini was a reader of *The Tribunal*, the No-Conscription Fellowship's newspaper. Her depiction of Dennis's appearance before the Central Tribunal in Westminster is a particularly clear echo of the paper's weekly accounts of the absurd and dangerous jingoism manifested in Tribunal hearings all over the country; Allatini, *Despised and Rejected*, 306–15.
22. Ethel Mannin, *Young in the Twenties*, 72; emphasis in the original.
23. Sylvia Pankhurst, *The Home Front*, 297.
24. RA, *Despised and Rejected*, 205–6.
25. In *The Home Front*, Sylvia Pankhurst recalls seeing a photograph of a pacifist poet dressed in a blanket on the front page of the *Daily Sketch* on April 14, 1916:

    Eric Chappelow! Eric Chappelow in a barrack yard, standing on the concrete with stockinged feet, a blanket fastened round him with a leather belt which strapped his arms tightly to his sides. A couple of soldiers stood on guard beside him. The yard bordered on the public street. . . . Undoubtedly he had refused to wear the khaki, and this was his punishment—to stand out there in a blanket, to be ridiculed, the target of whoever cared to throw at him an epithet or a missile! (316)

    This is the photograph *Eric Chappelow's First Day in the Army*; see figure 3, page 111 in this volume.

    Pat Barker recreates a similar scene rather more grimly in *The Eye in the Door* (261–66), but the conscientious objectors she depicts, unlike Allatini's, are of the working class.
26. RA, *Despised and Rejected*, 262.
27. May Sinclair, *The Tree of Heaven*, 384.
28. Sharon Ouditt, *Fighting Forces, Writing Women*, 106.
29. Sinclair, *The Tree of Heaven*, 375.
30. RA, *Despised and Rejected*, 318.
31. Ibid., 158.
32. Ouditt, *Fighting Forces, Writing Women*, 156.
33. Ibid., 107.
34. Suzanne Raitt, "Contagious Ecstasy," 67; RA, *Despised and Rejected*, 204, 234, 343.
35. RA, *Despised and Rejected*, 156.
36. Ibid., 157.
37. Ibid., 158.
38. Perhaps Allatini had read Vernon Lee's allegory of war, *The Ballet of the Nations* (1915), with its emphasis on the grotesque. The "dissonances and conflicting rhythms" produced by its Orchestra of the Passions might well have been a source of the nightmare music Dennis hears. Vernon Lee was also a pacifist, although she was involved with the Union for Democratic Control rather than the No-Conscription Fellowship: she was two generations older than Allatini and the conscientious objectors Allatini depicts.

    See also Jon Stallworthy, *Wilfred Owen*, 149, for an extraordinary account of the sounds of the Battle of the Somme, which he quotes from *The Westminster Gazette* of October 24, 1916:

    The sound was different. . . . It was not a succession of explosions or a continuous roar. . . . It was not a noise; it was a symphony. And it did not move. It hung over us. It seemed as though the air were full of a vast and agonized passion, bursting now with groans and sighs, now into shrill screaming and pitiful whimpering, shuddering beneath terrible blows, torn by unearthly whips, vibrating with the solemn pulses of enormous wings. And the supernatural tumult. . . . was poised in the air, a stationary panorama of sound, a condition of the atmosphere, not the creation of man.
39. RA, *Despised and Rejected*, 83–84.
40. Ibid., 131.
41. Allatini's debt to Carpenter, as opposed to other sexologists, is particularly clear in her refusal to make her gay man effeminate and her lesbian mannish. Carpenter states clearly

in *The Intermediate Sex* that although there are some examples of "the extreme type of the homogenic female" (30), most are "thoroughly feminine and gracious" in body. He does, however, opine that their "inner nature is to a great extent masculine [with] a temperament active, brave, originative, somewhat decisive" (35–36). Antoinette possesses these characteristics in the first half of the novel but later appears drained of energy, saddened by her unrequited love for Dennis and the events of the war.

42. RA, *Despised and Rejected*, 217.

43. Ibid., 37.

44. Ibid., 215, 277.

45. Ibid., 281.

46. This passage occurs at the end of Jonathan Cutbill's unpaginated introduction to the Gay Men's Press edition of *Despised and Rejected* (1988).

47. *Despised and Rejected* was Allatini's fourth novel; she published more than thirty more, under the pseudonyms Lucian Wainwright and Eunice Buckley as well as her own names, Allatini and Scott. Those that I have read, published between 1918 and 1973, are heterosexual romances. See Cutbill's introduction to *Despised and Rejected* for further details.

48. RA, *Despised and Rejected*, 347.

49. These words are particularly prominent in Carpenter's various characterizations of male "intermediate types." See Dilip Kumar Barua, *Edward Carpenter*, 174, on Carpenter's emphasis on tenderness rather than beauty or romance in his representation of homoerotic love in *Towards Democracy*.

50. "Despised and Rejected" is an allusion to Isaiah 53.3.

51. RA, *Despised and Rejected*, 348–49.

52. See Carpenter, *The Intermediate Sex*, 70–74, 114–16; and *Intermediate Types Among Primitive Folk*, 57–64.

53. See Lillian Faderman, *Surpassing the Love of Men*, 252. But see also chapter 1, note 15 above for Faderman's modification of this view.

54. VW, *Diary*, vol. 1, 246.

55. "A Pernicious Book" (*Times*).

56. "A Daniel Come to Judgment."

57. "'Despised and Rejected': Publisher of Pacifist Novel Fined."

58. "A 'Pernicious' Book" (*Daily News*).

59. Solomon Eagle, "Books in General" (October 12, 1918), 33.

60. See chapter 1 for an account of the Pemberton-Billing trial.

61. Eagle, "Books in General" (October 12, 1918), 33.

62. It seems fitting that J. C. Squire was succeeded on *The New Statesman* by Desmond MacCarthy, the "Affable Hawk" whose misogyny Woolf was to attack in letters to *The New Statesman* in October 1920; see note 121 below and Woolf's *Diary*, vol. 2, 339–42.

63. If Allatini knew Christopher St. John's autobiographical novel *Hungerheart: The Story of a Soul* (1915), no trace of its influence survives in her novel. Unlike Radclyffe Hall, who almost certainly knew this narrative of lesbian angst, Allatini may have wished to distance her lesbian from St. John's congenitally inverted protagonist. See chapter 2 for my reading of *Regiment of Women* as a work of eugenicist propaganda and lesbian panic.

64. See VW, *Letters*, vol. 2, 247.

65. See Tylee, *The Great War and Women's Consciousness*, 142–50. I agree with Tylee's condemnation of the way that "the distressing details of shell shock are glanced over by West" in *The Return of the Soldier*. She contrasts West's sketchy representation of shell shock with Rose Macaulay's explicitness in *Non-Combatants and Others* (1916).

66. West's first book, published in 1916, was a critical study of Henry James.

67. Rebecca West, *The Return of the Soldier*, 44.

68. Ibid., 68–70.

69. A similar murkiness occurs in James's and Conrad's fiction when they use unreliable narrators. Reading *The Return of the Soldier* as a precursor to *Mrs. Dalloway*, I am struck by the comparative clarity of Woolf's political stance in her complex stream-of-consciousness narrative.

70. West, *The Return of the Soldier*, 62.

71. Ibid., 79.

72. Ibid., 88.

73. Ibid., 90.

74. Ibid., 16, 19.

75. "Cure of Shell-Shock."
76. "War-Shaken Men."
77. The *Times* reported Collie's list of symptoms of shell shock as follows: "Disorderly action of the heart, epileptiform seizures, tremors, functional stiffness and functional loss of power of muscles, loss of flesh, and loss of hearing and speech" ("Cure of Shell-Shock"). It does not mention amnesia.

   In order to counter wartime scepticism about shell shock—the sufferers were often looked upon as malingerers—Collie focuses on its physical manifestations, its medical reality as a disease caused by the war, and the importance of telling soldiers disabled by shell shock that they cannot be reconscripted upon recovery. At no point does he blame the victims. He demonstrates an attitude to shell shock very different from the punitive recommendations of the postwar *Report of the War Office Committee of Enquiry into Shell-Shock* (1922) which Woolf probably read about in 1922.
78. West's 1916 series of articles in *The Daily Chronicle* about women's war work reflects her awareness of the cruelty of war; see West, *The Young Rebecca West*, 380–90. She was probably conscious of the escapist emphasis of her novel.
79. Carl Rollyson, *Rebecca West: A Life*, 66.
80. VW, *Diary*, vol. 2, 272.
81. Ibid., 207.
82. "Shell Shock"; emphasis added
83. For an unforgettable account of trench warfare, see Modris Eksteins, "Battle Ballet," in his *Rites of Spring*, 139–42.
84. Lord Southborough, "'Shell Shock': A Misleading Designation."
85. "Courage and Character"; emphasis added
86. VW, *Mrs. Dalloway*, 202.
87. Lord Southborough, "'Shell Shock': A Misleading Designation."
88. Sue Thomas, "Virginia Woolf's Septimus Smith," 50; see also Hermione Lee, *Virginia Woolf*, 183.
89. VW, *Mrs. Dalloway*, 110. Hermione Lee's chapter "Madness," 175–200, gives a valuable account of Woolf's experiences of the medical profession; she was particularly well informed about treatments for "hysteria" and "neurasthenia." Sue Thomas may be correct in her argument that Woolf read the *Report of the War Office Committee* itself, but I think the articles in the *Times* from which I quote, coupled with her own experience, would have been sufficient to ignite the rage with which she satirizes Sir William Bradshaw's dangerous, hypocritical will to power. That Bradshaw's jargon should resemble that of the *Report* is unsurprising: in his insistence that the "unfit" must be prevented from "propagating their views" (VW, *Mrs. Dalloway*, 110) and that "unsocial impulses" are "bred more than anything by the lack of good blood" (113), he is mouthing eugenicist clichés.
90. VW, *Mrs. Dalloway*, 202–3.
91. Lee, *Virginia Woolf*, 182. Lee writes that "Leonard considered putting her in a home" after her 1913 suicide attempt (330). It is not clear how such a "home" would have differed from Burley Park. Lee goes on to quote Vanessa Bell's account of a 1914 visit with Virginia and Leonard to the neurologist Maurice Craig: "he said that 'she wasnt [sic] in a state where she could possibly be certified and that she couldnt [sic] therefore be made to go into a home.'" This sounds as if Craig is reassuring Virginia that she cannot be put in what would have then been called an "asylum" against her will. One wonders who raised that subject.
92. VW, *Mrs. Dalloway*, 202.
93. Ibid., 129, 132, 127, 163.
94. Ibid., 69, 62, 57.
95. See Eksteins, *Rites of Spring*, 120–23, on "the sporting imagery of British social discourse" and its influence on the spirit in which the British entered the war.
96. VW, *Mrs. Dalloway*, 95. Due to the lengthy examination of *Mrs. Dalloway* that follows, page numbers will hereafter be cited parenthetically in the text.
97. George L. Mosse, *The Image of Man*, 3.
98. Septimus is suffering a clear case of "homosexual panic." Eve Kosofsky Sedgwick, in *Epistemology of the Closet*, argues that the armed services are a site of more than usually intense acting out of the double bind of male friendship: "In these institutions, where both men's manipulability and their potential for violence are at the highest possible premium, the *prescription* of the most intimate male bonding and the *proscription* of (the remarkably cognate) 'homosexuality' are both stronger than in civilian society" (186; emphasis in the

original). This double bind would be an additional motive for numbness and for veering from one intense emotion to its opposite as the repression wore off after the war. See Patricia Juliana Smith, *Lesbian Panic*, 48–53, for an analysis of Septimus's life in terms of Sedgwick's theory.

On emotional numbness as a necessity for survival in the trenches, see Eksteins, *Rites of Spring*, 172–74.

99. VW, *Diary*, vol. 1, 92.

100. See chapter 2 on the photographs of the Greeks in *Jacob's Room* and the importance of the ancient Greeks to the gay sexologists Edward Carpenter and John Addington Symonds. "Greek Love" was the subject of Symonds's *A Problem in Greek Ethics*. Woolf knew Symonds's daughters, Madge Vaughan and Katherine Furse, and would probably have heard about his "buggery" from Lytton Strachey or Roger Fry or other Cambridge/Bloomsbury men. Homosexuality is a primary connotation of "Greek words," Thessaly, and the "meadow of life beyond a river where the dead walk" in Septimus's visions.

In their readings of Septimus's madness, Hermione Lee, Stephen Trombley, and others focus on the birds singing in Greek that Woolf thought she heard while she was lying ill in 1904 in Violet Dickinson's house (see VW, "Old Bloomsbury," 162); see Lee, *Virginia Woolf*, 195–96. But "Old Bloomsbury" also includes an account of Woolf's introduction to "buggers" in Plato and growing experience of them among her brother Thoby's Cambridge friends (172–75). Both Greek Love and birds singing in Greek—including perhaps her love for Violet—were on Woolf's mind when she created Septimus's homosexuality and "madness."

101. See Emily Jensen, "Clarissa Dalloway's Respectable Suicide," 173, for another reading of these barking dogs. Jensen connects them to the earlier image of Evans and Septimus as "two dogs playing on a hearthrug" (VW, *Mrs. Dalloway*, 96), and argues that they represent "the body and its natural feelings" as opposed to conventional heterosexuality.

102. Christine M. Darrohn, "After the Abyss," 116. In her dissertation Darrohn emphasizes the ambiguity of Clarissa's identification with Septimus (109–11), drawing on the theory of "modernist undecidability" developed by Marianne DeKoven in *Rich and Strange*. Among other readings that connect Clarissa's meditation on Septimus's death with her memories of desire for Sally Seton, see especially Emily Jensen, "Clarissa Dalloway's Respectable Suicide"; Claire M. Tylee, *The Great War and Women's Consciousness*, 155–67; Elizabeth Abel, *Virginia Woolf and the Fictions of Psychoanalysis*, 36–41, and Julie Abraham, *Are Girls Necessary?* 146–52.

103. However, see Emily Jensen, "Clarissa Dalloway's Respectable Suicide"; 171, in which Jensen associates Imogen's cross-dressing with Clarissa, "who 'undoubtedly did feel what men felt.'" This quotation, however, is taken from the much-discussed "match burning in a crocus" passage about clitoral orgasm (36); Clarissa is thinking about sexual attraction to women, not dressing up to pass as a man. Her association of physical arousal with "what men felt" indicates her adoption of inversion theory along with the rest of her dominant cultural baggage.

See Teresa de Lauretis, *The Practice of Love*, 236–39, for an interesting analysis of Clarissa's desire.

104. See Reginald Abbott, "What Miss Kilman's Petticoat Means," 204.

105. Class privilege ensures that Lady Bruton, this novel's fourth lesbian, is much less distressed than Miss Kilman by her sartorial and sexual oddity. Bruton reveals her inversion by the formless, ungendered clothing she wears with impunity to Clarissa's party: "[A] spectral grenadier," she stands "draped in black," holding forth about India (199).

106. For a reading of *Mrs. Dalloway* through the lens of inversion theory, see Eileen Barrett, "Unmasking Lesbian Passion: The Inverted World of *Mrs. Dalloway*."

107. Reading other writers on *Mrs. Dalloway* makes it speedily apparent that I'm not the only reader whom Miss Kilman makes uncomfortable. Those critics who focus on Clarissa's lesbian romance—Sally Seton's kiss, the infinitely precious wrapped up diamond, the match burning in the crocus—tend to relegate Doris Kilman to a single paragraph or fail to mention her at all; those readers who emphasize Woolf's representation of the patriarchy, the war, the empire, commerce, and/or the class system generally write about Miss Kilman as a victim of social injustice, more or less erasing her sexuality. But see, as recent exceptions to this rule, Smith, *Lesbian Panic*, and Darrohn, "After the Abyss." See also Abraham, *Are Girls Necessary?* 152–53, for a succinct reading of Doris Kilman as lesbian historian that rescues her from abjection without sentimentalizing her. It is clear, however, that Doris's lesbianism can be an embarrassment: Claire Tylee refers to her as a spinster (160), and Kilman's

intense longing to grasp and clasp Elizabeth has been euphemized by Karen Levenback in *Virginia Woolf and the Great War*, 80, as "her seemingly unhealthy attachment." Some male critics, on the other hand, seem to have felt quite comfortable about Doris Kilman's discomfort: Stephen Trombley, in *All That Summer She Was Mad*, 67, says that she metaphorically consumes Elizabeth at tea in the Army and Navy Stores, while Kenneth Moon, in his "Doris Kilman and Recoil from the Flesh," 281, likens Kilman's chocolate éclair to Clarissa's match burning in the crocus.

108. Helena Michie, *The Flesh Made Word*, 12.

109. Pankhurst, *The Home Front*, 170. See Vera Brittain's war diary, *Chronicle of Youth*, 273, for a delighted account of the patriotic persecution of a German barber.

110. VW, *Diary* vol. 1, 135–36. See Levenback, *Virginia Woolf and the Great War*, 80.

111. "German Women in London."

112. Tylee, *The Great War and Women's Consciousness*, 160.

113. See Trudi Tate, *Modernism, History, and the First World War*, 147–70. Tate shows that although both Armenia and Albania had endured centuries of Turkish oppression, there was much more interest in and sympathy for the Armenians than for the Albanians in Britain. The *Times* gave extensive coverage to Turkish deportations and massacres of Armenians in 1915; during postwar negotiations over the dismantling of the Ottoman Empire, both the mainstream press and the British government appeared to support Armenian independence. Yet once the creation of the new state of Iraq had secured British interests in the region, the government simply dropped support for the fragile independent republic of Armenia that had briefly existed after the war. As Tate notes, "In *Mrs. Dalloway*, Richard Dalloway MP sits on the committee which is negotiating this final act of betrayal in June 1923. That is where he is going after giving Clarissa the roses" (159).

114. It is worth noting that Septimus Warren Smith, during his period of acute alienation and anxiety, associates the noisy, newly motorized vans of postwar London with brutality, too: "In the street, vans roared past him; brutality blared out on placards; men were trapped in mines; women burnt alive" (100); but Clarissa's wealth and charm have tamed and named "Durtnall's van" for her (6).

115. See Reginald Abbott, "What Miss Kilman's Petticoat Means," 193–216, for an account of the army and navy stores as a temple of imperialist commerce. See also Jeremy Tambling, "Repression in Mrs. Dalloway's London," 139, for the imperialist function of "the Stores," as Clarissa calls them with easy familiarity (VW, *Mrs. Dalloway*, 139).

116. See Kathy J. Phillips, *Virginia Woolf against Empire*, 3, on the nullity of Lady Bruton's conference with the prime minister. In *Modernism, History and the First World War*, Trudi Tate memorably describes the empty chairs that they have left "with no sign but the imprints of the buttocks of greatness" (165).

117. A version of the anonymous ballad can be found in W. H. Auden's 1938 edition of *The Oxford Book of Light Verse*, 289–90. I remember the first stanza (as well as a whole medley of shamelessly imperialist verse) from my childhood in London:

Some talk of Alexander, and some of Hercules,

Of Conon and Lysander, and some Miltiades;

But of all the world's brave heroes, there's none that can compare,

With a tow, row, row, row, row, to the British Grenadiers.

Everyone I know from England seems familiar with the tune.

118. Lewis Winstock, *Songs and Music of the Redcoats*, 27.

119. VW, *Diary*, vol. 2, 217, 325.

120. VW, *Letters*, vol. 2, 405; *Diary*, vol. 1, 315.

121. VW, letter to *New Statesman*, Oct. 16 1920; reprinted in VW, *Diary*, vol. 2, 341.

122. VW, *Essays*, vol. 3, 298.

123. Smyth, *Impressions That Remained*, 30.

124. See, however, the bitter satire in Warner's depiction of the aftermath of the war in a Dorset village in her satirical narrative poem, *Opus 7* (1931).

125. STW, *Letters*, 84.

126. STW, "My Shirt Is in Mexico," 81.

127. Ibid., 82.

128. Ibid., 83.

129. Ibid., 81.

130. Ibid., 82.

131. Ibid., 83.

132. Ibid., 84.
133. Ludwig Renn was of Warner's generation: he fought in the First World War and wrote a famous antiwar novel about it, *War* (*Krieg*, 1929). George L. Mosse cites Renn along with Siegfried Sassoon and Wilfred Owen as antiwar writers who "shared the consciousness of their masculinity with those who continued to support the war" in their writing as well as at the front (Mosse, *The Image of Man*, 108). Mosse neglects to point out that all three writers were gay. Of course, a masculine young soldier of 1918 could well have relaxed twenty years later into the campy waltzer on the lawn whom Warner remembers. Her fictional Renatus Leutner, freedom fighter and flirt, beautifully combines the masculine and the camp.

     Warner and Ackland first met Renn in Madrid at the 1937 Writers' Congress; in January 1939, after the fall of Barcelona, he was one of the International Brigade fighters who crossed the frontier to France and were promptly interned by the French government. Louis Aragon sent him to Warner and Ackland; they met his boat at Southampton in March, and he stayed with them until they sailed for New York together in May for the Third Congress of American Writers there. Warner and Ackland returned to England after the outbreak of war in September, while Renn went on to Mexico. After the war he became a professor of anthropology in Dresden.

     Renn and Warner had a lasting friendship: Warner dedicated her collection of political fables, *The Cat's Cradle Book*, to him in 1940; they were still corresponding as late as 1961 (letter from Ackland to Cunard, 1 January 1944, Nancy Cunard Papers; Sylvia Townsend Warner and Valentine Ackland, *I'll Stand By You*, 167–68; letters from Renn to Warner, Warner/Ackland Papers; and Warner, *Diaries*, 274).
134. Warner and Ackland, *I'll Stand By You*, 167.
135. STW, *Diaries*, 291.
136. STW, "A Love Match," 5–6.
137. It is interesting to compare "A Love Match" to the shell-shock episode in Rose Macaulay's 1916 pacifist novel, *Non-Combatants and Others*. Alix Sandomir is awakened by the nightmares of her cousin, who is sleepwalking and sleeptalking on the balcony that connects their rooms. At the time, she is too horrified to focus on what he is saying, but later she remembers that he had spoken about "the leg of a friend . . . pulling it out of the chaos of earth and mud and stones which had been a trench . . . thinking it led to the entire friend, finding it didn't, was a detached bit" (21). Such horrific events were commonplace in the trenches; perhaps Justin Tizard had a similar experience. But Warner's metaphorical "broth" is more nightmarish because broth is so commonplace, so nourishing: earth, fire, and flesh become soup. Modris Eksteins's account of the war in Flanders makes clear the lack of exaggeration in such imagery; see *Rites of Spring*, 139–69.

     It seems very likely that Warner read Macaulay's *Non-Combatants and Others* many years before she wrote "A Love Match." Celia's "vicarious endurance" of Justin's nightmares is similar to Alix's suffering after she overhears John. The Tizards' subsequent embrace is impossible to imagine in a Macaulay novel, however.
138. STW, "A Love Match," 8–9.
139. Ibid., 9.
140. See STW, *Diaries*, 70, and chapter 1, 32–33, for details about this event.
141. STW, "A Love Match," 12. See chapter 1, note 87, for the press's insistence on referring to Warner and Ackland as "literary ladies" in the Vicarage libel case in 1935.
142. STW, "A Love Match," 11.
143. Ibid., 12.
144. Ibid., 16–17.
145. Ibid., 17.
146. STW, "A Love Match," 18.
147. Ibid., 20.

5. WRITING AND REWRITING STEPHEN GORDON

1. RH, *Radclyffe Hall's 1934 Letter*, 2.
2. Another starting point for my interpretation of Stephen's sexual and gender difference was a conversation with Jay Prosser in 1995 about inversion, butchness, and transsexuality in *The Well of Loneliness* and in Leslie Feinberg's *Stone Butch Blues*.

     For lesbian-feminist critiques of *The Well of Loneliness*, see Blanche Wiesen Cook, "Women

Alone Stir My Imagination'": Lesbianism and the Cultural Tradition"; Lillian Faderman, *Surpassing the Love of Men*, 322–23; and Catharine R. Stimpson, "Zero Degree Deviancy." Esther Newton's "The Mythic Mannish Lesbian" first appeared in *Signs* in 1984.

True to lesbian-critical form, I want to state that my own response as a reader of *The Well* has been self-identification and embarrassment. I have always identified—and identified with—Stephen Gordon as a distressingly gender-dysphoric but sartorially enviable butch, finding her embarrassing not because of her butchness but because of her self-pity, her class and racial politics, and her patriotism. I persist in wanting my lesbian foremothers, whether fictional or historical, to be socialist.

3. Hall, *The Well of Loneliness*, 186–87.
4. Teresa de Lauretis, *The Practice of Love*, 283.
5. RH, *The Well of Loneliness*, 205. See Jean Radford, "An Inverted Romance," for an account of Hall's use of theories of inversion and Freudian repression.

I owe my connection of Puddle's "curious double insight" to Edward Carpenter's ideas in *The Intermediate Sex* to Laura Doan's "Radclyffe Hall's Sexual Science: A Passage in Modernity," given at the 1998 MLA convention in San Francisco. I think Hall had also read Carpenter's *Intermediate Types among Primitive Folk*. Puddle's speech here is very reminiscent of Carpenter's evolutionist theory that intermediate types—"the non-warlike men and the non-domestic women"—among "primitive" peoples "became medicine-men and healers, prophets and prophetesses; and so ultimately laid the foundation of the priesthood, and of science, literature, and art" (*Intermediate Types*, 58). Carpenter believed that in the future intermediates would lead humankind into a more spiritual, natural life in which the divisions of sex and gender would be transcended.

6. Judith Halberstam, *Female Masculinity*, 82.
7. Jay Prosser, *Second Skins*, 143.
8. Ibid., 159.
9. Halberstam, *Female Masculinity*, 85.
10. For Halberstam, the distinction that matters is the one between the forms of cross-gender identification that constitute female masculinity—including transsexuals, butches, and female husbands or passing women—and lesbianism, which, "since the rise of lesbian feminism refers to sexual preference" (153); but her definition is troubling because it erases the gender identity of the femme lesbian (lesbian femininity?).
11. Halberstam, *Female Masculinity*, 106.
12. RH, *The Well of Loneliness*, 150.
13. See Marianna Torgovnick, *Gone Primitive*, 8–11, on the tropes of primitivism.
14. RH, *The Well of Loneliness*, 52.
15. Ibid., 363.
16. See David Theo Goldberg, *Racist Culture*, 200–201, on the discourse of pollution that continues to depict the pathological Other as a degenerate.
17. Hall's story, "Miss Ogilvy Finds Herself," (written in 1926 but not published until 1934) is a primitivist fantasy that develops in greater detail the degeneration theory underlying these passages in *The Well*. Miss Ogilvy is an extremely masculine looking woman who lives in unhappy spinsterhood until she finds respect and acceptance leading an ambulance unit in the First World War, but after the war her old civilian life is insupportable. Strange memories of a former existence and a cave in a cliff drive her to visit a small island off the coast of Devon—significantly outside the perimeters of British nationality. Pacing her hotel room, she "becomes" a Paleolithic man, protective and peremptory toward an adoring and sexually submissive woman. Miss Ogilvy's fantasy is so overwhelming, or her desire to escape the present world so strong, that her dead body is found the following morning in a cave in the cliff. I find the story more open-ended than Judith Halberstam does: she reads Miss Ogilvy's death as suicide (83). But this story makes abundantly clear Hall's notion of the invert where s/he belongs, in the "turbulent age of transition" (see *The Well of Loneliness*, 52 and 150).
18. RH, *The Well of Loneliness*, 32.
19. The identification of the natural world at Morton with Anna and heterosexuality has been emphasized by several writers. See Gillian Whitlock, "'Everything Is out of Place': Radclyffe Hall and the Lesbian Literary Tradition," and Margot Gayle Backus, "Sexual Orientation in the (Post)Imperialist Nation."
20. RH, *The Well of Loneliness*, 186–87.
21. Ibid., 103.

22. Ibid., 437.
23. Ibid., 305. In "'Everything is out of Place,'" Gillian Whitlock shows how the Eden at Orotava is at best an ambiguous, illusory substitute for the Eden at Morton.

    Radclyffe Hall and Mabel Batten had visited Tenerife together in 1910. Their romantic visit there seems to have been blessedly cheerful and straightforward compared to the frustrated anguish endured by Stephen and Mary. See Diana Souhami, *The Trials of Radclyffe Hall*, 48–49.
24. RH, *The Well of Loneliness*, 308.
25. See Jean Radford, "An Inverted Romance," for an analysis of *The Well*'s mixture of genres and of the various plots and themes common in nineteenth-century and early twentieth-century romances.
26. RH, *The Well of Loneliness*, 11. In "Sexual Orientation in the (Post)Imperialist Nation," Margot Gayle Backus interestingly associates Hall's syntactic inversions in the first half of the novel with Anna Gordon's Anglo-Irish syntax: examples are "And himself the lovely young man" and "A lovely and most comfortable woman she had been" (*The Well*, 12, 80). Backus finds the inversions of word order later in the novel more "flamboyant," and she associates them with Stephen's congenital inversion. She maintains that Hall is "writing the lesbian body" according to inversion theory (259). I certainly think that Hall may have been reproducing Anglo-Irish syntax in the earlier examples that are associated with Anna, but in the second half of the novel the inversions of word order seem to me less controlled. They may well symbolize sexual inversion, just as the irritating frequency of the word *must* throughout the novel symbolizes the inevitability of congenitalism, but their significance is subsumed in the overwritten hodgepodge of Biblical phraseology and allusions, insistent repetitions, and "poetic" diction that is characteristic of Radclyffe Hall's melodrama.
27. RH, *The Well of Loneliness*, 341.
28. Ibid., 271.
29. See Claire M. Tylee, *The Great War and Women's Consciousness*, for details about women's war narratives in the twenties.
30. Hall's romanticized, superficial representation of the war probably reflects her guilt and regret that she did not serve in it. At the beginning of the war, she and Mabel Batten attended Red Cross lectures and learned first aid in Malvern—like Vera Brittain and her mother and most middle-class women in England. They offered two rooms of their house for the use of wounded soldiers, helped ferry them around in their car, and took library books to the hospitals. Hall also wrote fiery recruitment leaflets that they distributed, and at least once she made an impassioned patriotic speech at a recruiting meeting. But seven weeks into the war, their activity was curtailed when Batten was injured in a car accident; after that, Hall felt she couldn't leave her. Even Michael Baker, however, in his calmly tolerant biography *Our Three Selves*, admits that "in Malvern [Radclyffe Hall] could have occupied herself more usefully than she did" (56). She certainly managed to get away from Batten to spend time with Una Troubridge after they met in 1915.
31. RH, *The Well of Loneliness*, 387.
32. Ibid., 437.
33. RH, *Radclyffe Hall's 1934 Letter*, 7–8.
34. See Jonathan Dollimore, "The Dominant and the Deviant: A Violent Dialectic," and Sonja Ruehl, "Inverts and Experts: Radclyffe Hall and the Lesbian Identity."
35. Lucy Bland, *Banishing the Beast*, 256.
36. Diana Souhami, *The Trials of Radclyffe Hall*, 168.
37. Unable to bear Sir Chartres Biron's misrepresentation of her book during his verdict, Hall did once interrupt his hour-long monologue:

    > *Radclyffe Hall*: I protest. I am that writer.
    >   *Biron*: I must ask people not to interrupt the Court.
    > *Radclyffe Hall*: I am the authoress of this book.
    >   *Biron*: If you cannot behave yourself in court I shall have to have you removed.
    > *Radclyffe Hall*: It is shameful. (Transcript of Biron's judgment quoted in Baker, *Our Three Selves*, 243)

    Biron had focused on the representation of "vice" in Mrs. Breakspeare's Ambulance Unit; Hall maintained later that her protest had been "against that old man [who] sought to bring shame, not only on me as an author but upon the women of the British Empire" (quoted in Souhami, *The Trials of Radclyffe Hall*, 210). But her pathetic emphasis on her identity as author reveals the anguish that her loss of agency caused her.

    Souhami's quotation is taken from Hall's handwritten notes about the trial, which she made in preparation for a talk she gave to the Southend Young Socialists on January 25, 1929 (*The Trials*, 391, 395). This uncharacteristic choice of audience demonstrates again the urgency of Hall's need to express her sense of the injustice that had been done to her.

38. On Joynson-Hicks, see Baker, *Our Three Lives*, 227, and Souhami, *The Trials of Radclyffe Hall*, 179.

39. Leonard Woolf, "The New Censorship."

40. Souhami, *The Trials of Radclyffe Hall*, 187-88. See Leonard Woolf's editorial, "The New Censorship," and the ensuing correspondence over the following two weeks. Woolf was unaware, of course, of Cape's plan for publishing *The Well* in France, where it was enormously successful, especially among English tourists.

41. Memorandum from Joynson-Hicks to Stephenson, Public Records Office, 20 August, 1928; quoted in Souhami, *The Trials of Radclyffe Hall*, 181. The introduction to Souhami's book describes her own struggle with the Public Record Office and the Home Office to get access to government papers that were supposedly released to the general public in January 1998, seventy years after the ban of *The Well of Loneliness*. She was told that the material missing from the files was being retained "in the interests of national security" and that "the matter would be reviewed in 2007" (xi). After letters to cabinet members and members of Parliament and with the help of activists fighting for freedom of information and for gay and lesbian rights, Souhami eventually saw the private memoranda that she was after: they revealed how, in their determination to ban *The Well*, Sir William Joynson-Hicks and Sir Archibald Bodkin unscrupulously manipulated the law. There clearly has not been very much change in freedom of information in Britain during the last seventy years: the present bureaucracy continues to conceal the dirty linen of its predecessors.

Souhami's notes to *The Trials of Radclyffe Hall* are inexplicit. Whenever I have succeeded in identifying the new material she obtained about the prosecution of *The Well*, I indicate it by including her source, the Public Records Office, in my citations.

42. Quoted in Souhami, *The Trials of Radclyffe Hall*, 183; no source given.

43. Arnold Bennett, *The Journals of Arnold Bennett*, 271; his italics.

44. "Psychical Research."

45. Souhami, *The Trials of Radclyffe Hall*, 184.

46. I tend to agree with Diana Souhami that there was a misogynist conspiracy to prevent a fair trial for *The Well*. Souhami excoriates "the flawed men of power, gossiping with each other, plotting strategy, entrenching prejudice. It was not the state of literature that disturbed them. . . . It was passion between women. They feared its acceptance if Radclyffe Hall was heard. They had their view of a woman's place and they intended to legislate against this affront to it" (184). Virginia Woolf's fantasy in *A Room of One's Own* about Sir Chartres Biron behind the red curtain and Sir Archibald Bodkin in the cupboard spying on a meeting between women is ironic, of course, but nonetheless expresses a suspicion similar to Souhami's and mine (*A Room of One's Own*, 141, 194); Woolf snipes at Sir William Joynson-Hicks's well-known propensity for sniffing out illicit heterosexual relationships as well (149). See Jane Marcus, *Virginia Woolf and the Languages of Patriarchy*, 166.

Angela Ingram and Diana Souhami show a similar outrage at the often bizarre conduct of Joynson-Hicks and the other patriarchs who were fighting a fanatical rear-guard action against women's increased independence after the First World War. See Ingram's two articles about censorship, "'Unutterable Putrefaction' and 'Foul Stuff'" and "Un/Reproductions"; they trace the suppression between 1915 and 1930 of novels that suggest futures for women that don't include childbearing and marriage. There was a shortage of babies; the patriarchy was frightened that it could not reproduce itself fast enough to control the young women who had started to free themselves during the war and showed signs of continued independence during the 1920s. Ingram pays particular attention to the censorship trials of Rose Allatini's *Despised and Rejected*, Hall's *The Well of Loneliness*, and Norah James's *Sleeveless Errand* (1929). Two of these foreground lesbianism and/or homosexuality; see chapter 4 on *Despised and Rejected*. *Sleeveless Errand* is about a depressed young woman who uses a number of extremely prevalent swear words, has independent relationships with men and with her car, and eventually kills herself by driving very competently off a cliff.

See chapter 1 on Hall's 1920 slander suit against Fox-Pitt and the controversial proposal of a clause criminalizing lesbianism that succeeded in scuttling the 1921 Criminal Law Amendment Bill, thereby continuing men's legal access to the bodies of young girls and boys.

47. Public Records Office; quoted in Souhami, *The Trials of Radclyffe Hall*, 189.

48. Public Records Office; quoted in Souhami, *The Trials of Radclyffe Hall*, 190-91.

49. Souhami, *The Trials of Radclyffe Hall*, 191–92; Ingram, "'Unutterable Putrefaction' and 'Foul Stuff,'" 343.

50. Baker *Our Three Selves*, 243.

51. Souhami, *The Trials of Radclyffe Hall*, 209.

52. Ibid., 215.

53. Charles Carrington, *Rudyard Kipling*, 565.

54. See Leigh Gilmore, "Obscenity, Modernity, Identity: Legalizing *The Well of Loneliness* and *Nightwood*" and Adam Parkes, "Lesbianism, History, and Censorship: *The Well of Loneliness* and the Suppressed Randiness of Virginia Woolf's *Orlando*."

55. See later in this chapter for Evadne Price's ambivalently lesbophobic ambulance drivers in *Not So Quiet . . . Stepdaughters of War* and Rosemary Manning's World War I veterans in *The Chinese Garden*. Mary Renault provides an extreme and complicated example of lesbian panic in *The Friendly Young Ladies* (1944). This is an impressively bigoted book about two young women and a man; the "butch" ends up in a happy heterosexual marriage. Renault's afterword to the 1983 Virago edition is virulently hostile to latter-day gays and lesbians.

56. Elizabeth Lapovsky Kennedy and Madeline D. Davis, *Boots of Leather, Slippers of Gold*, 34, 29.

57. Ruth Ellis was born in Springfield, Illinois, on July 23, 1899, and died in Detroit on October 5, 2000. From 1941 to 1975 Ellis and her partner Ceciline "Babe" Franklin lived together in Detroit, where Ellis started her own printing business; they opened their house every weekend to the gay and lesbian community, providing a safe social environment at a time when gay bars did not welcome African Americans. In 1978, at the senior center where she lived, Ellis recognized a young self-defense teacher as a lesbian; Ellis "came out" to her and was welcomed into the multicultural gay and lesbian community of Detroit. For more details about this remarkable woman, see Yvonne Welbon's important film *Living with Pride: Ruth at 100*.

58. Winifred Young's diaries have not survived. See Jane Marcus, "Corpus/Corps/Corpse," 262–67, on Evadne Price's life and the genesis of *Not So Quiet*.

It seems impossible to ascertain whether or not Young's diaries are the source for the representation of lesbianism in *Not So Quiet*. There is no trace of lesbianism in the four sequels by and about Helen Zenna Smith that followed *Not So Quiet*. On the other hand, Evadne Price was a journalist who knew how to use the narrative of history: lesbianism and lesbophobia were hot topics when she was writing. Hall's friend, Toupie Lowther, who had received the Croix de Guerre for her leadership of an ambulance unit during the war, was both an aristocrat and a notorious lesbian; she may well have been a model for Tosh as she was for Stephen Gordon. Sir Chartres Biron's judgment of *The Well of Loneliness* in 1928 had emphasized Hall's delineation of "women of position and admirable character, who were engaged in driving ambulances during the course of the war, [and] were addicted to this vice" (quoted in Souhami, *The Trials of Radclyffe Hall*, 210). Hall's impassioned interruption at this point of the proceedings was prominent in the newspaper accounts of the trial.

The sequels to *Not So Quiet* are *Women of the Aftermath* (1931), *Shadow Women* (1932), *Luxury Ladies* (n.d.), and *They Lived with Me* (1934). They make clear how topical Price's representations of sexuality are. *Shadow Women* advocates birth control and the sterilization of a tubercular woman who has had eleven children and whose husband is called "Queer Joe." *They Lived with Me* also represents eugenics; by now, Nell has been a dance partner in a palais-de-danse and a girl in a chorus line, a "kept" woman, a shoplifter, a professional ex-WAAC beggar, and the owner of the House of the Helping Hand, a "doss-house," or hostel for the homeless. She has had three husbands and has now moved back, with a working-class woman friend, into the old house her family owned in Clapham before they became rich. In 1934, Nell is heterosexual, antisocialist, and probably a sympathizer with Oswald Mosley's fascists.

I have been unable to trace *Luxury Ladies* further than the listing of Helen Zenna Smith's previous works in *They Lived with Me*. Parts of Nell Smith's life that must have been covered in *Luxury Ladies*—the death of her third husband, the move from the House of the Helping Hand—are unaccounted for at the beginning of *They Lived with Me*. Jane Marcus reads *Not So Quiet* along with *All Quiet on the Western Front* as "textual deconstruction(s) of gender stereotypes." Her essay, "Corpus/Corps/Corpse" has been instrumental to my reading of *Not So Quiet* as a response to *The Well of Loneliness*.

On lesbian panic in relation to homosexual panic and to 1920s novels by women, see chapter 2.

59. RH, *The Well of Loneliness*, 282, 287–93.

60. Price, *Not So Quiet . . . Stepdaughters of War*, 69.

61. Ibid., 98–103.

62. Ibid., 119.

63. See Jane Marcus, "Corpus/Corps/Corpse," 295–96, on Sandra Gilbert and Susan Gubar's thesis in *Sexchanges* that "British women were empowered, psychologically, economically, and erotically, by World War I" (295). *Not So Quiet* certainly represents the psychological and erotic empowerment of women such as Mrs. Smith and the sadistic "Mrs. Bitch," commandant of the ambulàce unit, who profits economically, too. Nell's generation, however, are shown in alliance with the young men who are their brothers and lovers at home and who are sacrificed by power-hungry parents and politicians.

64. Price, *Not So Quiet . . . Stepdaughters of War*, 96.

65. Ibid., 148. Sylvia Townsend Warner briefly highlights war babies in *Opus 7*: "war-babies, too, now lost their pristine glamour, / and were as bastards bid to hold their clamour" (8). She returns to the subject during the Second World War in "Step This Way," a terse but remarkably poignant short story about abortion. An anxious mother accompanies her unmarried daughter to a midwife/abortionist. The abortionist takes her responsibilities seriously and "'[doesn't] like to hurry things'" (65); describing the joys of out-of-wedlock motherhood, she says, "'nowadays it's not like what it used to be. In the old days, I grant it freely, things were hard for a girl. People were so cruel and narrow-minded that you really couldn't blame a young lady for taking steps. But now everything's different. There's clinics, and welfare, and nurseries, and every baby's welcomed. Specially in wartime. Why, in wartime you might almost call it a duty'" (64).

66. See Modris Eksteins, "Battle Ballet," in his *Rites of Spring*, 139–42.

67. RH, *The Well of Loneliness*, 289.

68. Price, *Not So Quiet . . . Stepdaughters of War*, 11.

69. In "Corpus/Corps/Corpse," Jane Marcus reads the commandant as a phallic mother (274–75) and Tosh as heterosexual and "a large, imperialist, terrifying maternal figure" like Queen Victoria (281–87).

70. Price, *Not So Quiet . . . Stepdaughters of War*, 21.

71. Ibid., 125; emphasis added.

72. Ibid., 129.

73. Raymond Postgate, *Revolution from 1789 to 1906*, 179–80.

74. Sylvia Townsend Warner and Valentine Ackland, *I'll Stand By You*, 98, 106, 199, 40–41.

75. For varying responses to the intertextuality of *Summer Will Show* and *L'Éducation sentimentale*, see Terry Castle, "Sylvia Townsend Warner and the Counterplot of Lesbian Fiction"; Sandy Petrey, "Ideology, Écriture, 1848"; and Thomas Foster, "'Dream Made Flesh.'" Foster's reading of Warner through Lukàcs is particularly useful. See also Chris Hopkins, "Sylvia Townsend Warner and the Marxist Historical Novel"; Hopkins demonstrates that Ralph Fox, whom Warner knew, developed a theory similar to that of Lukàcs and used Flaubert as an example of the ahistorical writer in *The Novel and the People* (1937).

76. See Janet Montefiore, *Men and Women Writers of the 1930s*, and Terry Castle, *The Apparitional Lesbian*. In *Tragic Muse: Rachel of the Comédie-Française*, Rachel M. Brownstein identifies Minna as one of the great Jewish actress's fictional 'afterlives'—following Charlotte Brontë's Vashti, George Eliot's Mirah Lapidoth and Princess Halm-Eberstein, and Henry James's Miriam Rooth.

77. RH, *The Well of Loneliness*, 126.

78. Ibid., 388–89.

79. STW, *Summer Will Show*, 31.

80. Ibid., 93.

81. Ibid., 36.

82. I am indebted to Robin Hackett both for my reading of the lime-kiln man's part in *Summer Will Show* and for our ongoing discussions of the novel since 1994. Hackett places the lime-kiln man at the center of the representation of class and sexuality in *Summer Will Show*.

83. STW, *Summer Will Show*, 96–97.

84. Ibid., 98.

85. Ibid., 99.

86. STW, *Diaries*, 77.

87. D. H. Lawrence, "The Fox," 224.

88. STW, *Summer Will Show*, 52.

89. Lawrence, "The Fox," 223.

90. Ibid., 229.

91. Ibid., 300.
92. STW, *Summer Will Show*, 145.
93. Ibid., 156.
94. Ibid., 275.
95. Ibid., 279.
96. STW, *Summer Will Show*, 293.
97. Ibid., 299.
98. Ibid., 301.
99. STW, *Diaries*, 70.
100. Sophia shoots Caspar after he stabs Minna at the barricade (382). Caspar had been sent to England to Sophia's care; she placed him in a "moderate establishment where he could receive a sound commercial education," as her planter uncle had asked (34). But Caspar was taught only snobbery and anti-Semitism. At no point does Sophia place his welfare or her responsibility for his unhappiness above her personal convenience.
    For a detailed, up-to-date discussion of primitivism in the representation of Caspar, see Robin Hackett, *Sapphic Primitivism in Modern Fiction*.
101. Claire Harman, Introduction to *Summer Will Show*, viii.
102. In *Are Girls Necessary?* Julie Abraham uses Minna's death to categorize *Summer Will Show* with the "lesbian novels" that are doomed to an unhappy ending (6), a reading that involves a drastic oversimplification of Warner's narrative. Minna dies as a result of the class war and of Sophia's arrogant, racist refusal to take Caspar's infatuation seriously. Caspar kills Minna because Sophia loves her and neglects him and because he has absorbed the values of the patriarchal imperialism that brought him into the world.
103. Woolf practiced self-censorship quite consciously in 1928 and 1929. She was reading the proofs of *Orlando* in August, 1928, when James Douglas's article started the furor over *The Well of Loneliness*. See Hermione Lee, *Virginia Woolf*, 524, for the "dangerous details" about Sappho, Orlando's lusts, and her love affairs with women that were cut from the manuscript. See chapter 2, 40, for Woolf's editing of the manuscript of *A Room of One's Own*. Yet *Orlando* and *A Room of One's Own* are not merely subjected to censorship; censorship is also, ironically and satirically, their *subject*.
104. Such wartime novels as Allatini's *Despised and Rejected* were generally prosecuted under the Defense of the Realm Act rather than the Obscene Publications Act. For publication details about *Lady Chatterley's Lover*, see D. H. Lawrence, "Apropos of *Lady Chatterley's Lover*"; for Warner's and Ackland's outraged responses to the expurgated edition, see Warner, *Diaries*, 90, and Warner and Ackland, *I'll Stand By You*, 98. See Jeffrey Weeks, *Sex, Politics, and Society*, 263–68, on the liberalizing laws of the sixties; he includes the 1959 Obscene Publications Act; the 1967 Sexual Offences Act, which decriminalized private sexual activity between adult men; and the 1967 Abortion Act. In 1968 Lord Chamberlain's censorship of the theater was also abolished.
105. For the writing and publication history of *The Chinese Garden* and *A Time and a Time*, see Rosemary Manning, *A Corridor of Mirrors*, 139–40, 149, 152, and 159–61.
106. See STW, *Diaries*, 205–6 on "all this howdydoo about homosexuality." Warner's letters to Ian Parsons on this topic are a pleasure to read: she declines to remove Crusoe's declaration of love, suggests that Chatto might like to delay publication of *The Flint Anchor*, and says that she'll excise Ellen Barnard's mischief-making reference to "what dogs do in the street" (*Flint Anchor*, 197). But there it stands in the novel, in all its comic glory (Warner Ackland Papers).
107. STW, *Flint Anchor*, 204–5.

Bibliography

UNPUBLISHED SOURCES
Nancy Cunard Papers. Harry Ransom Humanities Research Center, University of Texas at Austin.
Warner/Ackland Papers. Dorset County Museum, Dorchester, England.

PUBLISHED SOURCES
Abbott, Reginald. "What Miss Kilman's Petticoat Means: Virginia Woolf, Shopping, and Spectacle." *Modern Fiction Studies* 38 (1992): 193–216.

Abel, Elizabeth. *Virginia Woolf and the Fictions of Psychoanalysis.* Chicago: University of Chicago Press, 1989

Abraham, Julie. *Are Girls Necessary? Lesbian Writing and Modern Histories.* New York: Routledge, 1996.

Achebe, Chinua. "An Image of Africa: Racism in Conrad's *Heart of Darkness.*" In Conrad, *Heart of Darkness.*

Ackland, Valentine. *Country Conditions.* London: Lawrence and Wishart, 1936.

———. *To Sylvia: An Honest Account.* New York: Norton, 1985.

Ackland, Valentine, and Sylvia Townsend Warner. *I'll Stand By You: Selected Letters of Sylvia Townsend Warner and Valentine Ackland.* Edited by Susanna Pinney. London: Pimlico, 1998.

———. *Whether a Dove or a Seagull.* New York: Viking, 1933.

Allatini, Rose. [A. T. Fitzroy, pseud.]. *Despised and Rejected.* New York: Arno, 1975.

"The Anatomy of Fear: Prevention of 'Shell-Shock.'" *Times* (London), 10 August 1922.

Anzaldúa, Gloria. *Borderlands/La Frontera: The New Mestiza.* San Francisco: Aunt Lute Books, 1987.

Apuleius, Lucius. *The Golden Ass.* Cambridge, Mass.: Harvard University Press, 1965.

Arnold, June. *The Cook and the Carpenter.* New York: New York University Press, 1995.

Ashton, Winifred. See Clemence Dane.

Auden, W. H., ed. *The Oxford Book of Light Verse.* Oxford: Clarendon Press, 1938.

Auerbach, Nina. *Our Vampires, Ourselves.* Chicago: University of Chicago Press, 1995.

Backus, Margot Gayle. "Sexual Orientation in the (Post)Imperial Nation: Celticism and Inversion Theory in Radclyffe Hall's *The Well of Loneliness.*" *Tulsa Studies in Women's Literature* 15, no. 22 (1996): 253–66.

Baker, Michael. *Our Three Selves: The Life of Radclyffe Hall.* New York: Morrow, 1985.

Bakshi, Parminder Kaur. "Homosexuality and Orientalism: Edward Carpenter's Journey to the East." In *Edward Carpenter and Late Victorian Radicalism,* edited by Tony Brown. London: Frank Cass, 1990.

Barkan, Elazar. "Victorian Promiscuity: Greek Ethics and Primitive Exemplars." In Barkan and Bush, eds., *Prehistories of the Future*.

Barkan, Elazar, and Ronald Bush, eds. *Prehistories of the Future: The Primitivist Project and the Culture of Modernism*. Stanford: Stanford University Press, 1995.

Barker, Pat. *The Eye in the Door*. London: Penguin, 1994.

Barnes, Djuna. *Ladies' Almanack*. 1928. Reprint, Elmwood Park, Ill.: Dalkey Archive Press, 1992.

Barrett, Eileen. "Unmasking Lesbian Passion: The Inverted World of Mrs. Dalloway." In *Virginia Woolf: Lesbian Readings*, edited by Eileen Barrett and Patricia Cramer. New York: New York University Press, 1997.

Barua, Dilip Kumar. *Edward Carpenter 1844–1929: An Apostle of Freedom*. Burdwan: The University of Burdwan Press, 1991.

Beer, Gillian. "The Dissidence of Vernon Lee: *Satan the Waster* and the Will to Believe." In Raitt and Tate, eds., *Women's Fiction and the Great War*.

Bell, Vanessa. *Selected Letters of Vanessa Bell*. Edited by Regina Marler. New York: Pantheon, 1993.

Bennett, Arnold. *The Journals of Arnold Bennett, 1921–1928*. Edited by Newman Flower. London: Cassell, 1933.

Benstock, Shari. *Women of the Left Bank: Paris, 1900–1940*. Austin: University of Texas Press, 1986.

Bland, Lucy. *Banishing the Beast: Sexuality and the Early Feminists*. London: Penguin, 1995.

———. "Trial by Sexology?: Maud Allan, *Salome*, and the 'Cult of the Clitoris' Case." In Bland and Doan, eds., *Sexology in Culture*.

Bland, Lucy, and Laura Doan, eds. *Sexology in Culture: Labeling Bodies and Desires*. Chicago: University of Chicago Press, 1998.

Brittain, Vera. *Chronicle of Youth: War Diary 1913–1917*. Edited by Alan Bishop and Terry Smart. London: Gollancz, 1981.

Broe, Mary Lynn, and Angela Ingram, eds. *Women's Writing in Exile*. Chapel Hill: University of North Carolina Press, 1989.

Brothers, Barbara. "Flying the Nets at Forty: *Lolly Willowes* as Female Bildungsroman." In *Old Maids to Radical Spinsters: Unmarried Women in the Twentieth-Century Novel*, edited by Laura L. Doan. Urbana: University of Illinois Press, 1991.

———. "Writing against the Grain: Sylvia Townsend Warner and the Spanish Civil War." In Broe and Ingram, eds., *Women's Writing in Exile*.

Brownstein, Rachel M. *Tragic Muse: Rachel of the Comédie-Française*. New York: Knopf, 1993.

Bryher. *Development*. London: Constable, 1920.

———. *The Heart to Artemis: A Writer's Memoir*. New York: Harcourt, Brace and World, 1962.

———. *The Player's Boy*. New York: Pantheon, 1953.

———. *Roman Wall*. New York: Pantheon, 1954.

Burstall, Sara A. *English High Schools for Girls: Their Aims, Organisation, and Management*. London: Longmans, Green, 1907.

Bush, Ronald. "The Presence of the Past: Ethnographic Thinking / Literary Politics." In Barkan and Bush, eds., *Prehistories of the Future*.

Bussy, Dorothy Strachey. *Olivia*. By Olivia. 1949. London: Virago, 1987.

Cahun, Claude (Lucy Schwob). "La 'Salomé' d'Oscar Wilde: Le Procès Billing et les 47,000 Pervertis du 'Livre Noir.'" *Mercure de France*, July 1, 1918.

Calder, Jenni. *Robert Louis Stevenson: A Life Study*. New York: Oxford University Press, 1980.

Carpenter, Edward. *From Adam's Peak to Elephanta: Sketches in Ceylon and India*. London: Swan Sonnenschein, 1892.

———. *Homogenic Love and Its Place in a Free Society*. Manchester: Labour Press, 1895.

———. *The Intermediate Sex: A Study of Some Transitional Types of Men and Women*. 1908. Reprint, London: Swan Sonnenschein, 1909.

———. *Intermediate Types among Primitive Folk: A Study in Social Evolution*. New York: Mitchell Kennerley, 1914.

———. *Love's Coming-of-Age: A Series of Papers on the Relations of the Sexes*. 1896. Reprint, London: Swan Sonnenschein, 1902.

———. *My Days and Dreams, Being Autobiographical Notes*. New York: Scribner's, 1916.

———. *The Story of Eros and Psyche: Retold from Apuleius*. London: George Allen and Unwin, 1923.

———. *Towards Democracy*. Complete edition, 1905. Reprint, London: George Allen and Unwin, 1918.

———. *An Unknown People*. 1897. Reprint, London: Bonner, 1905.

———, ed. *Iolaus: An Anthology of Friendship*. London: Swan Sonnenschein, 1902.

Carrington, Charles. *Rudyard Kipling: His Life and Work*. Rev. ed. London: Macmillan, 1978.

Caserio, Robert L. "Celibate Sisters-in-Revolution: Towards Reading Sylvia Townsend Warner." In *Engendering Men: The Question of Male Feminist Criticism*, edited by Joseph A. Boone and Michael Cadden. New York: Routledge, 1990.

———. *The Novel in England, 1900–1950: History and Theory*. New York: Twayne, 1999.

Castle, Terry. *The Apparitional Lesbian: Female Homosexuality and Modern Culture*. New York: Columbia University Press, 1993.

———. *Noël Coward and Radclyffe Hall: Kindred Spirits*. New York: Columbia University Press, 1996

———. "Sylvia Townsend Warner and the Counterplot of Lesbian Fiction." *Textual Practice* 4 (1990): 213–35.

Charke, Charlotte. *A Narrative of the Life of Mrs. Charlotte Charke*. London: W. Reeve, 1755.

Chauncey, George Jr. "From Sexual Inversion to Homosexuality: Medicine and the Changing Conceptualization of Female Deviance." *Salmagundi* 58–59 (1982–1983): 114–46.

Cherniavsky, Felix. *The Salome Dancer: The Life and Times of Maud Allan*. Toronto: McClelland and Stewart, 1991.

Clausen, Jan. *Beyond Gay or Straight: Understanding Sexual Orientation*. Philadelphia: Chelsea House, 1997.

Cline, Sally. *Radclyffe Hall: A Woman Called John*. Woodstock, N.Y.: Overlook Press, 1998.

Coleridge, Samuel Taylor. "Christabel." In *Selected Poetry and Prose* by Samuel Taylor Coleridge. London: Nonesuch Press, 1971.

Conrad, Joseph. *Heart of Darkness*. 1899. Reprint, New York: Norton, 1988.

———. *Victory*. 1915. Reprint, New York: Doubleday, 1957.

Cook, Blanche Wiesen. "'Women Alone Stir My Imagination': Lesbianism and the Cultural Tradition." *Signs: Journal of Women in Culture and Society* 4 (1979): 718–39.

Coombes, Annie E. *Reinventing Africa: Museums, Material Culture and Popular Imagination in Late Victorian and Edwardian England*. London: Yale University Press, 1994.

"Courage and Character." *Times* (London), September 2, 1922.

"The Cult of the Clitoris." *The Vigilante* (London), February 16, 1918.

"Cure of Shell-Shock: Organization of Homes of Recovery: Sir J. Collie's Scheme." *Times* (London), June 14, 1917.

Cutbill, Jonathan. Introduction to *Despised and Rejected*, by Rose Allatini. London: Gay Men's Press, 1988.

"Damages against Four People in Dorset Libel Action." *The Dorset County Chronicle and Somersetshire Gazette*, January 24, 1935.

Dane, Clemence. [Winifred Ashton]. *Legend*. 1919.

———. *Regiment of Women*. 1917. Reprint, London: Virago, 1995.

———. *The Women's Side*. 1926. Reprint, Freeport, N.Y.: Books for Libraries Press, 1970.

"A Daniel Come to Judgment." *Herald* (London), October 19, 1918.

Darrohn, Christine M. "After the Abyss: Class, Gender, and the Great War in British Fiction of the 1920s." Ph.D. diss., Rutgers University, 1996.

Darwin, Charles. *The Descent of Man and Selection in Relation to Sex*. 1871. Reprint, London: Murray, 1909.

———. *The Origin of Species by Means of Natural Selection*. 1859. New York: Collier, 1901.

Defoe, Daniel. *Robinson Crusoe*. 1719. Reprint, London: Dent, 1945.

DeKoven, Marianne. *Rich and Strange: Gender, History, Modernism*. Princeton: Princeton University Press, 1991.

De Lauretis, Teresa. *The Practice of Love: Lesbian Sexuality and Perverse Desire*. Bloomington: Indiana University Press, 1994.

DeSalvo, Louise. *Virginia Woolf: The Impact of Childhood Sexual Abuse on Her Life and Work*. New York: Ballantine, 1989.

"'Despised and Rejected': Publisher of Pacifist Novel Fined." *Times* (London), October 11, 1918.

Deutsch, Helene. "On Female Sexuality." Translated by Edith B. Jackson. *Psychoanalytic Quarterly* 1 (1932): 484–510.

Dickens, Charles. *Little Dorrit*. 1857. Reprint, Boston: Books, Inc., n.d.

Diderot, Denis. *La Religieuse*. 1796. Reprint, translated by Leonard Tancock, New York: Penguin, 1974.

Doan, Laura. "'Acts of Female Indecency': Sexology's Intervention in Legislating Lesbianism." In Bland and Doan, eds. *Sexology in Culture*.

———. "Passing Fashions: Reading Female Masculinities in the 1920s." *Feminist Studies* 24 (1998): 663–700.

Dollimore, Jonathan. "The Dominant and the Deviant: A Violent Dialectic." *Critical Quarterly* 28 (1986): 179–92.

Donoghue, Emma. *Passions between Women: British Lesbian Culture 1668–1801*. 1993. New York: Harper, 1996.

Douglas, Norman. *South Wind*. 1917; Reprint, New York: Modern Library, 1925.

Duberman, Martin Bauml, Martha Vicinus, and George Chauncey Jr., eds. *Hidden from History: Reclaiming the Gay and Lesbian Past*. New York: New American Library, 1989.

"Dying Author Carried into Assize Court." *News of the World* (London), January 20, 1935.

"Dying Author in Court Drama." *People* (London), January 20, 1935.

Eagle, Solomon [J. C. Squire]. "Books in General." *New Statesman*, October 12, 1918, 33.

———. "Books in General." *New Statesman*, October 26, 1918, 73.

Eksteins, Modris. *Rites of Spring: The Great War and the Birth of the Modern Age*. Boston: Houghton Mifflin, 1989.

Eliot, T. S. *Collected Poems 1909–1935*. London: Faber, 1936.

Ellis, Edith Lees. "Eugenics and Spiritual Parenthood." In *The New Horizon in Love and Life*. London: A. and C. Black, 1921.

———. "Personal Impressions of Edward Carpenter." In *Edward Carpenter: In Appreciation*, edited by Gilbert Beith. London: Allen and Unwin, 1931.

Ellis, Havelock, and John Addington Symonds. *Sexual Inversion*. 1897. Reprint, New York: Arno, 1975.

Faderman, Lillian. *Odd Girls and Twilight Lovers: A History of Lesbian Life in Twentieth-Century America*. New York: Penguin, 1992.

———. *Scotch Verdict: Miss Pirie and Miss Woods v. Dame Cumming Gordon*. 1983. Reprint, New York: Columbia University Press, 1993.

———. *Surpassing the Love of Men: Romantic Friendship and Love between Women from the Renaissance to the Present*. New York: Morrow, 1981.

Feinberg, Leslie. *Stone Butch Blues: A Novel*. New York: Firebrand Press, 1993.

Firbank, Ronald. *The Flower Beneath the Foot*. New York: Brentano, 1924.

"The First 47,000." *The Imperialist* (London), January 26, 1918.

Fitzroy, A. T. See Rose Allatini.

"£500 Damages in 'Ghost' Case." *Daily Mail* (London), 20 November 1920.

Flaubert, Gustave. *Sentimental Education*. Translated by Anthony Goldsmith. London: Dent, 1956.

Forster, E. M. *Maurice*. 1971. Reprint, New York: Norton, 1993.

———. *A Passage to India*. 1924. Reprint, New York: Harcourt, 1952.

———. *A Room with a View*. 1908. Reprint, Harmondsworth, England: Penguin, 1955.

———. *Where Angels Fear to Tread*. 1905. Reprint, New York: Vintage, 1958.

Foster, Thomas. "'Dream Made Flesh': Sexual Difference and Narratives of Revolution in Sylvia Townsend Warner's *Summer Will Show*." *Modern Fiction Studies* 41 (1995): 531–62.

Foucault, Michel. *The History of Sexuality*. Vol. 1. Translated by Robert Hurley. 1978. New York: Vintage, 1980.

Fox, Ralph. *The Novel and the People*. 1937. Reprint, New York: International Publishers, 1945.

Frazier, Adrian. *George Moore, 1852–1933*. New Haven: Yale University Press, 2000.

Fryer, Peter. *Staying Power: The History of Black People in Britain*. London: Pluto, 1984.

Garnett, David. *The Familiar Faces*. Vol. 3 of *The Golden Echo*. New York: Harcourt, 1962.

———. *Great Friends: Portraits of Seventeen Writers*. London: Macmillan, 1979.

———. *Lady into Fox*. 1922. Reprint, *Lady into Fox and A Man in the Zoo*. Garden City, N.Y.: Garden City Publishing, n.d.

———. *A Man in the Zoo*. 1924. Reprint, *Lady into Fox and A Man in the Zoo*. Garden City, N.Y.: Garden City Publishing, n.d.

———. *The Sailor's Return*. New York: Knopf, 1925.

Garrity, Jane. "Encoding Bi-Location: Sylvia Townsend Warner and the Erotics of Dissimulation." In Jay, ed., *Lesbian Erotics*.

"German Women in London." *Times* (London), May 13, 1915.

Gide, André. *If It Die . . . An Autobiography*. Translated by Dorothy Bussy. New York: Vintage, 1935.

———. *The Immoralist*. 1902. Translated by Dorothy Bussy. Harmondsworth, England: Penguin, 1960.

Gilbert, Sandra M., and Susan Gubar. *Sexchanges*. Vol. 2 of *No Man's Land: The Place of the Woman Writer in the Twentieth Century*. 3 vols. New Haven, Conn.: Yale University Press, 1988–1994.

Gilman, Sander L. "Black Bodies, White Bodies: Toward an Iconography of Female Sexuality in Late Nineteenth-Century Art, Medicine, and Literature." In *Race, Writing, and Difference*, edited by Henry Louis Gates Jr. New York: Routledge, 1986.

Gilmore, Leigh. "Obscenity, Modernity, Identity: Legalizing *The Well of Loneliness* and *Nightwood*." *Journal of the History of Sexuality* 4 (1994): 603–24.

Goldberg, David Theo. *Racist Culture: Philosophy and the Politics of Meaning*. Cambridge, Mass.: Blackwell, 1993.

Gould, Stephen Jay. *The Mismeasure of Man*. New York: Norton, 1981.

Greenaway, Judy. "It's What You Do with It That Counts." In Bland and Doan, eds., *Sexology in Culture*.

Gubar, Susan. "Sapphistries." *Signs: Journal of Women in Culture and Society* 10 (1984): 43–62.

Guénot, Marianne. "The Ambiguity of *Mr. Fortune's Maggot*." Unpublished paper.

Hackett, Robin. "Sapphic Primitivism in Modern Fiction: Virginia Woolf's *The Waves*, Sylvia Townsend Warner's *Summer Will Show*, and Willa Cather's *Sapphira and the Slave Girl*." Ph.D. diss., City University of New York, 2000.

Halberstam, Judith. *Female Masculinity*. Durham, N.C.: Duke University Press, 1998.

Hall, Radclyffe. "Miss Ogilvy Finds Herself." 1934. Reprinted in *The Penguin Book of Lesbian Short Stories*. Edited by Margaret Reynolds. New York: Penguin, 1993.

———. *Radclyffe Hall's 1934 Letter about* The Well of Loneliness. Edited by Polly Thistlewaite. New York: Lesbian Herstory Educational Foundation, 1994.

———. *The Unlit Lamp*. 1924. Reprint, London: Virago, 1981.

———. *The Well of Loneliness*. 1928. Reprint, New York: Anchor, 1990.

Hamer, Emily. *Britannia's Glory: A History of Twentieth-Century Lesbians*. London: Cassell, 1996.

Harman, Claire. Introduction to *Summer Will Show*, by Sylvia Townsend Warner. London: Virago, 1987.

———. Introduction to *The Diaries of Sylvia Townsend Warner*. London: Chatto, 1994.

———. *Sylvia Townsend Warner: A Biography*. London: Mandarin, 1991.

Hennegan, Alison. Introduction to *Regiment of Women* by Clemence Dane. London: Virago, 1995.

Hoare, Philip. *Oscar Wilde's Last Stand: Decadence, Conspiracy, and the Most Outrageous Trial of the Century*. New York: Arcade, 1998.

Hopkins, Chris. "Sylvia Townsend Warner and the Marxist Historical Novel." *Literature and History* 4 (1995): 50–64.

Ingram, Angela. "Un/Reproductions: Estates of Banishment in English Fiction after the Great War." In Broe and Ingram, eds., *Women's Writing in Exile*.

———. "'Unutterable Putrefaction' and 'Foul Stuff': Two 'Obscene' Novels of the 1920s." *Women's Studies International Forum* 9 (1986): 341–54.

Jay, Karla, ed. *Lesbian Erotics*. New York: New York University Press, 1995.

Jensen, Emily. "Clarissa Dalloway's Respectable Suicide." In Marcus, ed., *Virginia Woolf: A Feminist Slant*.

Joannou, Maroula. "Sylvia Townsend Warner in the 1930s." In *A Weapon in the Struggle: The Cultural History of the Communist Party in Britain*, edited by Andy Croft. London: Pluto Press, 1998.

Kennedy, Elizabeth Lapovsky, and Madeline D. Davis. *Boots of Leather, Slippers of Gold: The History of a Lesbian Community*. New York: Routledge, 1993.

Kettle, Michael. *Salome's Last Veil*. London: Granada, 1977.

Kipling, Rudyard. "The Gardener." In *Short Stories*, vol. 2: *Friendly Brook and Other Stories*. Harmondsworth, England: Penguin, 1971.

Knox, John. *The First Blast of the Trumpet against the Monstrous Regiment of Women*. 1558. Reprinted in *The Political Writings of John Knox: The First Blast of the Trumpet against the Monstrous Regiment*, edited by Marvin A. Breslow. Washington, D.C.: Folger, 1985.

Koestenbaum, Wayne. *Double Talk: The Erotics of Male Literary Collaboration*. New York: Routledge, 1989.

Krafft-Ebing, Richard von. *Psychopathia Sexualis with Especial Reference to the Antipathic Instinct: A Medico-Forensic Study*. 1886. Reprint, translated by Franklin S. Klaf, New York: Stein and Day, 1978.

Kuper, Adam. *The Invention of Primitive Society: Transformations of an Illusion*. London: Routledge, 1988.

Lanser, Susan S. "Queering Narratology." In *Ambiguous Discourse: Feminist Narratology and British Women Writers*, edited by Kathy Mezei. Chapel Hill: University of North Carolina Press, 1996.

Lawrence, D. H. "À Propos of *Lady Chatterley's Lover*." 1930. Reprinted in *À Propos of* Lady Chatterley's Lover *and Other Essays*. Harmondsworth, England: Penguin, 1961.

———. "The Fox." 1922. In *The Portable D. H. Lawrence*, edited by Diana Trilling. New York: Viking, 1947.

Leary, Lewis. *Norman Douglas*. New York: Columbia University Press, 1968.

Leduc, Violette. *La Bâtarde*. Translated by Derek Coltman. New York: Farrar, Straus and Giroux, 1965.

Lee, Hermione. *Virginia Woolf*. London: Chatto, 1996.

Lee, Vernon. *The Ballet of the Nations: A Present-Day Morality with a Pictorial Commentary by Maxwell Armfield*. London: Chatto, 1915.

———. *Satan the Waster: A Philosophic War Trilogy*. New York: John Lane, 1920.

LeFanu, Sheridan. "Carmilla" (1872). In *Best Ghost Stories of J. S. LeFanu*, edited by E. F. Bleiler. New York: Dover, 1964.

Lehmann, Rosamond. *Dusty Answer*. 1927. Reprint, Harmondsworth, England: Penguin, 1936.

Leperlier, François. *Claude Cahun: L'Écart et La Métamorphose*. Paris: Jean-Michel Place, 1992.

Levenback, Karen L. *Virginia Woolf and the Great War*. Syracuse, N.Y.: Syracuse University Press, 1999.

Lévy-Bruhl, Lucien. *How Natives Think*. Translated by Lilian A. Clare. 1926. Reprint, New York: Arno, 1979.

Lister, Anne. *I Know My Own Heart: The Diaries of Anne Lister 1791–1840*. Edited by Helena Whitbread. New York: New York University Press, 1992.

———. *No Priest But Love: Excerpts from the Diaries of Anne Lister, 1824–1826*. Edited by Helena Whitbread. New York: New York University Press, 1992.

Lucas, John. *The Radical Twenties: Aspects of Writing, Politics and Culture*. Nottingham, England: Five Leaves Publications, 1997.

Macaulay, Rose. *Non-Combatants and Others*. 1916. Reprint, London: Methuen, 1986.

Mackenzie, Compton. *Extraordinary Women: Theme and Variations*. New York: Macy-Masius, 1928.

MacKenzie, John M. *Propaganda and Empire: The Manipulation of British Public Opinion, 1880–1960*. Manchester: Manchester University Press, 1984.

———, ed. *Imperialism and Popular Culture*. Manchester: Manchester University Press, 1986.

Maine, Henry. *Ancient Law*. 1861. London: Dent, 1917.

Malinowski, Bronislaw. *The Sexual Life of Savages: An Ethnographic Account of Courtship, Marriage, and Family Life among the Natives of the Trobriand Islands, British New Guinea*. New York: Harcourt, 1929.

Mannin, Ethel. *Young in the Twenties*. London: Hutchinson, 1971.

Manning, Rosemary. *The Chinese Garden*. 1962. London: Brilliance Books, 1984.

———. *A Corridor of Mirrors*. London: The Women's Press, 1987.

———. *A Time and a Time: An Autobiography*. London, Calder and Boyars, 1971.

Marcus, Jane. "Alibis and Legends: The Ethics of Elsewhereness, Gender, and Estrangement." In Broe and Ingram, eds., *Women's Writing in Exile*.

———. *Art and Anger: Reading Like a Woman*. Columbus: Ohio State University Press, 1988.

———. "The Asylums of Antaeus: Women, War, and Madness: Is there a Feminist Fetishism?" In *The Difference Within: Feminism and Critical Theory*, edited by Elizabeth Meese and Alice Parker. Amsterdam: John Benjamins, 1989.

———. "Bluebeard's Daughters: Pretexts for Pre-Texts." In *Feminist Critical Negotiations*, edited by Alice Parker and Elizabeth Meese. Amsterdam: John Benjamins, 1992.

———. "Britannia Rules *The Waves*." In *Decolonizing Tradition: New Views of Twentieth-Century "British" Literary Canons*, edited by Karen R. Lawrence. Urbana: University of Illinois Press, 1992.

———. "Corpus/Corps/Corpse: Writing the Body in/at War." Afterword to *Not So Quiet . . . Stepdaughters of War*, by Helen Zenna Smith [Evadne Price]. New York: Feminist Press, 1989

———. "Registering Objections: Grounding Feminist Alibis." In *Reconfigured Spheres: Feminist Explorations of Literary Space*, edited by Margaret R. Higonnet and Joan Templeton. Amherst, Mass.: University of Massachusetts Press, 1994.

———. "Sylvia Townsend Warner." In *The Gender of Modernism: A Critical Anthology*, edited by Bonnie Kime Scott.

———. *Virginia Woolf and the Languages of Patriarchy*. Bloomington: Indiana University Press, 1987.

———. "A Wilderness of One's Own: Feminist Fantasy Novels of the Twenties: Rebecca West and Sylvia Townsend Warner." In *Women Writers and the City*, edited by Susan Squier. Knoxville: University of Tennessee Press, 1984.

———, ed. *Virginia Woolf: A Feminist Slant*. Lincoln: University of Nebraska Press, 1983.

———, ed. *The Young Rebecca: Writings of Rebecca West, 1911–17*. Bloomington: Indiana University Press, 1982.

Marsh, Joss Lutz. "In a Glass Darkly: Photography, the Premodern, and Victorian Horror." In Barkan and Bush, eds., *Prehistories of the Future*.

Michie, Helena. *The Flesh Made Word: Female Figures and Women's Bodies*. New York: Oxford University Press, 1987.

Miss Marianne Woods and Miss Jane Pirie against Dame Helen Cumming Gordon. New York: Arno, 1975.

Montefiore, Janet. *Men and Women Writers of the 1930s: The Dangerous Flood of History*. London: Routledge, 1996.

Moon, Kenneth. "Doris Kilman and Recoil from the Flesh in Virginia Woolf's *Mrs. Dalloway*." *College Language Association Journal* 23 (1980): 273–86.

Moore, George. *A Drama in Muslin*. 1886. Reprint, Belfast: Appletree Press, 1992.

Moore, Lisa L. *Dangerous Intimacies: Toward a Sapphic History of the British Novel*. Durham: Duke University Press, 1997.

Moorehead, Caroline. *Troublesome People: Enemies of War, 1916–1986*. London: Hamish Hamilton, 1987.

Mosse, George L. *The Image of Man: The Creation of Modern Masculinity*. New York: Oxford University Press, 1996.

Mulford, Wendy. *This Narrow Place: Sylvia Townsend Warner and Valentine Ackland: Life, Letters, and Politics, 1930–1951*. London: Pandora, 1988.

Newton, Esther. "The Mythic Mannish Lesbian: Radclyffe Hall and the New Woman." In Duberman, Vicinus, and Chauncey, eds., *Hidden from History*.

Nicolson, Nigel. *Portrait of a Marriage*. 1973. Reprint, New York: Atheneum, 1980.

Olivia, *Olivia*. See Dorothy Strachey.

Orwell, George. "Shooting an Elephant." In *Collected Essays*. London: Secker and Warburg, 1961.

Ouditt, Sharon. *Fighting Forces, Writing Women: Identity and Ideology in the First World War*. London: Routledge, 1994.

Owen, Wilfred. *Poems*. London: Chatto, 1955.

Pankhurst, Christabel. *The Great Scourge and How to End It*. London: E. Pankhurst, 1913.

Pankhurst, E. Sylvia. *The Home Front: A Mirror to Life in England During the First World War*. 1932. Reprint, London: Century Hutchinson, 1987.

Parkes, Adam. "Lesbianism, History, and Censorship: *The Well of Loneliness* and the Suppressed Randiness of Virginia Woolf's *Orlando*." *Twentieth-Century Literature* 39 (1994): 434–60.

Partridge, Eric. *A Dictionary of Slang and Unconventional English*. 1937. Reprint, edited by Paul Beale, London: Routledge, 1984.

"A 'Pernicious' Book." *Daily News* (London), October 11, 1918.

"A Pernicious Book." *Times* (London) September 27, 1918.

Petrey, Sandy. "Ideology, *Écriture*, 1848: Sylvia Townsend Warner Unwrites Flaubert." *Recherches Sémiotiques/ Semiotic Inquiry* 11, no. 2–3 (1991): 159–80.

Phillips, Kathy J. *Virginia Woolf against Empire*. Knoxville: University of Tennessee Press, 1994.

Postgate, Raymond. *Revolution from 1789 to 1906*. 1920. Reprint, New York: Harper, 1962.

Powys, T. F. "The Left Leg." *The Left Leg*. 1923. Reprint, London: Chatto, 1968.

———. *Mr. Tasker's Gods*. 1925. Reprint, London: Chatto, 1929.

———. *Mr. Weston's Good Wine*. 1927. Reprint, London: Chatto, 1930.

Price, Evadne [Helen Zenna Smith]. *Not So Quiet . . . Stepdaughters of War*. 1930. Reprint, New York: Feminist Press, 1989.

Prosser, Jay. *Second Skins: The Body Narratives of Transsexuality*. New York: Columbia University Press, 1998.

"Psychical Research." *Times* (London), November 19, 1920.

Radford, Jean. "An Inverted Romance: *The Well of Loneliness* and Sexual Ideology." In *The Progress of Romance: The Politics of Popular Fiction*, edited by Jean Radford. New York: Routledge, 1986.

Rae, John. *Conscience and Politics: The British Government and the Conscientious Objector to Military Service, 1916–1919*. New York: Oxford University Press, 1970.

Raitt, Suzanne. "'Contagious Ecstasy': May Sinclair's War Journals." In Raitt and Tate, eds., *Women's Fiction and the Great War*.

Raitt, Suzanne, and Trudi Tate, eds. *Women's Fiction and the Great War*. Oxford: Oxford University Press, 1997.

Rattenbury, Arnold. "Literature, Lying and Sober Truth: Attitudes to the Work of Patrick Hamilton and Sylvia Townsend Warner." In *Writing and Radicalism*, edited by John Lucas. London: Addison Wesley Longman, 1996.

———. "Plain Heart, Light Tether." *Poetry Nation Review* 8 (1981): 46–48.

Renault, Mary. *Fire from Heaven*. New York: Pantheon, 1969.

———. *The Friendly Young Ladies*. 1944. Reprint, London: Virago, 1984.

———. *The Last of the Wine*. New York: Pantheon, 1956.

———. *The Mask of Apollo*. 1966. Reprint, New York: Bantam, 1978.

———. *The Praise Singer*. New York: Pantheon, 1978.

Renn, Ludwig. *War*. (*Krieg*.) No translator. New York: Dodd, Mead, 1929.

Rich, Paul B. *Race and Empire in British Politics*. Cambridge: Cambridge University Press, 1986.

Rollyson, Carl. *Rebecca West: A Life*. New York: Scribner, 1996.

Rowbotham, Sheila, and Jeffrey Weeks. *Socialism and the New Life: The Personal and Sexual Life of Edward Carpenter and Havelock Ellis*. London: Pluto, 1977.

Royde-Smith, Naomi G. *The Tortoiseshell Cat*. New York: Boni and Liveright, 1925.

Rubin, Gayle. "The Traffic in Women: Notes on the 'Political Economy' of Sex." In *Toward an Anthropology of Women*, edited by Rayna R. Reiter. New York: Monthly Review Press, 1975.

Ruehl, Sonja. "Inverts and Experts: Radclyffe Hall and the Lesbian Identity." In *Feminism, Culture, and Politics*, edited by Rosalind Brunt and Caroline Rowan. London: Lawrence and Wishart, 1982.

Said, Edward W. *Orientalism*. New York: Pantheon, 1978.

St. John, Christopher. *Hungerheart: The Story of a Soul*. London: Methuen, 1915.

Sayers, Dorothy L. *Unnatural Death*. 1927. Reprint, New York: Harper, 1995.

Scott, Bonnie Kime. Introduction to *The Gender of Modernism: A Critical Anthology*, edited by Bonnie Kime Scott. Bloomington: Indiana University Press, 1990.

———, ed. *Refiguring Modernism*. 2 vols. Bloomington: Indiana University Press, 1995–1996.

Scott, Paul. *The Towers of Silence*. 1971. New York: Avon, 1979.

Sedgwick, Eve Kosofsky. *Between Men: English Literature and Male Homosocial Desire*. New York: Columbia University Press, 1985.

———. *Epistemology of the Closet*. Berkeley and Los Angeles: University of California Press, 1990.

Shakespeare, William. *Cymbeline*. London: Cambridge University Press, 1960.

———. *Twelfth Night*. The Kittredge Shakespeare. New York: Wiley, 1969.

"Shell Shock." *Times* (London), 10 August 1922.

Shelley, Mary. *The Last Man*. 1826. Reprint, Lincoln: University of Nebraska Press, 1965.

Shephard, Ben. "Showbiz Imperialism: The Case of Peter Lobengula." In MacKenzie, ed., *Imperialism and Popular Culture*.

Sinclair, May. *The Tree of Heaven*. 1917. Reprint, New York: Macmillan, 1918.

Smith, Helen Zenna. See Evadne Price.

Smith, Patricia Juliana. *Lesbian Panic: Homoeroticism in Modern British Women's Fiction*. New York: Columbia University Press, 1997.

Smyth, Ethel. *Impressions That Remained*. London: Longmans Green, 1919.

———. *The Memoirs of Ethel Smyth*. Edited by Ronald Crichton. New York: Viking, 1987.

———. *Streaks of Life*. London and New York: Longmans Green, 1921.

———. *What Happened Next*. London: Longmans Green, 1940.

Souhami, Diana. *Gluck: Her Biography*. London: Pandora, 1989.

———. *The Trials of Radclyffe Hall*. London: Weidenfeld and Nicolson, 1998.

Lord Southborough. "'Shell Shock': A Misleading Designation: Medical Experts' Conclusions." *Times* (London), September 2, 1922.

Spencer, Herbert. *The Principles of Sociology*. 1876–1906. Westport, Conn.: Greenwood Press, 1975.

"Spirits in a Slander Suit." *Daily Mail* (London), November 19, 1920.

Spraggs, Gillian. "'Exiled to Home': The Poetry of Sylvia Townsend Warner and Valentine Ackland." In *Lesbian and Gay Writing*, edited by Mark Lilly. Philadelphia: Temple University Press, 1990.

Stallworthy, Jon. *Wilfred Owen: A Biography*. London: Oxford University Press, 1974.

Stead, Christina. *The Man Who Loved Children*. 1940. Reprint, London: Penguin, 1970.

Steiner, Chistopher B. "Travel Engravings and the Construction of the Primitive." In Barkan and Bush, eds., *Prehistories of the Future*.

Stevenson, Robert Louis. "The Beach of Falesá." In *The Complete Short Stories*.

———. "The Bottle Imp." In *The Complete Short Stories*.

———. *The Complete Short Stories*. Edited by Ian Bell. Vol. 2. New York: Henry Holt, 1993.

———. "The Isle of Voices." In *The Complete Short Stories*.

———. *Treasure Island*. 1883. Reprint, New York: Dover, 1993.

———. *Vailima Letters*. 1895. Reprint, London: Methuen, 1904.

Stimpson, Catharine R. "Zero Degree Deviancy: The Lesbian Novel in English." In *Writing and Sexual Difference*, edited by Elizabeth Abel. Chicago: University of Chicago Press, 1982.

Stinton, Judith. *Chaldon Herring: The Powys Circle in a Dorset Village*. Woodbridge, Suffolk, England: Boydell Press, 1988.

Stoker, Bram. *Dracula*. 1897. New York: Bantam, 1981.

Summerfield, Penny. "Patriotism and Empire: Music-Hall Entertainment, 1870–1914." In MacKenzie, ed., *Imperialism and Popular Culture*.

Symonds, John Addington. *Male Love: A Problem in Greek Ethics and Other Writings*. Edited by John Lauritsen. New York: Pagan Press, 1983.

Tambling, Jeremy. "Repression in Mrs. Dalloway's London." *Essays in Criticism* 39 (1989): 137–55.

Tate, Trudi. *Modernism, History and the First World War*. Manchester: Manchester University Press, 1998.

Thomas, Sue. "Virginia Woolf's Septimus Smith and Contemporary Perceptions of Shell Shock." *English Language Notes* 25, no. 2 (1987): 49–57.

Torgovnick, Marianna. *Gone Primitive: Savage Intellects, Modern Lives*. Chicago: University of Chicago Press, 1990.

Travis, Jennifer. "Clits in Court: *Salome*, Sodomy, and the Lesbian 'Sadist.'" In Jay, ed., *Lesbian Erotics*.

Trombley, Stephen. *All That Summer She Was Mad: Virginia Woolf, Female Victim of Male Medicine*. New York: Continuum, 1982.

Tsuzuki, Chushichi. *Edward Carpenter 1844–1929: Prophet of Human Fellowship*. Cambridge: Cambridge University Press, 1980.

Tylee, Claire M. *The Great War and Women's Consciousness: Images of Militarism and Womanhood in Women's Writings, 1914–64*. Iowa City: University of Iowa Press, 1990.

Ulrichs, Karl Heinrich. *The Riddle of Man-Manly Love: The Pioneering Work on Male Homosexuality*. 1864. Reprint, translated by Michael A. Lombardi-Nash. Buffalo, N.Y.: Prometheus Books, 1994.

Vicinus, Martha. "Distance and Desire: English Boarding School Friendships, 1870–1920." In Duberman, Vicinus, and Chauncey, eds., *Hidden from History*.

———. *Independent Women: Work and Community for Single Women, 1850–1920*. Chicago: University of Chicago Press, 1985.

———. "Lesbian History: All Theory and No Facts or All Facts and No Theory?" *Radical History Review* 60 (1994): 57–75.

———. "'They Wonder to Which Sex I Belong': The Historical Roots of the Modern Lesbian Identity." In *The Lesbian and Gay Studies Reader*, edited by Henry Abelove, Michèle Aina Barale, and David M. Halperin. New York: Routledge, 1993.

Walker, Alice. "In Search of Our Mothers' Gardens." In *In Search of Our Mothers' Gardens*. San Diego: Harcourt, 1983.

———. *Meridian*. 1976. New York: Pocket Books, 1977.

Warner, George Townsend. "Civilian Control in War." *Blackwoods Edinburgh Magazine*, February 1915, 186–201.

———. "Divergent Operations in War." *Blackwoods Edinburgh Magazine*, June 1915, 756–71.

———. "From a Voluntary System to Compulsion: The Precedent of '63." *Blackwoods Edinburgh Magazine*, January 1916, 92–111.

———. "Improvised Armies." *Blackwoods Edinburgh Magazine*, October 1914, 547–61.

———. "Recruiting in War-Time." *Blackwoods Edinburgh Magazine*, December 1915, 757–80.

———. "The Spirit of the War." *The Living Age*, July–September 1915, 728–35.

———. "Two Great Blockades: Their Aims and Effects." *Blackwoods Edinburgh Magazine*, April 1916, 504–21.

———. "The United States as a Neutral." *Blackwoods Edinburgh Magazine*, August 1916, 230–41.

Warner, Sylvia Townsend. *After the Death of Don Juan*. 1938. Reprint, London: Virago, 1989.

———. "Battles Long Ago." In *Scenes of Childhood*.

———. "Behind the Firing Line: Some Experiences in a Munitions Factory." *Blackwoods Edinburgh Magazine*, February 1916, 191–207.

———. "Being a Lily." 1970. In *Scenes of Childhood*.

———. *The Cat's Cradle Book*. 1940. Reprint, London: Chatto, 1960.

———. *Collected Poems*. Edited by Claire Harman. New York: Viking, 1982.

———. *Diaries*. Edited by Claire Harman. London: Chatto, 1994.

———. "East Chaldon and T. F. Powys." *The Powys Review* 2, no. 3 (1980): 59–70.

———. "Elphenor and Weasel." In *Kingdoms of Elfin*.

———. *The Espalier*. London: Chatto, 1925.

———. *The Flint Anchor*. New York: Viking, 1954.

———. "The Foregone Conclusion." In *Selected Stories*.

———. *A Garland of Straw*. London: Chatto, 1943.

––––––. *Kingdoms of Elfin*. New York: Viking, 1977.

––––––. *Letters*. Edited by William Maxwell. London: Chatto, 1982.

––––––. *Lolly Willowes*. 1926. Reprint, London: Chatto, 1928.

––––––. "A Love Match," first published as "Between Two Wars," *New Yorker*, October 31, 1964, 51–60. Reprinted as "A Love Match" in *Selected Stories*.

––––––. *Mr. Fortune's Maggot*. New York: Viking, 1927.

––––––. *The Museum of Cheats and Other Stories*. London: Chatto, 1947.

––––––. "My Shirt Is in Mexico." In *A Garland of Straw*.

––––––. "Notation: The Growth of a System." In *The Oxford History of Music*. Edited by Percy C. Buck. Introductory Volume. London: Oxford University Press, 1929.

––––––. *One Thing Leading to Another*. London: Chatto, 1984.

––––––. *Opus 7*. London: Chatto, 1931.

––––––. "The Salutation." In *The Salutation*.

––––––. *The Salutation*. London: Chatto, 1932.

––––––. *Scenes of Childhood*. New York: Viking, 1982.

––––––. *Selected Stories*. London: Virago, 1990.

––––––. *Some World Far from Ours and 'Stay, Corydon, Thou Swain.'* London: Elkin Mathews and Marrot, 1929.

––––––. "A Spirit Rises." In *Selected Stories*.

––––––. "Step This Way." In *The Museum of Cheats*.

––––––. *Summer Will Show*. 1936. London: Virago, 1987.

––––––. "Sylvia Townsend Warner In Conversation." Interview with Val Warner and Michael Schmidt, 1975. *Poetry Nation Review* 8, no. 3 (1981): 35–37.

––––––. "Theodore Powys and Some Friends at East Chaldon, 1922–1927: A Narrative and Some Letters." *The Powys Review* 2, no. 1 (1979): 13–26.

––––––. *The True Heart*. London: Chatto 1929.

––––––. "The Way by Which I Have Come." *Countryman*, July 1939, 472–86.

Warner, Sylvia Townsend, and Valentine Ackland. *I'll Stand By You: Selected Letters of Sylvia Townsend Warner and Valentine Ackland*. Edited by Susanna Pinney. London: Pimlico, 1998.

––––––. *Whether a Dove or a Seagull*. New York: Viking, 1933.

Warner, Sylvia Townsend, and David Garnett. *Sylvia and David: The Townsend Warner/Garnett Letters*. Edited by Richard Garnett. London: Sinclair-Stevenson, 1994.

"War-Shaken Men." *Times* (London), November 27, 1916.

Webb, Mary. *Gone to Earth*. New York: Dutton, 1917.

Weeks, Jeffrey. *Sex, Politics, and Society: The Regulation of Sexuality since 1800*. 2nd ed. London: Longman Group, 1989.

Welbon, Yvonne. *Living with Pride: Ruth Ellis at 100*. Videotape, 60 mins. Written, directed, and produced by Yvonne Welbon. Our Film Works, P.O. Box 267848, Chicago, IL 60626 (1–800–343–5540); stills and quotations can be viewed at http://www.sistersinthelife.com.

West, Rebecca. *Henry James*. London: Nisbet, 1916.

––––––. *The Return of the Soldier*. 1918. Reprint, New York: Penguin, 1998.

––––––. *The Young Rebecca West: Writings of Rebecca West 1911–1917*. Edited by Jane Marcus. Bloomington: Indiana University Press, 1982.

White, Antonia. *Frost in May*. 1933. Reprint, London: Penguin, 1992.

Whitlock, Gillian. "'Everything Is out of Place': Radclyffe Hall and the Lesbian Literary Tradition." *Feminist Studies* 13 (1987): 555–82.

Wilde, Oscar. "The Ballad of Reading Gaol." In *The Picture of Dorian Gray and Other Writings*. Edited by Richard Ellmann. New York: Bantam, 1982.

––––––. *The Importance of Being Earnest*. In Ellmann, ed., *The Picture of Dorian Gray and Other Writings*. New York: Bantam, 1982.

Williams, Raymond. "Social Darwinism." In *Problems in Materialism and Culture*. London: Verso, 1980.

Winsloe, Christa. *The Child Manuela*. 1934. Trans. Agnes Neill Scott. London: Virago, 1994.

Winstock, Lewis. *Songs and Music of the Redcoats: A History of the War Music of the British Army 1642–1902*. Harrisburg, Penn.: Stackpole Books, 1970.

Winterson, Jeanette. *Written on the Body*. New York: Knopf, 1993.

Woolf, Leonard. "The Well of Loneliness." *Nation and Athenaeum*, 4 August 1928, 593.

––––––. "The New Censorship." *Nation and Athenaeum*, 1 September 1928, 696.

Woolf, Virginia. *Between the Acts*. 1941. Reprint, London: Hogarth Press, 1969.

––––––. *The Diary of Virginia Woolf*. Edited by Anne Olivier Bell. 5 vols. New York: Harcourt, 1977–84.

————. *The Essays of Virginia Woolf*. Edited by Andrew McNeillie. 4 vols. to date. New York: Harcourt, 1986—.

————. *Jacob's Room*. 1922. Harmondsworth, England: Penguin, 1965.

————. *The Letters of Virginia Woolf*. Edited by Nigel Nicolson and Joanne Trautmann. 6 vols. New York: Harcourt, 1975–1980.

————. *Moments of Being*. New York: Harcourt, 1976.

————. *Mrs. Dalloway*. 1925. Harmondsworth, England: Penguin, 1964.

————. "Old Bloomsbury." In *Moments of Being*.

————. *Orlando: A Biography*. 1928. Reprint, New York: Harcourt, n.d.

————. *The Pargiters*. New York: Harcourt, 1977.

————. *A Room of One's Own*. 1929. Reprint, New York: Harcourt, n.d.

————. "A Sketch of the Past." In *Moments of Being*.

————. *To the Lighthouse*. 1927. New York: Harcourt, n.d.

————. *Women and Fiction: The Manuscript Versions of* A Room of One's Own. Edited by S. P. Rosenbaum. Oxford: Blackwell, 1992.

————. *The Years*. 1937. Reprint, New York: Harcourt, n.d.

Woollacott, Angela. *On Her Their Lives Depend: Munition Workers in the Great War*. Berkeley and Los Angeles: University of California Press, 1994.

Wylie, Elinor. *The Venetian Glass Nephew*. 1925. London: Heinemann, 1926.

Yourcenar, Marguerite. *The Abyss*. Translation of *L'Oeuvre au Noir*, 1968, by Grace Frick in collaboration with the author. New York: Noonday Press, 1990.

————. "Anna, Soror." 1935. Reprinted in *Comme L'Eau Qui Coule*, 1982; published in English as *Two Lives and a Dream*, translated by Walter Kaiser, 1987. Reprint, Chicago: University of Chicago Press, 1994.

————. *Memoirs of Hadrian*. Translated by Grace Frick in collaboration with the author. New York: Farrar, Straus and Giroux, 1963.

————. "Reflections on the Composition of *Memoirs of Hadrian*." Translated by Grace Frick in collaboration with the author. In *Memoirs of Hadrian*.

Index

About the Author

Gay Wachman is an associate professor in the English Language Studies Department at the State University of New York, Old Westbury. She has published articles on Sylvia Townsend Warner and Virginia Woolf and reviews in *The Women's Review of Books*, *The Nation*, and *American Book Review*. She emigrated from Britain to New York City in 1977.